CELTIC MYTHOLOGY

PLATE I

Brug na Boinne

The tumulus at New Grange is the largest of a group of three at Dowth, New Grange, and Knowth, County Meath, on the banks of the Boyne in the plain known to Irish tales as Brug na Boinne, the traditional burial-place of the Tuatha Dé Danann and of the Kings of Tara. It was also associated with the Tuatha Dé Danann as their immortal dwelling-place, e. g. of Oengus of the Brug (see pp. 50–51, 66–67, 176–77). The tumuli are perhaps of the neolithic age (for plans see Plate VI, A and B).

CELTIC MYTHOLOGY

J. A. MacCulloch

ACADEMY

CHICAGO

This edition published in 1996 by Academy Chicago Publishers
An imprint of Chicago Review Press Incorporated
814 North Franklin Street
Chicago, Illinois 60610
ISBN 978-0-89733-433-4

Cover design: Julia Anderson-Miller

Printed in the United States of America

CONTENTS

                                                                PAGE

Author's Preface   5

Introduction   7

Chapter I. The Strife of the Gods   23

II. Tuatha Dé Danann and Milesians. . . .   42

III. The Division of the Síd   49

IV. Mythic Powers of the Gods.   54

V. Gods Helping Mortals   62

VI. Divine Enmity and Punishment   68

VII. The Loves of the Gods   78

VIII. The Myths of the British Celts   92

IX. The Divine Land   114

X. Mythical Animals and Other Beings. . .   124

XI. Myths of Origins   135

XII. The Heroic Myths — I. Cúchulainn and his Circle   139

XIII. The Heroic Myths — II. Fionn and the Féinn   160

XIV. The Heroic Myths — III. Arthur   184

XV. Paganism and Christianity.   206

ILLUSTRATIONS

PLATE   FACING PAGE

  I   Brug na Boinne . . . . *Frontispiece*

 II   Gaulish Coins 8

             1. Horse and Wheel-Symbol

             2. Horse, Conjoined Circles and S-Symbol

             3. Man-Headed Horse and Wheel

             4. Bull and S-Symbol

             5. Bull

             6. Sword and Warrior Dancing Before it

          7-8. Swastika Composed of Two S-Symbols (?)

       9-10. Bull's Head and two S-Symbols; Bear Eating a
                  Serpent

            11. Wolf and S-Symbols

 III   Gaulish Coins 14

             1. Animals Opposed, and Boar and Wolf (?)

             2. Man-Headed Horse and Bird, and Bull Ensign

             3. Squatting Divinity, and Boar and S-Symbol or Snake

             4. Horse and Bird

             5. Bull and Bird

             6. Boar

             7. Animals Opposed

 IV   God with the Wheel 20

  V   Smertullos 40

 VI   A. Plan of the Brug na Boinne 50

       B. Plan of the Brug na Boinne 50

 VII   Three-Headed God 56

VIII   Squatting God 72

 IX   A. Altar from Saintes 86

       B. Reverse Side of the same Altar 86

  X   Incised Stones from Scotland 94

             1. The "Picardy Stone"

             2. The "Newton Stone"

PLATE		FACING PAGE
XI	Gauls and Romans in Combat	106
XII	Three-Headed God	112
XIII	Sucellos	116
XIV	Dispater and Aeracura (?)	120
XV	Epona	124
XVI	Cernunnos	128
XVII	Incised Stones from Scotland	134
	1. The "Crichie Stone"	
	2. An Incised Scottish Stone	
XVIII	Menhir of Kernuz	140
XIX	Bulls and S-Symbols	152
	1, 6. Carvings of Bulls from Burghhead	
	2–5. S-Symbols	
XX	A. Altar from Notre Dame. Esus	158
	B. Altar from Notre Dame. Tarvos Trigaranos	158
XXI	Altar from Trèves	166
XXII	Page of an Irish Manuscript	176
XXIII	Artio	186
XXIV	Boars	188
XXV	Horned God	204
XXVI	Sucellos	208

TO

DR. JAMES HASTINGS

EDITOR OF THE *Encyclopædia of Religion and Ethics*,
THE *Dictionary of the Bible*, ETC.

WITH THE GRATITUDE AND RESPECT OF THE AUTHOR

AUTHOR'S PREFACE

IN a former work * I have considered at some length the religion of the ancient Celts; the present study describes those
Celtic myths which remain to us as a precious legacy from
the past, and is supplementary to the earlier book. These
myths, as I show, seldom exist as the pagan Celts knew them,
for they have been altered in various ways, since romance,
pseudo-history, and the influences of Christianity have all
affected many of them. Still they are full of interest, and it
is not difficult to perceive traces of old ideas and mythical
conceptions beneath the surface. Transformation allied to
rebirth was asserted of various Celtic divinities, and if the
myths have been transformed, enough of their old selves remained for identification after romantic writers and pseudo-
historians gave them a new existence. Some mythic incidents
doubtless survive much as they were in the days of old, but
all alike witness to the many-sided character of the life and
thought of their Celtic progenitors and transmitters. Romance
and love, war and slaughter, noble deeds as well as foul, wordy
boastfulness but also delightful poetic utterance, glamour and
sordid reality, beauty if also squalid conditions of life, are found
side by side in these stories of ancient Ireland and Wales.

The illustrations are the work of my daughter, Sheila Mac-
Culloch, and I have to thank the authorities of the British
Museum for permission to copy illustrations from their publica-
tions; Mr. George Coffey for permission to copy drawings and
photographs of the Tumuli at New Grange from his book *New
Grange (Brugh na Boinne) and other Inscribed Tumuli in Ireland;* the Librarians of Trinity College, Dublin, and the Bod-

* *The Religion of the Ancient Celts,* Edinburgh, 1911.

leian Library, Oxford, for permission to photograph pages from well-known Irish MSS.; and Mr. R. J. Best for the use of his photographs of MSS.

In writing this book it has been some relief to try to lose oneself in it and to forget, in turning over the pages of the past, the dark cloud which hangs over our modern life in these sad days of the great war, sad yet noble, because of the freely offered sacrifice of life and all that life holds dear by so many of my countrymen and our heroic allies in defence of liberty.

J. A. MACCULLOCH.

BRIDGE OF ALLAN, SCOTLAND,
May, 16, 1916.

INTRODUCTION

IN all lands whither the Celts came as conquerors there was an existing population with whom they must eventually have made alliances. They imposed their language upon them — the Celtic regions are or were recently regions of Celtic speech — but just as many words of the aboriginal vernacular must have been taken over by the conquerors, or their own tongue modified by Celtic, so must it have been with their mythology. Celtic and pre-Celtic folk alike had many myths, and these were bound to intermingle, with the result that such Celtic legends as we possess must contain remnants of the aboriginal mythology, though it, like the descendants of the aborigines, has become Celtic. It would be difficult, in the existing condition of the old mythology, to say this is of Celtic, that of non-Celtic origin, for that mythology is now but fragmentary. The gods of the Celts were many, but of large cantles of the Celtic race — the Celts of Gaul and of other parts of the continent of Europe — scarcely any myths have survived. A few sentences of Classical writers or images of divinities or scenes depicted on monuments point to what was once a rich mythology. These monuments, as well as inscriptions with names of deities, are numerous there as well as in parts of Roman Britain, and belong to the Romano-Celtic period. In Ireland, Wales, and north-western Scotland they do not exist, though in Ireland and Wales there is a copious literature based on mythology. Indeed, we may express the condition of affairs in a formula: Of the gods of the Continental Celts many monuments and no myths; of those of the Insular Celts many myths but no monuments.

The myths of the Continental Celts were probably never

committed to writing. They were contained in the sacred verses taught by the Druids, but it was not lawful to write them down;[1] they were tabu, and doubtless their value would have vanished if they had been set forth in script. The influences of Roman civilization and religion were fatal to the oral mythology taught by Druids, who were ruthlessly extirpated, while the old religion was assimilated to that of Rome. The gods were equated with Roman gods, who tended to take their place; the people became Romanized and forgot their old beliefs. Doubtless traditions survived among the folk, and may still exist as folk-lore or fairy superstition, just as folk-customs, the meaning of which may be uncertain to those who practise them, are descended from the rituals of a vanished paganism; but such existing traditions could be used only with great caution as indexes of the older myths.

There were hundreds of Gaulish and Romano-British gods, as an examination of the Latin inscriptions found in Gaul and Britain[2] or of Alfred Holder's *Altceltischer Sprachschatz*[3] will show. Many are equated with the same Roman god, and most of them were local deities with similar functions, though some may have been more widely popular; but we can never be sure to what aspect of the Roman divinity's personality a parallel was found in their functions. Moreover, though in some cases philology shows us the meaning of their names, it would avail little to speculate upon that meaning, tempting as this may be — a temptation not always successfully resisted. This is also true of the symbols depicted on monuments, though here the function, if not the myth, is more readily suggested. Why are some deities horned or three-headed, or why does one god carry a wheel, a hammer, or an S-symbol? Horns may suggest divine strength or an earlier beast-god, the wheel may be the sun, the hammer may denote creative power. Other symbols resemble those of Classical divinities, and here the meaning is more obvious. The three *Matres*, or "Mothers," with their symbols of fertility were Earth Mothers; the horned deity with a bag of

1

2

3

4

5

6

7

8

9

10

11

PLATE II

Gaulish Coins

1. Coin of the Nervii, with horse and wheel-symbol (cf. Plates III, 4, IV, XV).

2. Gaulish coin, with horse, conjoined circles, and S-symbol (cf. Plates III, 3, IV, XIX, 2–5).

3. Coin of the Cenomani, with man-headed horse (cf. Plate III, 2) and wheel.

4. Coin of the Remi (?), with bull (cf. Plates III, 5, IX, B, XIX, 1, 6, XX, B, XXI), and S-symbol.

5. Coin of the Turones, with bull.

6. Armorican coin, showing sword and warrior dancing before it (exemplifying the cult of weapons; cf. pp. 33–34).

7, 8. Gaulish coins, with swastika composed of two S-symbols (?).

9, 10. Gaulish coin, showing bull's head and two S-symbols; reverse, bear (cf. Plate XXIII) eating a serpent.

11. Coin of the Carnutes, showing wolf (cf. Plate III, 1) and S-symbols.

grain was a god of plenty. Such a goddess as Epona was a divinity of horses and mules, and she is represented as riding a horse or feeding foals. But what myths lie behind the representation of Esus cutting down a tree, whose branches, extending round another side of the monument, cover a bull and three cranes — *Tarvos Trigaranos?* Is this the incident depicted on another monument with a bull's head among branches on which two birds are perched?[4]

Glimpses of myths are seen in Classical references to Celtic gods. Caesar, whose information (or that of his source) about the gods of Gaul is fragmentary, writes: "They worship chiefly the god Mercury. Of him there are many *simulacra;*[5] they make him inventor of all arts and guide of journeys and marches, and they suppose him to have great power over the acquiring of money and in matters of merchandise. After him come Apollo, Mars, Jupiter, and Minerva. Concerning these they hold much the same opinions as other nations — Apollo repels diseases, Minerva teaches the beginnings of arts and crafts, Jupiter sways celestial affairs, Mars directs wars."[6] There is no evidence that all the Gauls worshipped a few gods. Many local deities with similar functions but different names is the evidence of the inscriptions, and these are grouped collectively by Caesar and assimilated to Roman divinities. There are many local Mercuries, Minervas, Apollos, and the like, each with his Celtic name attached to that of the Roman god. Or, again, they are nameless, as in the case of the Yorkshire inscription, "To the god who invented roads and paths" — an obvious Mercury. Caesar adds, "The Gauls declare that they are descended from Dispater, and this, they say, has been handed down by the Druids."[7] If, as the present writer has tried to show elsewhere,[8] Dispater is the Roman name of a Celtic god, whether Cernunnos, or the god with the hammer, or Esus, or all three, who ruled a rich underworld, then this myth resembles many told elsewhere of the first men emerging from the earth, the autochthones. The parallel Celtic myth has not survived. In Ireland, if it ever existed there, it gave place to stories of descent from fictitious personages, like Mile, son of Bile, invented by the early scribes, or from Biblical patriarchs.

Apollonius, writing in the third century B. C., reports a Celtic myth about the waters of Eridanus. Apollo, driven by his father's threats from heaven because of the son whom Karonis bore to him, fled to the land of the Hyperboreans; and the tears which he shed on the way formed the tossing waters.[9] Some Greek myth is here mingled with a local legend about the origin of a stream and a Celtic god, possibly Belenos, who had a neighbouring temple at Aquileia. In an island of the Hyperboreans (a Celtic people dwelling beyond the Rhipaean Mountains whence Boreas blew) was a circular temple where Apollo was worshipped. Every year near the vernal equinox the god appeared in the sky, harping and dancing, until the rising of the Pleiades.[10] It is natural that this "circular temple" should have been found in Stonehenge.

Lucian (second century A. D.) describes a Gaulish god Ogmios, represented as an old man, bald-headed and with wrinkled and sun-burnt skin, yet possessing the attributes of Hercules — the lion's skin, the club, the bow, and a sheath hung from his shoulder. He draws a multitude by beautiful chains of gold and amber attached to their ears, and they follow him with joy. The other end of the chains is fixed to his tongue, and he turns to his captives a smiling countenance. A Gaul explained that the native god of eloquence was regarded as Hercules, because he had accomplished his feats through eloquence; he was old, for speech shows itself best in old age; the chains indicated the bond between the orator's tongue and the ears of enraptured listeners.[11]

Lucian may have seen such a representation or heard of a Gaulish myth of this kind, and as we shall see, an Irish god Ogma, whose name is akin to that of Ogmios, was a divine warrior and a god of poetry and speech. Ogma is called *grianainech* ("sun-faced," or "shining-faced"), perhaps a parallel to Lucian's description of the face of Ogmios. The head of Ogmios occurs on Gaulish coins, and from one of his eyes proceeds a ray or nail. This has suggested a parallel with the Ulster hero Cúchulainn in his "distortion," when the *lón láith* (?"champion's light") projected from his forehead thick and long as a man's fist. Another curious parallel occurs in the *Táin Bó Cúalnge*, or "Cattle-Spoil of Cúalnge," where, among the Ulster forces, is a strong man with seven chains on his neck, and seven men dragged along at the end of each, so that their noses strike the ground, whereupon they reproach him. Is this a distorted reminiscence of the myth of Ogmios?

A British goddess Sul, equated with Minerva at Bath, is mentioned by Solinus (third century A. D.) as presiding over warm springs. In her temple perpetual fires burned and never grew old, for where the fire wasted away it turned into shining globes.[12] The latter statement is travellers' gossip, but the "eternal fires" recall the sacred fire of St. Brigit at Kildare, tended by nineteen nuns in turn, a day at a time, and on the twentieth by the dead saint herself. The fire was tabu to males, who must not even breathe on it.[13] This breath tabu in connexion with fire is found among Parsis, Brāhmans, Slavs, in Japan, and formerly in Rügen. The saint succeeded to the myth or ritual of a goddess, the Irish Brigit, or the Brigindo or Brigantia of Gaulish and British inscriptions, who was likewise equated with Minerva.

A tabued grove near Marseilles is mythically described by Lucan, who wrote in the first century of our era, and doubtless his account is based on local legends. The trees of the grove were stained with the blood of sacrifices, and the hollow caverns were heard to roar at the movement of the earth; the yew trees bent down and rose again; flames burned but did not consume the wood; dragons entwined surrounded the oaks. Hence people were afraid to approach the sacred grove, and the priest did not venture within its precincts at midnight or midday, lest the god should appear — "the destruction that wasteth at noonday."[14] In Galatia Artemis was thought to wander with demons in the forest at midday, tormenting to death those whom she met; while Diana in Autun was regarded as a midday demon who haunted cross-roads and forests. Whether these divinities represent a Celtic goddess is uncertain, and their fateful midday aspect may have been suggested by the "midday demon" of the Septuagint version of Psalm xc. 6. Both accounts occur in lives of saints.

Several references suggest that the gods punished the taking of things dedicated to themselves, and therefore tabu to men. Caesar says that this was a criminal action punished by torture and death,[15] and Irish myth also discloses the disastrous results of breach of tabu. The awe of the priest of the grove is paralleled by incidents of Celtic history. After the battle of Allia in 390 B. C., where the Celts saw divine aid in the flight of the Romans and stood awestruck before it, they were afraid of the night.[16] After the battle of Delphi (279 B. C.) "madness from a god" fell on them at night, and they attacked each other, no longer recognizing each other's speech.[17] Another fear based on a myth is referred to in Classical sources, that of the future cataclysm. The Celts did not dread earthquakes or high tides, which, indeed, they attacked with weapons; but they feared the fall of the sky and the day when fire and water must prevail. An Irish vow perhaps refers to this: something would be done if the sky with its showers of stars did not fall or the earth burst or the sea submerge the world. Any untoward event might be construed as the coming of this catastrophe or analogous to it. How, then, was the sky meanwhile supported? Perhaps on mountain-peaks like that near the source of the Rhône, which the native population called "the column of the sun," and which was so lofty that it hid the northern sun from the southern folk.[18] Gaidoz says that "the belief that the earth rests on columns is the sole *débris* of ancient cosmogony of which we know in Irish legends, but we have only the reflexion

of it in a hymn and gloss of the *Liber Hymnorum*. In vaunting
the pre-eminence of two saints who were like great gods of old
Christian Ireland, Ultán says of Brigit that she was 'half of
the colonnade of the kingdom (of the world) with Patrick the
eminent.' The gloss is more explicit — 'as there are two pillars
in the world, so are Brigit and Patrick in Ireland.'" [19] In some
of the romantic Irish voyages islands are seen resting on pillars,
and an echo of these myths is found in the Breton tradition that
the church at Kernitou stands on four columns, resting on a
congealed sea which will submerge the structure when it becomes liquid.[20]

Divine help is often referred to in Irish myths, and a parallel
instance occurs in Justin's allusion to the guidance of the
Segovesi by birds to the Danubian regions which they conquered.[21] Such myths are depicted on coins, on which a horse
appears led by a bird, which sometimes whispers in its ear.
Heroes were also inspired by birds to found towns. Birds were
objects of worship and divination with the Celts, and divinities
transformed themselves into the shape of birds, or birds formed
their symbols.

The birth of heroes from a god and a human mother occurs in
Irish myth. One Classical parallel to this is found in the account of the origin of the northern Gauls given by Diodorus.
They were descended from Hercules and the beautiful giant
daughter of the King of Celtica, and hence they were taller and
handsomer than other peoples.[22] This is perhaps the Greek
version of a native myth, which is echoed in the Irish tale of
the gigantic daughter of the king of Maidens' Land and her
love for Fionn.[23] Again, when Diodorus speaks of Hercules as-
sembling his followers, advancing into Celtica, improving the
laws, and founding a city called Alesia, honoured ever since by
the Celts as the centre of their kingdom, he is probably giving
a native myth in terms of Greek mythology.[24] Some native
god or hero was concerned, and his story fitted that of Hercules, who became popular with the Celts.

The Celts had beliefs resembling those of the Greeks and Romans about *incubi*. Demons called *dusii* sought the couches of women out of lust, a belief reported by sub-Classical authors. The Classical evidence for Celtic belief in divine descent is also furnished by the form of several proper names which have been recorded, while lineage from a river or river-god is associated with the Belgic Viridomar.[25]

A legend reported by Pliny concerns some natural product, perhaps a fossil *echinus*, in explanation of the origin of which this myth was current, or to it an existing serpent-myth had been attached. Numerous serpents collected on a day in summer and, intertwining, formed a ball with the foam from their bodies, after which their united hissings threw it into the air. According to the Druids, he who would obtain it must catch it on a mantle before it touched the ground and must escape hastily, putting running water between himself and the pursuing serpents. The ball was used magically.[26]

Classical observers cite vaguely some myths about the otherworld and they admired profoundly the Celtic belief in immortality, which, if Lucan's words are correct, was that of the soul animating a new body there. Diodorus also affirms this, though he compares it with the Pythagorean doctrine of transmigration;[27] yet in the same passage he shows that the dead passed to another world and were not reborn on earth. Irish mythology tells us nothing about the world of the dead, though it has much to say of a gods' land or Elysium, to which the living were sometimes invited by immortals. This Elysium was in distant islands, in the hollow hills, or under the waters. Plutarch, on the authority of Demetrius, who may have been a Roman functionary in Britain, reports that round Britain are many desert islands, named after gods and heroes. Demetrius himself visited one island lying nearest these, inhabited by a people whom the Britons regarded as sacred, and while he was there, a storm arose with fiery bolts falling. This the people explained as the passing away of one of the mighty, for when a

1

2   4

5   3   6

7

PLATE III

Gaulish Coins

1. Coin of the Senones, showing on one side two animals opposed, and on the reverse a boar and a wolf (?) opposed (cf. Plates II, 11, XXIV).

2. Gaulish coin, with man-headed horse and bird, and, below, a bull ensign (cf. Plates II, 3–5, 9, IX, B, XIX, 1, 6, XX, B, XXI).

3. Coin of the Remi, showing squatting divinity with a torque in the right hand (cf. Plates VIII, IX, XXV), and on the reverse a boar and S-symbol or snake.

4. Armorican coin, with horse and bird.

5. Coin of the Carnutes, with bull and bird.

6. Gaulish coin from Greek model, with boar.

7. Gaulish coin of the Senones, with animals opposed.

great soul died, the atmosphere was affected and pestilences were caused. Demetrius does not say whither the soul went, either to the islands or elsewhere, but islands named after gods and heroes suggest the Irish divine Elysium, and this is confirmed by what Demetrius adds, and by what Plutarch reports in another work. On one of the islands Kronos is imprisoned, and Briareos keeps guard over him,[28] along with many deities (δαίμονας) who are his attendants and servants. What Celtic divinities or heroes lurk under these names is unknown, but the myth resembles traditions of Arthur in Avalon (Elysium), or of Fionn or Arthur sleeping in a hollow hill, waiting to start up at the hour of their country's need. Elsewhere Plutarch speaks of an island in which the barbarians say that Kronos is imprisoned by Jupiter in a cavern. There Kronos sleeps, fed by birds with ambrosia, while his son lies beside him as if guarding him. The surrounding sea, clogged with earth, appears to be solid, and people go to the island, where they spend thirteen years waiting on the god. Many remain, because there is no toil or trouble there, and devote their time to sacrificing, singing hymns, or studying legends and philosophy. The climate is exquisite, and the island is steeped in fragrance. Sometimes the god opposes their departure by appearing to them along with those who minister to him, and these divine ministrants themselves prophesy or tell things which have been revealed to them as dreams of Saturn when they visit his cave. Plutarch's alleged informant had waited on the god and studied astrology and geometry, and before going to another island he carried with him golden cups.[29] In this latter story the supposed studies and ritual of the Druids are mingled with some distorted tradition of Elysium, and the reference to cups of gold carried from the island perhaps points to the myth of things useful to man brought from the land of the gods.[30]

The sixth century Byzantine historian Procopius has a curious story about the island of "Brittia," which was divided by a wall from north to south. West of the wall none could live, so foul was the air, so many the vipers and evil beasts; but in its inhabited part dwelt Angles, Frisians, and Britons. The island lay between Britannia and Thule. Thule is probably Scandinavia; Britannia, which is, strictly speaking, Britain, is confused with the region lying between Brittany and the mouths of the Scheldt and Rhine. Brittia is Britain; the wall is the Roman Wall, shown on Ptolemy's map running north and south at the present Scottish border, because Scotland was represented as lying at right angles to England. The region beyond the wall, mountainous, forest-clad, and inaccessible, was easily conceived as a sinister place by those who heard of it only vaguely. Procopius then says that on the coast of the Continent fishermen and farmers are exempt from taxation because it is their duty to ferry souls over to Brittia, doing this in turn. At midnight they hear a knocking at their door and muffled voices calling; but when they reach the shore, they see only empty boats, not their own. In these they set out and presently perceive that the boats have become laden, the gunwale being close to the water; and within an hour Brittia is reached, though ordinarily it would take a day and a night to cross the sea. There the boats are invisibly unladen, and although no one has been seen, a loud voice is heard asking each soul his name and country.[31] The Roman poet Claudian, writing toward the close of the fourth and the beginning of the fifth century of our era, had perhaps heard such a story, though he confuses it with that of Odysseus and the shades.[32] At the extremity of the Gaulish coast is a place protected from the tides, where Odysseus by sacrifice called up the shades. There is heard the murmur of their complaint, and the inhabitants see pale phantoms and dead forms flitting about.[33] This strictly concerns the Homeric shades, for Classical testimony to the Celtic other-world, as well as Irish stories of the return of the dead, never suggests "pale phantoms." Claudian may have heard some story like that of Procopius, though it is by no means certain that the latter is reporting a Celtic belief for other peoples than the Celts dwelt in his time opposite Britain. Possibly, however, the Celts believed that the dead went to distant islands. Even now the Bretons speak of the "Bay of Souls" at Raz, at the extreme point of Armorica, while folk-lore tells how the drowned are nightly conveyed by boat from Cape Raz to the isle of Tevennec.[34] If the Celtic dead went to an island, this may explain the title said by Pliny, quoting Philemon (second century B. C.), to have been given by the Cimbri to the northern sea, *Morimarusam = Mortuum Mare* or possibly *Mortuorum Mare* ("Sea of the Dead") — the sea which the dead crossed. The title may refer, however, to an unchangeably calm sea, and such a sea has always been feared, or to the ice-covered sea, which Strabo [35] regarded as an impassable spongy mixture of earth, water, and air. The supposed Celtic belief in an island of the dead might also explain why, according to Pliny, no animal or man beside the Gallic ocean dies with a rising tide [36] — a belief still current in Brittany; the dead could be carried away only by an outflowing tide. But whether or not the Celts believed in such an island, it is certain that no Irish story of the island Elysium connects that with them, but associates it only with divine beings and favoured mortals who were lured thither in their lifetime.

In Wales and Ireland, where Roman civilization was unknown, mythology had a better chance of survival. Yet here, as in Gaul, it was forced to contend with triumphant Christianity, which was generally hostile to paganism. Still, curiously enough, Christian verity was less destructive of Celtic myths than was Roman civilization, unless the Insular Celts were more tenacious of myth than their Continental cousins. Sooner or later the surviving myths, more often fragments than finished entities, were written down; the bards and the *filid* (learned poets) took pride in preserving the glories of their race; and even learned Christian monks must have assisted in keeping the old stories alive. Three factors, however, played their part in corrupting and disintegrating the myths. The first of these was the dislike of Christianity to transmit whatever directly preserved the memory of the old divinities. In the surviving stories their divinity is not too closely descried; they are made as human as possible, though they are still superhuman in power and deed; they are tolerated as a kind of fairy-folk rather than as gods. Yet they are more than fairies and they have none of the wretchedness of the decrepit, skin-clad Zeus of Heine's *Gods in Exile*. Side by side with this there was another tendency, natural to a people who no longer worshipped gods whose names were still more or less familiar. They were regarded as kings and chiefs and were brought into a genealogical scheme, while some myths were reduced to annals of supposititious events. Myth was transmuted into pseudo-history. This euhemerizing [37] process is found in all decaying mythologies, but it is outstanding in that of the ancient Irish. The third factor is the attempt of Christian scribes to connect the mythical past and its characters with persons and events of early Scriptural history.

These factors have obscured Irish divine legends, though enough remains to show how rich and beautiful the mythology had been. In the two heroic cycles — those of Cúchulainn and Fionn respectively — the disturbance has been less, and in these the Celtic magic and glamour are found. Some stories of the gods escaped these destructive factors, and in them these delectable traits are also apparent. They are romantic tales rather than myths, though their mythical quality is obvious.

Two mythical strata exist, one older and purely pagan, in which gods are immortal, though myth may occasionally have spoken of their death; the other influenced by the annalistic scheme and also by Christianity, in which, though the unlikeness of the gods to humankind is emphasized, yet they may be overcome and killed by men. The literary class who rewrote the myths had less simple ideals than even the Greek mythographers. They imagined some moving situations and majestic episodes or borrowed these from the old myths, but they had little sense of proportion and were infected by a vicious rhetorical verbosity and exaggeration. Many tales revel monotonously in war and bloodshed, and the characters are spoiled by excessive boastfulness. Yet in this later stratum the mythopœic faculty is still at work, inasmuch as tales were written in which heroes were brought into relation with the old divinities.

The main sources for the study of Irish mythology are the documents contained in such great manuscripts as the *Book of Leinster* and the *Book of the Dun Cow (Leabhar na hUidhre)*,[38] written in the eleventh and twelfth centuries, but based on materials of older date. Later manuscripts also contain important stories. Floating tales and traditions, fairy- and folklore, are also valuable, and much of this material has now been published.[39]

Among the British Celts, or those of them who escaped the influence of Roman civilization, the mythological remains are far less copious. Here, too, the euhemerizing process has been at work, but much more has the element of romance affected the old myths. They have become romantic tales arranged, as in the *Mabinogion*, in definite groups, and the *dramatis personae* are the ancient gods, though it is difficult to say whether the incidents are myths transformed or are fresh romantic inventions of a mythic kind. Still, the Welsh *Mabinogion* is of great importance, as well as some parts of Arthurian romance, the poems about Taliesin, and other fragments of Welsh literature. The euhemerizing process is still more evident in those portions of Geoffrey of Monmouth's *History* which tell of the names and deeds of kings who were once gods.

Thus if materials for Irish and British mythology are copious, they must be used with caution, for we cannot be certain that any one story, however old, ever existed as such in the form of a pagan myth. As the mountain-peaks of Ireland or Wales or the Western Isles are often seen dimly through an enshrouding mist, which now is dispersed in torn wisps, and now gathers again, lending a more fantastic appearance to the shattered crags, so the gods and their doings are half-recorded and half-hidden behind the mists of time and false history and romance. Clear glimpses through this Celtic mist are rare. This is not to be wondered at when we consider how much of the mythology has been long forgotten, and how many hands have worked upon the remainder. The stories are relics of a dead past, as defaced and inexplicable as the battered monuments of the old religion. Romancers, would-be historians, Christian opponents of paganism, biographers of saints, ignorant yet half-believing folk, have worked their will with them. Folk-tale incidents have been wrought into the fabric, perhaps were originally part of it. Gods figure as kings, heroes, saints, or fairies, and a new mythical past has been created out of the *débris* of an older mythology. There is little of the limpid clearness of the myths of Hellas, and yet enough to delight those who, in our turbulent modern life, turn a wistful eye upon the past.

To make matters worse, modern writers on Celtic tradition have displayed a twofold tendency. They have resolved every story into myths of sun, dawn, and darkness, every divinity or hero into a sun-god or dawn-goddess or ruler of a dark world. Or those with a touch of mysticism see traces of an esoteric faith, of mysteries performed among the initiate. In mediaeval Wales the "Druidic legend" — the idea of an esoteric wisdom transmitted from old priests and philosophers — formed itself among half-crazy enthusiasts and has been revived in our own time by persons of a similar *genus*. Ireland and the West Highlands have always been remarkably free of this nonsense, though some Celts with a turn for agreeing with their interlocutor seem to have persuaded at least one mystic that he was on the track of esoteric beliefs and ritual there.[40] He did not know his Celt! The truth is that the mediaeval and later Welsh Druidists were themselves in the mythopœic stage — crude Blakes or Swedenborgs — and invented stories of the creed of the old Druids which had no place in it and are lacking in any document of genuine antiquity, Welsh or Irish. This is true

PLATE IV

GOD WITH THE WHEEL

This deity, who carries S-symbols as well as the wheel, was probably a solar divinity (see p. 8; for the wheel as a symbol cf. Plate II, 1, 3, and for the S-symbol Plates II, 2, 4, 7–9, 11, III, 3, XIX, 2–5). The statue was found at Chatelet, Haute-Marne, France.

also of the modern "mythological" school. Not satisfied with
the beautiful or wild stories as they stand, they must mytholo-
gize them still further. Hence they have invented a pretty but
ineffectual mythology of their own, which they foist upon our
Celtic forefathers, who would have been mightily surprised to
hear of it. The Celts had clearly defined divinities of war, of
agriculture, of the chase, of poetry, of the other-world, and they
told romantic myths about them. But they did not make all
their goddesses dawn-maidens, or transform every hero into a
sun-god, or his twelve battles into the months of the solar year.
Nor is it likely that they had mystic theories of rebirth, if that
was a wide-spread Celtic belief; and existing examples of it
always concern gods and heroes, not mere mortals. They are
straightforward enough and show no esoteric mystic origin or
tendency, any more than do similar myths among savages, nor
do they set forth philosophic theories of retribution, such as were
evolved by Pythagorean and Indian philosophy. Modern inves-
tigators, themselves in the mythopœic stage, easily reflect back
their ideas upon old Celtic tales. Just as little had the Celts an
esoteric monotheism or a secret mystery-cult; and such genuine notices of their ancient religion or its priests as have reached
us know nothing of these things, which have been assumed to
exist by enthusiasts during the last two centuries.

CELTIC MYTHOLOGY

CHAPTER I

THE STRIFE OF THE GODS

THE annalistic account of the groups of people who successively came to Ireland, some to perish utterly, others to remain as colonists, represents the unscientific historian's attempt to explain the different races existing there in his time, or of whom tradition spoke. He wrote, too, with an eye upon Biblical story, and connected the descendants of the patriarchs with the folk of Ireland. Three different groups of Noah's lineage arrived in successive waves. The first of these, headed by Noah's granddaughter, Cessair, perished, with the exception of her husband. Then came the Fomorians, descendants of Ham; and finally the Nemedians, also of the stock of Noah, arrived. According to one tradition, they, like Cessair's people and another group unconnected with Noah — the race of Partholan (Bartholomew) — died to a man, although another legend says that they returned to Spain, whence they had come. Spain figures frequently in these annalistic stories, and a close connexion between it and Ireland is taken for granted. This may be a reminiscence of a link by way of trade between the two countries in prehistoric days, of which, indeed, archaeology presents some proof. Possibly, too, early Celtic colonists reached Ireland directly from Spain, rather than through Gaul and Britain. Still another tradition makes Nemedian survivors wander over the world, some of their descendants becoming the Britons, while others returned to Ireland as a new colonizing group — Firbolgs, Fir-Domnann, and Galioin. A third group of their descendants who had learned magic came to Ireland — the

Tuatha Dé Danann. Finally the Milesians, the ancestors of the Irish, arrived and conquered the Tuatha Dé Danann, as these had defeated the Fomorians.[1]

Little of this is actual history, but how much of it is invention, and how much is based on mythic traditions floating down from the past, is uncertain. What is certain is that the annalists, partly as a result of the euhemerizing process, partly through misunderstanding, mingled groups of gods with tribes or races of men and regarded them as more or less human. These various traditions are introductory to the story of the two battles of Mag-Tured, enlarged from an earlier tale of a single conflict. An interval of twenty-seven years elapsed between the two battles, and they were fought in different parts of Ireland bearing the same name, one in Mayo and the other in Sligo, the first battle being fought against the Firbolgs, and the second against the Fomorians, by the Tuatha Dé Danann.

Having reached Ireland, the Tuatha Dé Danann established themselves at Mag-Rein in Connaught. The Firbolgs sent a huge warrior, Sreng, to parley with them, and to him approached Bres, son of Elatha, of the Tuatha Dé Danann. The warriors gazed long upon each other; then they mutually admired their weapons, and finally exchanged them, Bres receiving the heavy, broad-pointed spears of the Firbolg, and Sreng the light, sharp-pointed lances of Bres. The demand of the invaders was surrender of the half of Ireland, but to this the Firbolgs would not agree. Meanwhile the Tuatha Dé Danann, terrified at the heavy Firbolg spears, retreated to Mag-Tured, Badb, Morrígan, and Macha, three of their women, producing frogs, rain of fire, and streams of blood against the Firbolgs. By mutual agreement an armistice was arranged for preparation, and some from each side even engaged in a hurling match. Such were the tactics of the time! Each party prepared a healing well for the wounded, in which medicinal herbs were placed. Dagda led the forces on the first day, when the Tuatha Dé Danann were defeated; but under the command of Ogma,

Midir, Bodb Dearg, Diancecht, Aengaba of Norway, Badb, Macha, Morrígan, and Danann, they were successful on the second day. On the third day Dagda again led, "for in me you have an excellent god"; on the fourth day *badba*, *bledlochtana*, and *amaite aidgill* ("furies," "monsters," "hags of doom") cried aloud, and their voices resounded in the rocks, waterfalls, and hollows of the earth. Sreng severed the arm of Nuada, king of the Tuatha Dé Danann; Bres was slain by Eochaid, who, overpowered by thirst, sought water throughout Ireland, but the wizards of the Tuatha Dé Danann hid all streams from him, and he was slain. The Firbolgs, reduced to three hundred, were still prepared to fight, but when the Tuatha Dé Danann offered them peace and the province of Connaught, this was accepted.[2]

As we shall see, the Tuatha Dé Danann were gods, and their strife against the Firbolgs, a non-Celtic group, is probably based on a tradition of war between incoming Celts and aborigines. Meanwhile the Tuatha Dé Danann made alliance with the Fomorians. Ethne, daughter of Balor, married Cian, son of Diancecht, her son being the famous Lug. Nuada's mutilation prevented his continuing as King, for no maimed person could reign; and the women insisted that the Fomorian Bres, their adopted son, should receive the throne, since he was son of Elatha, the Fomorian King. Eri, sister of Elatha, was counted of the Tuatha Dé Danann, perhaps because their mother was also of them, an instance of succession through the female line; and this would account for Bres becoming King, though these genealogies are doubtless inventions of the annalists. Bres was son of Elatha and Eri. Such unions of brother and sister (or half-sister) are common in mythology and were not unknown in royal houses, e. g. in Egypt and Peru, as a means of keeping the dynasty pure. One day Eri saw a silver boat approaching. A noble warrior with golden locks stepped ashore, clad in an embroidered mantle and wearing a jewelled golden brooch, and five golden torques round his neck. He carried two silvery pointed spears with bronze shafts, and a golden-hilted sword inlaid with silver. Eri was so overcome by his appearance that she easily surrendered to him and wept bitterly when he rose to leave her. Then he drew from his finger a golden ring and bade her not part with it save to one whose finger it should fit. Elatha was his name, and she would bear a son Eochaid Bres, or "the Beautiful." At seven years old Bres was as a boy of fourteen.[3]

Bres was miserly and caused much murmuring among the Tuatha Dé Danann. "Their knives were not greased by him; and however often they visited him their breaths did not smell of ale." No poets, bards, or musicians were in his household, and no champions proved their prowess, save Ogma, who had the slavish daily task of carrying a load of fuel, two-thirds of which were swept from him by the sea, because he was weak through hunger.[4] Bres claimed the milk of all brown, hairless cows, and when these proved to be few in number, he caused the kine of Munster to pass through a fire of bracken so that they might become hairless and brown,[5] this tale being possibly connected with the ritual passing of cattle through fires at Beltane (May-Day). Another version of the tale, however, makes it less pleasant for Bres. He demanded a hundred men's drink from the milk of a hornless dun cow or a cow of some other colour from every house in Ireland; but by the advice of Lug and Findgoll, Nechtan, King of Munster, singed the kine in a fire of fern and smeared them with a porridge of flax-seed. Three hundred wooden cows with dark brown pails in lieu of udders were made, and the pails were dipped in black bog-stuff. When Bres inspected them, the bog-stuff was squeezed out like milk; but since he was under *geis*, or tabu, to drink whatever was milked, the result of his swallowing so much bog-stuff was a gradual wasting away, until he died when traversing Ireland to seek a cure. Stokes conjectures that Bres required the milk of one-coloured cows as a means of removing his wife's barrenness.[6]

Another account of Bres's death tells how Corpre the poet came to his house. It was narrow, dark, and fireless, and for food the guest received only three small unbuttered cakes. Next morning, filled with a poet's scorn, he chanted a satire:

"Without food quickly on a dish,
Without a cow's milk whereon a calf grows,
Without a man's abode under the gloom of night,
Without paying a company of story-tellers,
Let that be the condition of Bres."

This was the first satire made in Ireland, but it had all the effect which later belief attributed to satire, and Bres declined from that hour. Surrendering his sovereignty and going to his mother, he asked whence was his origin; and when she tried the ring on his finger, she found that it fitted him. Bres and she then went to the Fomorians' land, where his father recognized the ring and upbraided Bres for leaving the kingdom. Bres acknowledged the injustice of his rule, but asked his father's help, whereupon Elatha sent him to Balor, grandson of Nét, the Fomorian war-god, and to Indech, who assembled a huge force in order to impose their rule on the Tuatha Dé Danann.[7]

Some curious incidents may be mentioned here. While Bres ruled, the Fomorian Kings, Indech, Elatha, and Tethra, bound tribute on Ireland and reduced some of the Tuatha Dé Danann to servitude. The Fomorians had formerly exacted tribute of the Nemedians, and it was collected by one of their women in an iron vessel — fifty fills of corn and milk, of butter, and of flour. This may be a memory of sacrifice. Ogma had to carry fuel, and even Dagda was obliged to become a builder of *raths*, or forts. In the house where he lived was a lampooner named Cridenbél who demanded from him the three best bits of his ration, and thus Dagda's health suffered; but Oengus, Dagda's son, hearing of this, gave him three gold coins to put into Cridenbél's portion. These would cause his death, and Bres would be told that Dagda had poisoned him. Then he must tell the story to Bres, who would cause the lampooner's stomach to be opened; and if the gold were not found there, Dagda would have to die. In the sequel Oengus advised Dagda to ask as reward for his *rath*-building only a black-maned heifer; and although this seemed weakness to Bres, the astuteness of Oengus was seen when, after the second battle, the heifer's lowing brought to Dagda the cattle exacted by the Fomorians.[8]

This mythical story of Bres's sovereignty, and of the servitude of beings who are gods, is probably parallel to other myths of the temporary eclipse of deities, as when the Babylonian high gods were afraid of Tiāmat and her brood, or cowered in terror before the flood. It may also represent an old nature dualism — the apparent paralysis of gods of sunshine and fruitfulness in the death and cold of winter; or it may hint at some temporary defeat of Celtic invaders, which even their gods seemed to share. Whatever the Fomorians be, their final defeat was at hand.

When Bres retired, Nuada was again made King because his hand was restored. Diancecht (a divinity of leechcraft), assisted by Creidne, god of smith-work, made for him a silver hand, but Miach, Diancecht's son, not content with this, obtained the mutilated hand and by means of such a spell as is common to many races — "joint to joint, sinew to sinew" — he set it to the stump, caused skin to grow, and restored the hand. In another version he made a new arm with a swineherd's arm-bone.[9] Through envy Diancecht struck Miach four blows, three of which Miach healed, but the fourth was fatal. His father buried him, and from his grave sprang as many herbs as he had joints and sinews. Airmed, his sister, separated them according to their properties, but Diancecht confused them so that none might know their right values.[10] These incidents reflect beliefs about magico-medical skill, and the last may be a myth of divine jealousy at man's obtaining knowledge. Nuada now made a feast for the gods, and as they banqueted, a warrior, coming to the portal, bade the doorkeepers announce him as Lug, son of Cian, son of Diancecht, and of Ethne, Balor's daughter. He was also known as *samil-dánach* ("possessing many arts"), and when asked what he practised, he answered that he was a carpenter, only to hear the door-keeper reply, "Already we have a carpenter." In succession he declared himself smith, champion, harper, hero, poet, magician, leech, cup-bearer, and brazier, but the Tuatha Dé Danann possessed each one of these. Lug, however, because he knew all these arts, gained entrance and among other feats played the three magic harp-strains so often referred to in Irish texts — sleep-strain, wail-strain, and laughter-strain, which in turn caused slumber, mourning, and joy.[11]

In another version of Lug's coming, from *The Children of Tuirenn* (*Aided Chlainne Tuirenn*), as he approached, "like the setting sun was the splendour of his countenance," and none could gaze on it. His army was the fairy cavalcade from the Land of Promise,[12] and with them were his foster-brothers, Manannan's sons. Lug rode Manannan's steed, Enbarr, fleet as the spring wind, and on whose back no rider could be killed; he wore Manannan's *lorica* which preserved from wounds, his breastplate which no weapon could pierce, and his sword, the wound of which none survived, while the strength of all who faced it became weakness. When the Fomorians came for tribute, Lug killed some of them, whereupon Balor's wife, Céthlionn, told him that this was their grandson and that it had been prophesied that when he arrived, the power of the Fomorians would depart. As Lug went to meet the Fomorians, Bres was surprised that the sun seemed rising in the west, but his Druids said that this was the radiance from the face of Lug, who cast a spell on the cattle taken for tribute, so that they returned to the Tuatha Dé Danann. When his fairy cavalcade arrived, Bres begged his life on condition of bringing over the Fomorians, while he offered sun, moon, sea, and land as guarantees that he would not again fight; and to this Lug agreed. The guarantee points to an animistic view of nature, for it means that sun, etc., would punish Bres if he was unfaithful.[13]

To return to the other account, Nuada gave Lug his throne, and for a year the gods remained in council, consulting the wizards, leeches, and smiths. Mathgen the wizard announced that the mountains would aid them and that he would cast them on the Fomorians; the cup-bearer said that through his power the Fomorians would find no water in lough or river; Figol the Druid promised to rain showers of fire on the foe and to remove from them two-thirds of their might, while increase of strength would come to the Tuatha Dé Danann, who would not be weary if they fought seven years; Dagda said that he would do more than all the others together. For seven years weapons were prepared under the charge of Lug.[14]

At this point comes the episode of Dagda's assignation with the war-goddess Morrígan, who was washing in a river, one foot at Echumech in the north, the other at Loscuinn in the south. This enormous size is a token of divinity in Celtic myths, and the place where Dagda and Morrígan met was now known as "the couple's bed." She bade him summon the men of knowledge and to them she gave two handfuls of the blood of Indech's heart, of which she had deprived him, as well as valour from his kidneys. These men now chanted spells against the Fomorians — a practice invariably preceding battle among the Celts.[15]

Another incident shows that the Celts, like other races, could recount irreverent stories about their gods. Dagda had been sent to spy out the Fomorians' camp and to ask a truce. Much porridge was made for him, boiled with goats, sheep, and swine, and the mess being poured into a hole in the ground, he was bidden to eat it under pain of death. Taking a ladle big enough for a man and woman to lie in, he began his meal and ate it all, after which sleep overcame him, and the Fomorians mocked his distended paunch. When he rose, uneasy was his movement, but he bravely bore his huge branched fork or club, dragging it till its track was like a boundary-ditch, so that men call that "the track of Dagda's club." An obscene story follows regarding his amour with Indech's daughter, who agreed to practise magic against her father's army.[16]

Before the battle each chief promised Lug prodigies of valour, craftsmanship, or magic — weapons, and armour in unfailing abundance, enfeeblement and destruction of the enemy, the power of satire upon them, magical healing of wounded or slain. Lug's two witches said, "We will enchant the trees and the stones and the sods of the earth so that they shall become a host under arms against the foe"; but Lug was prevented from going to the fray, because "they feared an early death for the hero owing to the multitude of his arts." Preliminary combats occurred in which the superior magic of the Tuatha Dé Danann was apparent. Weapons were restored or new ones made in a twinkling by Goibniu, Luchtine, and Creidne. Goibniu (cf. Old Irish *goba*, "smith") had promised that though the battle lasted seven years, he would replace every broken sword or spear-head; no spear-head forged by him would miss, and none whom it pierced would continue in life. He kept his promise, making weapons by three turns in his forge, and renewed the blunted or broken instruments of war. Elsewhere we learn that Goibniu's immortal ale, like nectar and soma, made the divinities immortal,[17] so that he is the equivalent of the Greek Hephaistos, god of craftsmen, who poured out nectar for the gods at their banquet, and of the Vedic deity Tvaṣṭṛ, who made the cup from which the gods drank.[18] Why divine smiths should be associated with the drink of the gods is not clear, but probably we have here different forms of a myth common to the Indo-European peoples. Goibniu is still remembered in Irish folk-tales.

Creidne, the *cerd*, or brazier, promised to supply rivets for the spears, hilts for the swords, and bosses and rims for the shields; he made the rivets in three turns and cast the rings to them. Creidne, whom euhemerizing tradition described as having been drowned while bringing golden ore from Spain to Ireland, may be compared with Lén Linfiaclach, *cerd* of the god Bodb, who lived in Loch Léin, making the bright vessels of Fand, daughter of Flidais. Every evening he threw his anvil eastward as far as a grave-mound at Indeóin na nDése and it in turn cast three showers toward the grave, of water, of fire, and of purple gems.[19]

Luchta the carpenter (*saer*) promised to supply all the shields and javelin-shafts required for the battle. These shafts he made with three chippings, the third completing them and setting them in the rings of the spears, or he threw them with marvellous accuracy at the sockets of the spear-heads stuck by Goibniu in the door-lintels, this being precisely paralleled by the art of Caoilte, the survivor of the Féinn.[20]

The mortally wounded were placed in a well over which Diancecht and his children sang spells, or into which he put healing herbs; and thus they became whole.[21] The Fomorians sent Ruadan, son of Bres and of Brig, daughter of Dagda, to discover the reason of these things; and a second time he was sent to kill one of the divine craftsmen. He obtained one of the magic spears and wounded Goibniu, who slew Ruadan and then entered the healing well, while Brig bewailed her son with the first death-keen heard in Ireland. Here, as so often, the origin of mourning chants and runes is ascribed to divinities.[22]

Before the battle Lug escaped from his guards and heartened the host by circumambulating them on one foot with one eye closed, chanting a spell for their protection — the attitude of the savage medicine-man, probably signifying concentration. Then came the clash of battle, "gory, shivering, crowded, sanguineous, the river ran in corpses of foes." Nuada and Macha were slain by Balor, who possessed an evil eye, or was a personification of the evil eye, so much feared by the Celts. Once when his father's Druids were concocting magic potions, the fumes gave his eye poisonous power, and his eyelid was raised by four men, but only on the battle-field, where no army could resist it. When Lug appeared, Balor desired it to be lifted, but Lug cast a stone at the eye, so that it was carried through his head, blasting some of his own men.[23] In a ballad account of this, Balor was beheaded by Lug, but asked him to set the head upon his own and earn his blessing. Fortunately for himself, however, Lug set it on a hazel, and it dropped poison which split the hazel in two. The tree became the abode of vultures and ravens for many years, until Manannan caused it to be dug up, when a poisonous vapour from its roots killed and wounded many of the workmen. Of the wood Luchta made a shield for Manannan, which became one of the famous shields of Erin. It could not be touched in battle and it always caused utter rout. Finally it became Fionn's shield.[24]

The war-goddess Morrígan sang a magic rune to hearten the host, and the battle became a rout for the Fomorians, though not before Ogma and Indech had fallen in single combat. Bres was found unguarded by Lug and others, and made three offers for his life; but two of these — that Ireland's kine should always be in milk, and that corn would be reaped every quarter — were rejected. Life was offered him, however, if he would tell how the men of Erin should plough, sow, and reap; and when Bres said that these things should always be done on a Tuesday, he was set free.[25] In another account four Fomorians escaped, ruining corn, milk, fruit, and sea produce; but on November Eve (Samhain) they were expelled by Bodb, Midir, Oengus, and the Morrígan, so that never more should their depredations occur.[26] This points to the conception of the Fomorians as powers of blight; that of Bres suggests rather that they were pre-Celtic gods of fertility.

Two curious incidents, revealing the magic powers of weapons, which were worshipped by the Celts, and of musical instruments, occur here. Ogma captured the sword of the war-god Tethra, and when unsheathed it told the deeds it had done, as was the custom with swords in those days, for, as the Christian compiler adds, "the reason why demons spake from weapons was because weapons were then worshipped and acted as safe-guards." The other incident tells how Dagda's harp was carried off and was found by Lug, Ogma, and Dagda in the house where Bres and his friends were. No melody would sound from it until Dagda uttered a charm; but then the harp came to him, killing nine men on its way, after which he played the three magic strains of sleep, mourning, and laughter.[27] This harp resembles that of Teirtu in the Welsh tale of *Kulhwch and Olwen*, which played or stopped playing of itself when so desired.[28]

Thus the Tuatha Dé Danann conquered, and the Morrígan proclaimed the victory to the royal heights of Ireland, its hosts of the *síde*, its chief waters, and its river-mouths — a reminiscence of the animistic view or the personalization of nature. Then she sang of the world's end and of the evils to come — one of the few eschatological references in Irish mythology, though it is most likely of Christian origin.[29]

This curious story is undoubtedly based on old myths of divine wars, but what these denoted is uncertain. Both Tuatha Dé Danann and Fomorians are superhuman. Vaguely we discern behind the legend a strife of anthropomorphic figures of summer, light, growth, and order, with powers of winter, darkness, blight, and disorder. Such powers agree but ill. There is strife between them, as, to the untutored eye, there is strife in the parts of nature for which they stand; and this apparent dualism is reflected on the life of the beings who represent the powers of nature. All mythologies echo the strife. The Babylonian Marduk and the gods battle with Tiāmat and her brood; gods and Titans (or Jötuns), Rê' and 'Apop, fight, and those hostile to gods of light and growth, gods dear to man's heart, are represented in demoniac guise. If Tuatha Dé Danann and Fomorians were both divine but hostile groups of the Irish Celts, the sinister character of the latter would not be forgotten by the annalists, who regarded both with puzzled eyes and sought vainly to envisage them as mortals. Or, again, the two may be hostile sets of deities, because divinities respectively of Celts and aborigines. The Fomorians are, in fact, called gods of the menial Firbolgs, who are undoubtedly an aboriginal race, while Fomorians are described in later Christian times as ungracious and demoniac, unlike the Tuatha Dé Danann; and the pagan Celts must already have regarded them as evil. The gods of a conquering race are often regarded as hostile to those of the aborigines, and *vice versa*, and now new myths arise. In either case the close relationship in which the groups stand by marriage or descent need not be an invention of the compiler. Pagan mythology is inconsistent, and compromise is inevitable. Conquerors and conquered tend to coalesce, and this is true of their gods; or, as different tribes of one race now intermarry, now fight, so also may their evil and their friendly divinities. Zeus was son of the Titan Kronos, yet hostile to him. Vile, Ve, and Odin, father of the gods, were sons of a giant, and the gods fought with giants. Other parallels might be cited; but what is certain is that gods of an orderly world — of growth, craftsmanship, medicine, poetry, and eloquence, if also of magic and war — are opposed to beings envisaged, on the whole, as harmful. In this combat some of the gods are slain. If this were told of them in the old myths, probably it did not affect the continuance of their cult. Pagan gods are mortal and immortal; their life is a perennial drama, which ever begins and ends, and is ever being renewed — a reflexion of the life of nature itself.

In another story the strife of powers of light and growth with those of darkness and blight is suggested, though the latter are euhemeristically described as mortals. Three men came from Athens with their mother Carman—Valiant, Black, and Evil, sons of Extinction, who was son of Darkness, and he son of Ailment. By her incantations Carman ruined every place where she came, while her sons destroyed through plundering and dishonesty. They came to Ireland to blight the corn of the Tuatha Dé Danann, who sent against them Ai, a poet, Cridenbél the lampooner, Lugh Laebach, a wizard, and Béchuille, a witch, some of whom have already played a part in the story of Mag-Tured. By spells they drove the men oversea, but not until they gave the Seven Things which they served as security that they would not return, and left their mother as a hostage. She died of grief, begging the gods to hold an annual festival at her burial-place and to call it by her name; and as long as they kept it the Leinstermen were promised plenty of corn, fruit, milk, and fish.[30] No explanation is given as to what the mysterious " Seven Things " were.

In other tales groups of gods are seen at strife with each other and in their conflict they were sometimes not too mighty to seek the help of heroes. An example of this occurs in the story of Cúchulainn's visit to Elysium. In spite of the prowess of the god Labraid, sung by the goddesses Fand and Liban, the time has come when he must give battle to supernatural foes — Senach the Unearthly, Eochaid, Eol, and Eogan the Stream, the last mentioned in the *Book of Invasions* (*Leabhar Gabála*) as hostile to the Tuatha Dé Danann.[31] These were united, apparently, with Manannan, whose consort Fand, Labraid's sister, had left him.[32] Labraid was afraid, for the contest would be of doubtful issue. Glad indeed would he be of the hero Cúchulainn's aid, and for that assistance he was willing to give him his sister Fand. When Cúchulainn arrived in the gods' domain and was welcomed by Labraid, they gazed on the vast armies of the foe, while two ravens, skilled in Druidic secrets, announced the hero's presence to the hosts. Next morning Eochaid went to wash at a stream, when Cúchulainn slew him; and a great fight followed between Cúchulainn and Senach, who also was slain. Cúchulainn then put forth all his might, and so great was the carnage that Labraid himself entreated him to end it; and then Labraid sang:

"A mighty host, with multitudes of horses,
　　Attacked me on every side;
　　They were the people of Manannan, son of the sea,
　　Whom Eogan had called to his aid."

Another instance occurs in the story of Loegaire, son of the King of Connaught. The people of Connaught were met in assembly near the Loch of the Birds in the plain of Ai, when a stranger approached them through the mist which rose from the lake. He wore a purple cloak, and his yellow hair fell upon his shoulders. A golden-hilted sword hung at his side; in his right hand he carried a five-pointed spear, and on his left arm a shield with a golden boss. Loegaire welcomed him, and he told how he had come from the gods' land to seek the aid of warriors. Fiachna was his name, and he had slain his wife's ravisher, but had been attacked by his nephew, Goll, son of the king of the fort of Mag Mell, and in seven battles had been vanquished, so that in view of a new conflict he had come for succour. He sang of the beauty of the land and of the bloody combats fought there among the people of majestic race, and how silver and gold awaited those who would help him. Beautiful were the divine warriors, with blue eyes of powerful sight, teeth brilliant as glass, and red lips. Mighty in conflict, in their assemblies they sang in melodious verse of learned matters.[33] Fiachna disappeared into the lake, and now Loegaire appealed to his men. Fifty warriors plunged with him into the water and in the divine land under the loch joined Fiachna against his foe, besieging the fort of Mag Mell, where his wife was a prisoner. The defenders released her, and she followed the vanquishers, singing of her love for Goll. Fiachna gave his daughter, Sun Tear, to Loegaire, and each of his men also received a wife. For a year they remained in the divine land, until they became home-sick; and as they left him Fiachna bade them mount on horseback and not alight on the earth if they wished to return to him. The people of Connaught rejoiced to see them again, for sorely had they mourned them, but now Loegaire announced their return to the gods' land, nor would he remain, although his father offered him the kingdom, its gold, and its women. The unmoved son sang of the divine land, where beer fell in showers, and every army was of a hundred thousand warriors, while as one went from kingdom to kingdom, the melodious music of the gods was heard. He told of his goddess wife and those of his comrades and of the cauldrons and drinking-horns taken from the fort; for one night of the nights of the *sid* he would not accept his father's kingdom. With these words he quitted the king for ever and returned to Mag Mell, there to share the sovereignty with Fiachna — a noble divine reward to a mortal.[34] In the heroic cycle of Fionn other instances of heroes helping gods will be found.

War between different divine groups is also found in the story of Caibell and Etar, Kings of the *side* (divine or fairy-folk), each of whom had a beautiful daughter. Two Kings who sought the maidens in marriage were offered battle for them. If, however, the combat was fought in the *sid*, the *sid* would be polluted — an idea contrary to that of these other instances of war in the gods' land; and if the *sid*-folk were seen among men, they would no longer be invisible at will. The fight, therefore, took place at night, lest there should be no distinction between them and men; and the *side* took the form of deer. So terrible was the struggle that four hillocks were made of the hoofs and antlers of the slain; and to quell it, water broke forth from a well and formed Loch Riach, into which if white sheep are cast every seventh year at the proper hour, they become crimson. Etar alone of the kings survived.[35]

The Christian scribes were puzzled over the Tuatha Dé Danann. The earliest reference to them says that because of their knowledge they were banished from heaven, arriving in Ireland in clouds and mists — the smoke of their burning ships, says an euhemerizing tradition. Eochaid ua Flainn, in the tenth century, calls them "phantoms" (*siabhra*) and asks whether they came from heaven or earth; were they demons or men. They were affiliated to Japhet, yet regarded as demons in the *Book of Invasions*. Another tradition makes them a branch of the descendants of Nemed who, after being in the Northern isles learning wizardry, returned to Ireland. The annalists treated them more or less as men; official Christianity more or less as demons; popular belief and romance as a kind of beautiful fairy race with much of their old divine aspect.

D'Arbois translates *Tuatha Dé Danann* as "people of the god whose mother is called Danu"; [36] Stokes renders it "folk or folks of the goddess Danu"; [37] Stern prefers to regard *Danann* as a later addition and to take the earlier name as *Tuatha Dé* or *Fir Dea* — "the divine tribe," or "the men of the god." [38] Three insignificant members of the group, Brian, Iuchar, and Iucharba, are sometimes called "three gods of Danu"; and hence also, perhaps, the whole group is designated "men of the three gods." Brian, Iuchar, and Iucharba are also termed *tri dée dána*, or "three gods of *dán*," i. e. "knowledge," or "fate." Danand (Danu) is mentioned with Béchuille as a separate goddess, and both are called foster-mothers of the gods. Cormac's *Glossary* knows nothing of Danu, but speaks of a goddess Anu, *mater deorum hibernensium* — "It was well she nursed the gods" — while he refers to two hills in Kerry as "the paps of Anu," which a later glossary calls "the paps of Danu." Ireland is called Iath n'Anann, and Anu is mentioned with Macha, Morrígan, and Badb, the war-goddesses, though other passages give Danu along with these. Possibly Danu is a mistake for Anu, through confusion with *dán*, "knowledge," knowledge as a function of Brian, Iuchar, and Iucharba being personified as Danu, so that they would then be called gods or sons of Danu, though they were actually sons of Brigit. As Stern points out, Danu can scarcely be mother of the whole group, since she herself is daughter of Delbaeth, who was brother of Dagda, Ogma, Bres, etc. If Anu was mother of the group, the likeness of her name to Danu would also lead to the mistake; and Anu as goddess is perhaps a personification of Ireland, a kind of earth mother. On the whole, the general relationship of the euhemerized gods evolved by the annalists is as mythical as the pagan stories themselves.

In the story of *The Children of Tuirenn* Brian, Iuchar, and Iucharba are sons of Tuirenn, son of Ogma. One day Cian, at enmity with them, saw them approaching. Striking himself with a Druidic wand, he became a pig, but Brian noticed this and changed himself and his brothers into hounds which chased and killed Cian with stones, because he said that weapons would tell the deed to his son. They buried his body seven times ere the earth ceased to reject it. Lug, Cian's son, was told of this deed by the earth, and he forced the children of Tuirenn to bring many magical treasures, in getting which danger was incurred. By their father's advice they crossed the sea in Manannan's canoe and succeeded in obtaining the treasures, but now had to give "three shouts on Cnoc Miodh-chaoin," a hill on which Miodhchaoin and his sons prohibited all shouting. Here, then, they were wounded by these men, and their father asked Lug for the magic pig's skin which healed all wounds. He refused it, even when Brian was carried before him, and thus the murderers perished miserably.[39]

Most of the names of the chief gods have already been mentioned — Dagda or Eochaid Ollathair, who in one place is called an "earth god" to the Tuatha Dé Danann, and also their "god of wizardry" — probably a deity of fruitfulness and fertility; Oengus; Nuada; Ogma, god of poetry; Goibniu, god of smiths; Creidne, of braziers; Diancecht, of medicine; Manannan, son of Ler; Midir; Bodb Dearg; Lug, perhaps a sun-god; and other lesser divinities. Of goddesses there are Anu or Danu; Brigit, goddess of poetry and primitive culture; Etain; and the war-goddesses — Morrígan, Macha, and Neman, while Badb constitutes a fourth or sometimes takes the place of one of the triple group. The Tuatha Dé Danann had power over agriculture and cattle, but they had other functions, while all of them had great magic potency. Unfortunately few myths about these functions exist, and their precise nature must be matter of conjecture. The mythico-magical nature of the gods' possessions survives even in records which regard them

PLATE V

Smertullos

This deity is perhaps a god of the underworld, particularly as the serpent is a chthonian creature. See p. 158. From an altar found at Notre Dame, Paris. For other Celtic deities of Elysium see Plates VII–IX, XII–XIV, XVI, XXV–XXVI.

as mortals. The preface to the story of the battle of Mag-Tured tells how from Falias was brought the stone of Fal, which roared under every king who would assume the sovereignty. From Gorias was brought Lug's spear; no battle was ever won against it or against him who bore it. From Findias came Nuada's sword, which none could escape when it was drawn. From Murias came Dagda's cauldron, from which no company ever went away unthankful.[40] Their magic food and other possessions will be mentioned later. Some things of which no myths remain are said to have been in the Brug na Boinne — the bed of Dagda, the two paps of Morrígan, the comb and casket of Dagda's wife (i. e. two hills), the stone wall of Oengus, the shot of Midir's eye, and the like.

CHAPTER II

TUATHA DÉ DANANN AND MILESIANS

THE annalistic account of the conquest of the Tuatha Dé Danann by the Milesians cannot conceal the divinity of the former nor the persistence of the belief in Druidic magic and supernatural power. M. d'Arbois has shown that the scheme which makes the Tuatha Dé Danann masters of Ireland for one hundred and sixty-nine years until the Milesians came is the invention of Gilla Coemain, who died in 1072. The *Book of Invasions* adopted it, and it assumes that the gods reigned in succession as kings until 1700 B. C. Even in Gilla Coemain's time, however, this scheme was not always accepted, for Tigernach in his *Annals* knows no *historic* Irish date before 305 B. C., while current tales showed that the gods were still alive at a much later date, e. g. in the time of Conchobar and Cúchulainn, alleged Irish contemporaries of Christ.[1]

When the Milesians arrived, three Kings of the Tuatha Dé Danann ruled — MacCuill ("Son of the Hazel"), MacCecht ("Son of the Plough"), and MacGréine ("Son of the Sun"), married respectively to Banba, Fotla, and Ériu, whose names are ancient names of Ireland, the last still surviving as "Erin." Were these old eponymous goddesses, from whom parts of Ireland were supposed to have taken their names, or were they inventions of the annalists, derived from titles given to the country? The former is suggested by an incident in the story. The three Kings may have been gods of nature and agriculture, and in fighting the Milesians they were respectively slain by Eber, Airem ("Ploughman"), and Amairgen, singer of spells and giver of judgements. The Milesians were descendants of a

Scythian noble expelled from Egypt, who came to Spain, where his descendant Bregon built a tower and was father or grandfather of Mile, whose father is sometimes called Bile. Another son, Ith, gazing one evening from the tower, saw the coast of Ireland. With ninety followers he sailed thither and was welcomed by the Kings, who begged him to settle a dispute. Very different was his fate from that of folk-tale heroes called in to adjust quarrels. While bidding the Kings act according to justice, he so praised the fertility of the land that they suspected him of designs upon it and slew him. His followers carried his body to Spain, and the chiefs of the Milesians, resolving to avenge him, sailed to Ireland, but the Tuatha Dé Danann made a magic mist, so that the island appeared like a hog's back — hence its name Muic-Inis, or "Pig Island." At last they landed, and the poet Amairgen, son of Mile, sang: —

> "I am a wind at sea,
> I am a wave of the sea,
> I am a roaring of the sea,
> I am an ox in strength,
> I am a bird of prey on a cliff,
> I am a ray of the sun,
> I am an intelligent navigator,
> I am a boar of fierceness,
> I am a lake on a plain,
> I am an effective artist,
> I am a giant with a sharp sword hewing down an army," etc.[2]

Some see in this a species of Celtic pantheism, but if so it is pantheism of a curious kind, for it is, rather, the vain-glorious bombast of the Celt, to which there are parallels in Welsh poems, where Taliesin speaks of the successive forms which he has assumed. The comparison should not be made with the pantheism of the Irishman Erigena, but with the bragging utterances of savage medicine-men.

The Milesians met in succession Banba, Fotla, and Ériu, each of whom asked that they would call the isle after her name. The Kings then begged an armistice, ostensibly to discuss the question of battle or capitulation, but really in order to give their Druids time to prepare incantations; while they agreed to accept the judgement of Amairgen, save that, if it were false, he must die. Amairgen then told the Milesians that they must embark for the magic distance of nine waves; and if they succeeded in returning, the land would be theirs. This was the first judgement ever given in Ireland. The Milesians now returned to their ships, but no sooner had they gained the desired distance than the Druids and poets of the gods raised a storm. Eber recognized it as a Druidic storm, which did not rage beyond the top of the masts; and Amairgen now invoked the aid of the natural features of Erin — an archaic animistic rune, embedded in the later story, and one which preserves a primitive stage of thought:

> "I invoke thee, Erin,
> Brilliant, brilliant sea,
> Fertile, fertile hill,
> Wood with valleys,
> Flowing, flowing stream," etc.

Now the storm ceased, and Eber joyfully boasted that he would strike the people of Erin with spear and sword; but that moment the tempest burst forth again, scattering and wrecking the ships, and drowning many. The survivors landed at the Boyne and gave battle to the Tuatha Dé Danann. The three queens are said to have created a magic army which was a delusion to the Milesians,[3] as Lug's witches had done to the Fomorians; but in spite of this the Tuatha Dé Danann were defeated.

> "We boldly gave battle
> To the sprites (*siabhra*) of the isle of Banba,
> Of which ten hundred fell together
> By us, of the Tuatha Dé Danann."

At another conflict a further rout took place, in which the three Kings and Queens were slain; and it was now that the survivors of the Tuatha Dé Danann took refuge in the underground *síd*, the Milesians remaining masters of Ireland.[4]

On whatever this account is based, it is not itself an ancient pagan myth, for gods worshipped by men are not defeated by them or by their supposititious ancestors. By the annalists, real races, imaginary races, and divine groups were regarded more or less from one standpoint; all were human and might be made to fight each other. Next came the question — How were the old gods abandoned, and why had they been, or were even now, supposed popularly to live in the *sid?* It was known that the Christianized tribes had forsaken the gods, though these had come to be regarded by them as a kind of fairy race living out of sight, to whom in time of need and *sub rosa* they might appeal. Obviously, then, Christianity must have caused their defeat. To this idea we may trace one source of the account just summarized. It is, in effect, what is said in the *Colloquy with the Ancients* (*Acallamh na Senórach*), in which, regardless of the annalistic scheme, the gods are powerful long after their supposed defeat. Caoilte, survivor of the Féinn into the days of St. Patrick, says that soon the Tuatha Dé Danann will be reduced in power, for the saint "will relegate them to the foreheads of hills and rocks, unless that now and again thou see some poor one of them appear as transiently he revisits the earth," i. e. the haunts of men.[5] Hence, perhaps, the *Colloquy* elsewhere represents them as possessing not so much land as will support themselves.[6] In St. Patrick's *Life* this victory is dramatically represented. He went to Mag Slecht, where stood an image of Cenn Crúaich ("Head of the Mound"), covered with gold and silver, and twelve others covered with bronze. The chief image bowed downward when he raised his crozier, and the earth swallowed the others, while their indwelling demons, cursed by the saint, fled to the hill.

Why, then, was the defeat ascribed to the Milesians? Of the different hostile Celtic groups dwelling in different parts of Ireland, two at last became pre-eminent shortly before St. Patrick's time, governed by great dynastic families and reigning respectively at Cashel and Tara. It was for their aggran-

dizement that the legend of descent from Mile and his ancestors was invented; but as the gods had come to be regarded as
a powerful race who had conquered earlier races in Ireland,
so it became necessary to show that the Milesians had overcome them. This pushed the Milesians back to remote antiquity and showed that they had been masters of Ireland since
1700 B.C., while the Tuatha Dé Danann, whose power had
passed at the coming of Christianity, were now alleged to have
been conquered by them. Thus the central theory of those
mediaeval reconstructors of Irish history was "that Ireland
had been subjected to the Milesian race for ages before the
Christian era." Later, the Ulster heroes were brought into
relationship with Mile, as at last were all the Irish aristocracy.[7]

Mile (Latin *miles*, "soldier") and Bile are men of straw
with no place in the older mythology, and hence the attempts
of Rhŷs and d'Arbois to equate Bile with Balor and with a
Celtic Dispater, as god of death and ancestor of the Celts, are
nothing but modern mythologizing. The account of the conquest doubtless made use of earlier conceptions of supernatural
power and magic, while still apt to consider the Tuatha Dé
Danann as somehow different from men (*siabhra*, "sprites"),
this being the popular view and also current in literary tales
embodying older myths. The gods were a superhuman race,
the *side*, helping men on occasion; and this influenced the
official view, for euhemeristic documents tell how, after their
defeat, the Tuatha Dé Danann retired to subterranean palaces, emerging now and then to help or to harm mortals. Even
the Milesians were not yet free of their power, especially that
of Dagda. Their corn and milk were being destroyed by the
Tuatha Dé Danann, and to prevent this in future they made
friends with Dagda, so that now these things were spared to
them.[8] This story seems to be the late form of the earlier
mythic idea that corn and milk depend on the gods, who, when
offended by men, withhold these gifts. They were also obtained
by sacrifice, e. g. by offerings of children and animal firstlings

to Cenn Crúaich;[9] and elsewhere we find that the Fomorians exacted two-thirds of their corn and milk annually from the Nemedians.[10] Perhaps there is here a mingling of the idea of destruction by gods of blight with that of the withholding of such gifts and with that of the offering of these things. A survival of such sacrifices occurs in the food and milk left out for the fairies in Ireland and in the West Highlands.

The functions of some of the divinities as controllers of fertility are suggested by references of this character, as well as by the symbols on Gaulish monuments; and some folk-lore collected by Mr. D. Fitzgerald in Limerick shows how the memory of these functions vaguely persisted under a romantic dress. Cnoc Aine (*Knockainy*, or "Aine's Hill") has always been considered the dwelling of Aine, queen of the fairies of South Munster and daughter of Eogabal, of the Tuatha Dé Danann. Aine, "the best-hearted woman that ever lived," is still seen in Loch Guirr or on Cnoc Aine. She married Lord Desmond after he had captured her — the usual fairy bride incident — and bore him a son. Both she and the son left him, but appeared from time to time afterward, the son becoming Earl of Desmond in due course. Once he spoke to his mother about the barrenness of the hill, and next morning it was planted with pease set by her at night — a significant hint of her functions. Remnants of the agricultural ritual survived into last century in the form of a procession round the hill on St. John's Eve with *cléars* — bunches of straw tied on poles and lit, these being afterward carried through fields and cattle to bring luck to both. One year this was neglected, but a mysterious procession, with *cléars*, headed by Aine, was seen on the hill. On another occasion girls who had remained after the usual procession had gone met Aine, who thanked them for the honour done to her but begged them to depart as "they wanted the hill to themselves," "they" being Aine's retinue, seen by the girls through a ring which she produced.[11] Aine was thus obviously associated with fertility-rites.

It now remains to be seen how, according to the annalistic account, after their defeat and retirement to the hollow hills or *síd*, the gods divided these among themselves, while at the same time one of their number acted as king.

CHAPTER III

THE DIVISION OF THE SÍD

CELTIC deities may have been associated in pagan times with hills and pre-historic *tumuli*, especially those near the Boyne; and within these was the subterranean land of the gods, who also dwelt on distant islands. If this were the case, it would help to explain why mounds were regarded as the retreats of the Tuatha Dé Danann, and why they are still supposed to emerge thence as a kind of fairies. If the folk believed that the old gods had always been associated with mounds, it was easy for the euhemeristic writers to evolve a legend of their having retired there after being defeated by the Milesians.

Within these hills and mounds were their gorgeous palaces, replete with all Elysian joys. These hollow hills were known as *síd*, a word possibly cognate with Latin *sedes*, and hence perhaps meaning "seats of the gods"; and their divine inhabitants were the *áes síde, fir síde, mná síde*, "the people [*or* "men" *or* "women"] of the *síd*," or simply "the *síde*." These are everywhere regarded as the Tuatha Dé Danann or their descendants. Men used to worship the *síde*, says St. Fiacc's hymn, while the daughters of King Loegaire regarded St. Patrick and his white-robed bishops as *áes síde*, appearing on earth.[1] In later times the *síde* were held to be fairies and were called by various names, but these fairies closely resemble the earlier *síde*, the Tuatha Dé Danann, while they are not necessarily of small stature. In this they are very like the *fées* of mediaeval French belief — romantic survivals of earlier goddesses.

In some stories the *síde* are associated both with the *síd* and with the island Elysium, these being regarded as synonymous — the goddess with whom Connla elopes is of the *áes síde*, yet she comes from the island overseas. The confusion may be due to the fact that the gods were supposed to have various dwelling-places, not necessarily to the priority of one belief over the other. On the other hand, the *Mesca Ulad*, or *Intoxication of the Ulstermen*, says that after their defeat the Tuatha Dé Danann went underground to speak with the *síde*,[2] although this may be only the confused notion of an annalist who knew of the *síde*, yet regarded the Tuatha Dé Danann as human.

The mingled romantico-annalistic view was that the Tuatha Dé Danann retired to the *síd*. An early text, *The Conquest of the Síd* (*De Gabail int sída*), tells how Dagda apportioned the *síd* among them, his son Oengus, who was absent, being omitted. This story is clearly based upon an earlier myth which narrates how the chief god divided their various spheres among the divinities, as the Babylonian Marduk prepared the mansions of the deities and made them inhabit these as their strongholds. Of Dagda's *síd* another document says:

> "Behold the *síd* before your eyes,
> It is manifest to you that it is a king's mansion
> Which was built by the firm Dagda;
> It was a wonder, a court, an admirable hill."[3]

This was the Brug na Boinne. Oengus Mac Ind Óc, or "Son of the Young Ones," viz. Dagda and Boann, was then with his foster-father Midir, but soon claimed his abode as Esau did his blessing. The claim, however, could not be granted, whereupon Oengus asked to spend the night in Dagda's palace, to which his father agreed, granting him also the next day. When this had elapsed, Oengus was bidden to go, but refused, because, time being composed of day and night, his tenancy must be perpetual. Thus Dagda was dispossessed; and the *síd*, passing to Oengus, took his name, Brug Maic Ind Óc.[4]

In another version of this story from the *Book of Fermoy*, in-

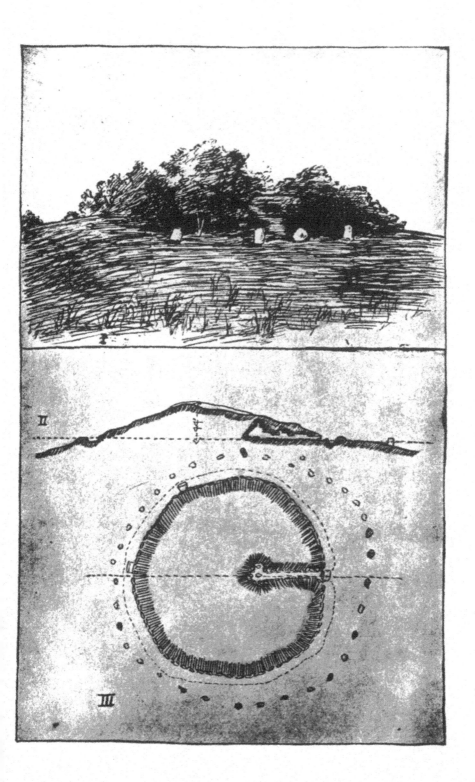

PLATE VI

A and B

Plan of the Brug na Boinne

1. General view of the tumulus.
2. Cross-section of the mound.
3. Plan of the central chamber.
4. View of the stone-work of the Brug and its entrance, after the removal of the earth.
5. General ground-plan of the Brug.

See also Plate I and cf. pp. 66–67, 176–77.

4

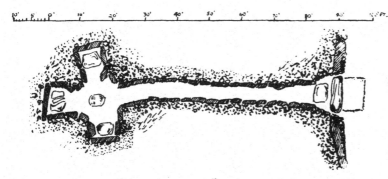

5

fluenced by the view that some of the Tuatha Dé Danann had died as mortals, Dagda has long since passed away, and the mounds are places of sepulture, perhaps a reflection of the fact that kings were interred there. Yet they are apportioned by the chief survivors, Bodb Dearg and Manannan, the latter having the task of selecting concealed dwellings. These he found in beautiful hills and valleys, and drew round them an invisible and impenetrable wall, though the Tuatha Dé Danann themselves could see and pass through it. He gave them Goibniu's ale, which preserved them from old age, disease, and death, and his own swine, which, killed and eaten one day, were alive the next and fit again for use. Thus even from this euhemeristic narrative the real divinity of its personages appears.[5]

In this account Bodb Dearg is made sovereign of the Tuatha Dé Danann, as he is also in the story of *The Children of Ler* (*Aided Chlainne Lir*). Ler, disgusted at the choice, retired, whereupon the others resolved to punish him, but were overruled by Bodb, who gave Ler his daughter Aobh as wife, provided he would pay allegiance to him. Aobh bore him two daughters and two sons before her death, and to comfort him Bodb now gave him her sister Aoife who, jealous of her stepchildren, transformed them into swans — a shape which they must keep for nine hundred years, though they retained speech and reason and the power of exquisite song. As a punishment Bodb changed Aoife into a "demon of the air." Not till the time of St. Patrick and St. Mochaomhog did Ler's children resume their own form. Withered and old, they now accepted the Christian faith and died, after having found their father's palace a roofless ruin.[6]

In the version given in the *Book of Fermoy* Elcmar, fosterfather of Oengus, received the Brug na Boinne, and Manannan advised Oengus to ask it from him. Through Manannan's magic power Elcmar was expelled, and Oengus gained the *síd*, where he dwells invisibly, eating the swine and drinking the ale of immortality. In still another version a curious account of the origin of Oengus is given. He was a natural son of Dagda, by Elcmar's wife. Dagda sent Elcmar on a journey and wrought spells, bringing darkness and "strayings" upon him, and warding off hunger and thirst from him. He obtained access to the goddess, perhaps because, like Uther and Manannan on like occasions, he assumed the appearance of the real husband. Elcmar was still absent when Oengus was born, but he may later have discovered the truth, for Oengus was taunted, as Merlin was, with having no parents. He went in tears to the god Midir, who took him to Dagda, and the latter acknowledged him as his son, bidding him go to Elcmar's *sid* and threaten him with death if he would not promise him "the sovereignty of a day and night in his land" — the same trick which Oengus played on Dagda in the first version.[7] This story is introductory to the beautiful myth of Etain, to be told later; but here it should be noted that in a poem by the euhemerizing monk, Flann Manistrech, Elcmar slew Midir and was himself slain by Oengus.[8] This, however, need be no part of an earlier myth.

Still another account is given in verse by the tenth century poet, Cináed úa hArtacáin. Boann, Nechtain's wife, came to stay with her brother Elcmar, vassal of Dagda, who sought her love in vain. His Druids advised him to send Elcmar on a mission, but the latter bargained that it should not keep him away over night, whereupon Dagda "kept the sun in the lofty ridge of the heavens till the end of nine months." Elcmar thought that only a day had passed, but on his return he saw by the change in the flowers how long the time had been. Meanwhile Dagda and Boann had deceived him, but now they were afraid, and birth-pangs seized the faithless wife. They left her child Oengus by the road-side near Midir's *sid*, and there he was brought up until his companions jeered at his unknown origin. Taxed by Oengus, Midir told the truth, and taking him to Dagda's *sid*, obtained it for him for a day and a night, thus tricking him.[9]

Whether the earliest story told of Dagda's or of Elcmar's dispossession, Oengus is a god who tricks his father or his foster-father, and perhaps the latter was the sufferer in the primitive form. Rhŷs makes Dagda an equivalent of Kronos and Oengus of Zeus; but apart from the disinheriting incident, which is not exactly parallel in the respective Greek and Celtic stories,[10] Dagda and Oengus have no clear traits in common with Kronos and Zeus, nor is there the slightest evidence that Dagda, like Kronos, ruled over the dead, either before or after his expulsion. The possible basis of the story, as the present writer has suggested elsewhere, is a myth explaining why the cult of one god came to supersede that of another.[11]

CHAPTER IV

MYTHIC POWERS OF THE GODS

AS in most mythologies, the Celtic deities have powers which reflect those supposed to be possessed by medicine-men, as well as others peculiar to themselves. These were the subject of myths taught by the Druids, who knew many things concerning the might of the immortal gods.[1] The gods were undying, and their abode was that of "the ever-living ones," where none ever died. Caoilte describes the Tuatha Dé Danann to St. Patrick as beings "who are unfading, and whose duration is perennial" in contrast with himself or men;[2] or they are "fairies or sprites with corporeal forms, endowed with immortality." Yet immortality is said to have been given them by Manannan through their drinking Goibniu's immortal beer, so that "no disease nor sickness ever attacks them," nor "decay nor old age comes upon them."[3] The daughter of Bodb Dearg was asked by St. Patrick what it was which maintained the gods in form and comeliness, and her answer was, "All such of us as partook of Goibniu's banquet, nor pain nor sickness troubles them."[4] Elsewhere this immortality seems to be dependent upon the eating of certain fragrant berries, of which it is said that "no disease attacks those who eat them, but they feel the exhilaration of wine and old mead; and were it at the age of a century, they would return again to be thirty years old." Once the Tuatha Dé Danann had played a match with the Féinn and brought from the Land of Promise crimson nuts, catkin apples, and these fragrant berries; but one of them fell to earth, and from it grew a quicken (rowan) tree, whose berries possessed these virtues. The gods sent one of their people to guard the tree — a savage, one-eyed giant, Searbhan Loch-lannach, who could not be slain until struck with three blows of his iron club; and around the tree he made a wilderness, sleeping in it by night, and watching at its foot by day. Fionn demanded as *eric*, or fine, from two warriors either the head of Diarmaid or a handful of these berries; but Diarmaid overcame them, and then asked the giant for the berries. Searbhan refused them, but by skill and strength the hero seized his club and slew him.[5]

Yet, even in their own immortal land, gods are slain. Perhaps this was not altogether the result of the annalistic view of the gods, for myth may have told of their death, as it did of gods elsewhere — Dionysus, Attis, Balder, Osiris. The analistic view did not hinder the continuance of myths, and divinities whose death is recorded in the *Annals* are found to be alive long after, while gods and goddesses born in pagan times appear thousands of years later to persons living in the Christian period. In spite of this perennial duration, they remained youthful and beautiful. Yet while the gods' land was pictured as a deathless, peaceful place, men still gave it certain of the traits of human life. War, wounds, and death were there, according to some stories; gods might even be slain by men; and as gods have human passions, so they may also have human weaknesses. Such is always the inconsistency of myth.

Invisibility was another divine power, innate, or acquired by donning a mantle, or from Manannan's spell, *Féth Fiada*, which was known also to Druids, poets, and Christian saints, who by it became unseen or took other forms. When the sons of Midir, assisted by the Féinn, fought against Bodb, Midir's son and Caoilte went to the *sid* of Oengus for a physician to heal Oscar's wounds; and then "there arose a *Féth Fiada* around us, so that we were invisible." In one passage Dagda is invisible, and Midir said, "We behold and are not beheld." When Manannan came to fetch his consort Fand, none saw him but the goddess, and when Lug arrived to assist Cúchulainn, he was unseen by the hero's foes. Divinities sometimes hid in a magic mist, as the Tuatha Dé Danann did on arriving in Ireland; they could appear to such mortals as they pleased, remaining unseen by others. Gods were probably not regarded as spiritual beings. Like the dead in Celtic belief, they had resplendent corporeal forms and ate and drank; but their bodily form differed from men's in that it could become invisible and was not subject to the laws of gravitation. The gods travelled through the air or appeared above men's heads.

How, then, did they appear when visible? Sometimes in the magnificence of divinity, yet still in anthropomorphic form. Sometimes they were of vast size, like the Morrígan or the Welsh Bran, while a goddess who sought the aid of Fionn was enormous compared even with the gigantic Féinn. Sometimes they appear merely as mortals and are not recognized as gods. Instances of this are found in the story of Cúchulainn's birth, where Lug is seen as a mortal host in a mysterious house, and in that of Merlin's father; invisible to all but his mother, and later taking human shape. Sometimes a disguise was assumed. Oengus and Midir appeared to Rib and Eochaid in the shape of hospitallers, with a haltered pack-horse, and bade them begone. Gods also took the appearance of particular mortals, as when Midir appeared to Etain as her lover Ailill, or Manannan as Fiachna to the latter's wife, or as when Pwyll and Arawn exchanged forms.[6]

Animal forms were also assumed. Of these one favourite shape was that of birds. Morrígan appeared to Cúchulainn as a bird; so also do Devorgilla and her handmaid, the former being in love with the hero. Llew took the form of an eagle; Bude and his foster-brother that of birds when the former wished to visit his paramour, whose husband Nár slew them. Midir and Etain, Fand and Liban were seen as birds linked together. The gods, or *síde*, appear as deer in one story. Again, the idea of divine shape-shifting, expressed, however, in the well-known folk-tale formula of the "Transformation Com-

PLATE VII

THREE-HEADED GOD

This triple-headed divinity (cf. p. 8) may possibly be another form of Cernunnos (see Plate XVI). For another representation see Plate XII, and for a three-headed deity of the Elbe Slavs cf. pp. 284–85 and see Plate XXXIV, 3. From a block of stone found at Paris, now in the Musée Carnavalet in that city.

bat," is combined with the Celtic idea of rebirth in Welsh and Irish tales; and the Welsh story, *Hanes Taliesin*, a sixteenth century tale, is based on earlier poems in which this formula is already prefixed to the rebirth incident. Shape-shifting is so commonly ascribed to Taliesin that it is no wonder that the formula was attached to his story, as it also was to the Greek myth of Proteus and the Hindu story of Vikramāditya: In the poem Taliesin describes his transformations and adds,

> "I have been a grain discovered
> Which grew on a hill . . .
> A hen received me
> With ruddy claws and parting comb.
> I rested nine nights
> In her womb a child." [7]

The *Hanes Taliesin* represents earlier myths about the hero and Cerridwen, the latter being a Brythonic goddess. Cerridwen, who dwelt below a lake, became hostile to Gwion Bach because he obtained the inspiration which she had intended for her son. The goddess pursued him, but he changed himself to a hare, and she took the form of a greyhound, after which the pair successively became fish and otter, bird and hawk, grain of wheat and hen. Cerridwen as a hen swallowed the grain, and gave birth to a beautiful child, whom she cast into the sea, but he was rescued by Elphin and obtained the name of Taliesin. [8]

In most versions of the Transformation Combat the opponents are males, and therefore one cannot give birth to the other; but by an ingenious device the compiler of the Irish myth of *The Two Swine-Herds* (*Cophur in dá muccida*), an introductory story to the *Táin Bó Cúalnge*, surmounted this difficulty. The swine-herds were subordinate divinities — Friuch, herd of the god Bodb, king of the *sid* of Munster, and Rucht, herd of Ochall Oichni, king of the *sid* of Connaught. They could take any shape, and there was friendship between them. When there was mast in Munster, Rucht fed his swine there; and Friuch brought his herd to Connaught in the same way.

People stirred up a quarrel between them, however, and Friuch put spells on Rucht's swine so that they should not eat the mast of Munster, while Rucht did the same to Friuch's pigs. When the swine became thin, the gods took their office from the herds, and Friuch and Rucht turned themselves into ravens and for a year reviled each other in Connaught and for a year in Munster. Resuming their own shape, they announced that there would yet be many corpses and much wailing because of them. Now they took the form of water-beasts and were seen for a year in the Suir and for another in the Shannon, devouring each other, and appearing as large as hills, until they came ashore as men, telling Ochall that they must still take other shapes to test their strength. They became champions, one of Bodb's host, the other of Fergna, King of the *sid* of Nento-fo-hiuscne, their term in this form ending with a fight which lasted three days and nights, and in which they gave such wounds that their lungs were visible. Next they became demons, a third of the people dying with fright at seeing them; while in another version transformations into stags and dragons are added. Finally they became worms, one in a spring in Connaught, the other in the river Cruind in Ulster. Queen Medb came one day to the spring to draw water, and the little animal, speckled with all colors, jumped into her dish. She spoke to it, and it told her that it had been in many shapes, and bade her take Ailill as her husband, after which it returned into the spring. That day Fiachna washed in the river Cruind and was frightened at seeing a tiny beast which told him of the luck about to befall him, and how it was Bodb's swine-herd. It besought Fiachna to feed it for a year, as the other had begged of Medb, and later it told him of a future combat with the other beast. Next day one of Fiachna's cows would swallow it when drinking, as one of Medb's kine would swallow the other; and as a result Medb's cow bore Findbennach ("White-Horn"), and Fiachna's the Donn or Brown Bull of Cúalnge. No bull dared bellow before either, and great war was caused in Ireland on their account.[9] The *Dindsenchas* speaks of seven shapes which the swine-herds took, but describes five only — swine-herds, birds, wolves, trout, and worms — and it also tells how a bull-calf of the Donn's was killed by White-Horn.[10]

A folk-tale analogy to this myth occurs in a West Irish collection. Two heroes at enmity fought until they were old men, then as puppies until they were old dogs, then as young bulls, as stallions, and as birds, until one was slain, his body falling on the other and killing him. The rebirth incident is lacking here.[11]

In the story which narrates how King Mongan recovered his wife from the King of Leinster his feats were originally those of a divine namesake. Taking the form of a cleric, he gave that of another cleric to his attendant and won entrance to the King's fort and to his wife. He kissed her, but when the attendant hag cried out, he sent a magic breath at her, and what she had seen was no longer clear in her mind, after which he shaped a sharp spike on which she fell and was killed. His attempt to recover his wife failed, however, and at a later time he took the guise of Aed, son of the King of Connaught, transforming a hag into the shape of Aed's beautiful wife, Ibhell. The King of Leinster fell in love with her and exchanged Mongan's wife to the pretended Aed for her; but the pair escaped, and great was the King's disgust to find Ibhell in the form of a hag. Mongan also made a river with a bridge over it, where none had ever been before, and in it he set the two clerics whose shapes he had borrowed.[12]

The gods could likewise transform each other. Etain was changed by Fuamnach into an insect, as a preliminary to her rebirth, and we have seen how the children of Ler were transformed into swans by their jealous step-mother. Ler heard them singing, yet god though he was, he could not disenchant them, just as Manannan was unable to change Aoife from the shape of a crane into which the jealous Iuchra had turned her.[13] The gods remained for three hundred years listening to the

music of the swans, which caused happiness to all who heard
it; and after many sufferings the birds met the sons of Bodb,
who spoke to them of the divinities, while Fionnghula sang of
her former happiness when she enjoyed the guileless teaching
of Manannan, the convocations of Bodb, the voice of Oengus,
and the sweetness of his kisses. We have seen how the children, after their disenchantment, died in the Christian faith.
This old and touching myth has received a Christian ending:
how it originally told the further fate of Ler's children is
unknown.

The gods also transformed mortals. Morrígan brought a
bull to a cow over which Odrus watched, and which followed
the bull when Morrígan went into the cave of Cruachan. Odrus
pursued through the cave to the *síd* within, but there she fell
asleep, and the goddess awoke her, sang spells over her, and
made of her a pool of water.[14] This is partly paralleled by
another story in which elves, or *siabhra*, transformed Aige into
a fawn and sent her round Ireland. Later she was killed, and
nothing remained of her but a bag of water which was thrown
into a river, thenceforward named after her.[15] A more curious
transformation is that by which the god Oengus changed his
four kisses into as many birds, in order that they might satirize
the nobles of Erin, until a Druid by a stratagem stopped
them.[16] As has been seen, the kisses of Oengus were dear to
Fionnghula. The souls of the righteous appear sometimes as
white birds, and those of the wicked as ravens, in Christian
documents — a conception which is probably of pagan origin.[17]

Finally, to show how the memory of the Tuatha Dé Danann
and their powers survived into later centuries the story of
O'Donnell's Kern may be cited. In this, Manannan appears
as a kern, or serving-man, at the houses of historic personages
of sixteenth century Ireland. He plays such music as never
was heard, bewitching men to slumber; he is a marvellous
conjuror, producing out of his bag hound, hare, dog-boy, and
lady, who all climb a silken thread which he tosses upward to a

cloud; he performs miracles of healing; he takes off a man's head and puts it on again; and from each place where he goes he suddenly disappears from human sight, none knowing whither he has vanished.[18] Folk-memory thus preserved much of the old conception of the gods.

CHAPTER V

GODS HELPING MORTALS

IN Greek mythology the gods were represented as coming to man's help, and in Christian legend saints were seen hovering above an army in battle and giving it substantial aid. So in Celtic myth deities were often kindly disposed toward men or assisted them, sometimes for ends of their own.

Such a myth is associated with the historic King Mongan of Ulster in the sixth and seventh centuries. He is shown to be son of the god Manannan by a mortal mother, and as has been seen, he had powers of shape-shifting, and besides being brought up in the divine land, had free access to it. He was also regarded as a rebirth of the hero Fionn; hence the stories told of this king of the Christian historic period must already have been narrated of some far earlier mythic king or god, perhaps possessed of the same name. Two of these legends narrate how the god assisted Mongan's putative father out of desire for his wife. In the shorter story Fiachna, King of Ulster, had gone to help Aedan in Scotland against Saxon hosts who had with them a terrible warrior, and during the fight a noble stranger appeared to Fiachna's wife and asked her love. She refused him with scorn, but later relented in order to save her husband's life, which, said the visitant, was in danger from the terrible warrior. "Our son will be famous, and his name will be Mongan. I shall tell thy husband our adventures, and that thou didst send me to his help." This the stranger did, afterward slaying the warrior and giving victory to Fiachna; and when Mongan was born, he was known as Manannan's son, for Manannan had announced his name when leaving the Queen at dawn.[1]

In the longer version Fiachna had become security for the exchange of four kine offered by the King of Lochlann to a Black Hag for her cow, the flesh of which alone could cure his disease. Later the hag compelled Fiachna to fight with the King, who had broken his promise to her; but all went well until the King of Lochlann let loose venomous sheep, before which Fiachna's men fell in hundreds. A warrior in a green cloak fastened by a silver brooch, with a circlet of gold on his head and golden sandals on his feet, appeared and asked what reward Fiachna would give him who would drive off the sheep. Fiachna replied that he would give anything he had, whereupon the warrior begged his ring "as a token for me when I go to Ireland to thy wife to sleep with her," to which the complacent Fiachna assented. The stranger — Manannan — announced that he would beget a glorious child, called Mongan Finn, or the "Fair"; "and I shall go there in thy shape, so that thy wife shall not be defiled by it." Fiachna would also become King of Lochlann. Taking a venomous hound from his cloak, Manannan launched it successfully at the sheep and then appeared to the Queen as Fiachna. On the night of Mongan's birth the Queen's attendant had a son, Mac an Daimh, while the wife of Fiachna's opponent, Fiachna the Black, bore a daughter, Dubh Lacha, these possibly also being children of the amorous god. When Mongan was three days old, Manannan took him to the Land of Promise and brought him back when he was sixteen. Meanwhile Fiachna Dub having killed the other Fiachna, the Ulstermen bargained that Mongan should retain half the province, with Dubh Lacha as his wife. One day when he and his Queen were playing together, "a dark, black-tufted little cleric" reproached Mongan for his inactivity and offered to help him to regain his land. Mongan went with him; they slew Fiachna; and all Ulster became Mongan's. The cleric was Manannan, though his transformation, in this as in the other version, is the result of the revision of the story by a Christian scribe. At a later time Mongan exchanged Dubh Lacha for the kine of the King of Leinster, but she, while living in the King's house, persuaded him to wait a year ere she was his.[2] How Mongan regained her through his magic powers learned in the divine land has already been described. A prophecy about Mongan is put into Manannan's mouth in *The Voyage of Bran*, where he tells Bran how he will go to Fiachna's Queen, that by her he will have a son who will delight the folk of the *síd*, will make known secrets and take all forms — dragon, wolf, stag, salmon, seal — and how the god will place the valiant hero with princes and will be his tutor.

Apart from the Christian colouring in these tales, they are of pagan origin and reflect pagan ideas about semi-divine sons of gods and the help given by gods to men. The late Mr. Nutt maintained that the story of Mongan was one form of a Celtic myth which might be fitted to any real or imaginary hero — that of a wonder-child, born of a mortal mother and a supernatural father, gifted magically by him, associated with him in the divine land, and passing thence at death. He assumed that Mongan had finally gone there, basing this assumption on verses which mention Mongan's wandering with Manannan in "the land with living heart," and his coming thence to see St. Columba. Mongan was the hero of such a myth in Ulster; Fionn of another local myth, later popular all over Ireland; Arthur of a similar Brythonic myth.[3]

The myth of the help given by gods to mortals is seen again in the story of Cúchulainn, son of the god Lug, who assists him in time of need. Cúchulainn stood alone against Medb's hosts, because she invaded Ulster when its men were in their periodic sickness.[4] He had slain hundreds of them and was now distorted with fury and in sore distress, when Loeg, his charioteer, announced that he saw a warrior approaching, fair, tall, with yellow hair, clad in a green mantle with a silver brooch. Shield, five-pointed spear, and javelin were in his hands. He plied these as he came, but "no one attacks him and he attacks no one," for he was invisible to Medb's warriors. Cúchulainn cried that this must be one of his friends of the *síde* coming to his aid, and so it turned out, for the warrior was his father Lug from the *síd*. "My wounds are heavy," said Cúchulainn, "it is time they were healed." Lug bade him sleep for three days while he himself fought the hosts; and as he sang a charm, the hero slept. Lug not only battled for him, but as he had claimed the power of healing in the story of the battle of Mag-Tured, so now he cured his son's wounds with medicinal herbs; and when Cúchulainn awoke, he was refreshed and strong. The god, however, would not stay to help him further, lest the fame of the deeds wrought by both should accrue to Cúchulainn; and the hero now donned a dress of invisibility given him by Manannan, a precious garment of the Land of Promise. Manannan is also called his foster-father in Druidism or wizardry,[5] and Cúchulainn's "friends of the *síde*" may be compared with the *leannan sighe*, fairies who befriend mortals when human powers fail them.[6] His opponent, Ferdia, reproached him for not telling him how his friends of the *síde* came to his aid when he thought of them, but Cúchulainn replied that since the *Féth fiada* was shown to all by the sons of Mile, the Tuatha Dé Danann could not use invisibility or work magic.[7] This passage, however, from the Stowe manuscript of the *Táin Bó Cúalnge* is, in its final statement, inconsistent with the incidents of the other manuscripts.

Other heroes were helped by Manannan. In *The Tragic Death of the Sons of Usnech* (*Longes mac nUsnig*) Naisi has a sword given to him by the god, its virtue being that it leaves no trace of stroke or blow behind it;[8] and some of his weapons were possessed by the Féinn. Diarmaid had his *crann buidhe* — a yellow-shafted spear — but its properties were less powerful than another magic spear with a red shaft, the *gai dearg*. It could do nothing against the boar which slew Diarmaid, and he lamented that he had not taken with him the *gai dearg*, as Grainne advised. With the shafts of these spears he twice leaped beyond the ring of his surrounding enemies and escaped them, and he also used "Manannan's magic staves" on another occasion to leap up a precipice. Besides these he possessed the *moralltach*, the sword of Manannan or of Oengus.[9]

Of Diarmaid it is said that "with most potent Manannan mac Ler thou studiedst and wast brought up in the Land of Promise and in the bay-indented coasts; with Oengus too, the Dagda's son, thou wast most accurately taught."[10] Oengus freely helped Diarmaid when he and Grainne were pursued by Fionn. Oengus learned that they were surrounded in a wood, and passing through the foe, unknown to the Féinn, he bade the eloping pair come under his mantle, when he would remove them without their pursuer's knowledge. Diarmaid refused to go, but asked the god to take Grainne, which Oengus did, reaching a distant wood unseen. There Diarmaid came to them and found a fire and a meal prepared by Oengus, who ere he left them warned Diarmaid of the places into which he must not go. When Diarmaid and Grainne took refuge in the quicken-tree of Dubhros, Oengus came invisibly as before, but now as each warrior in succession climbed the tree to take Diarmaid's head, he gave them the hero's form as he threw them down. When the Féinn cut the heads off, however, their true form was restored, and the ruse was discovered. Oengus would fain have carried both away, but again had to be satisfied with taking Grainne, bearing her invisibly in his magic cloak to the Brug na Boinne, where Diarmaid joined them, carrying the head of the witch whom Fionn had sent against him. Oengus now made peace between Diarmaid and Fionn, arranging the conditions which his foster-son demanded. Finally, when Diarmaid's death was caused by Fionn's craft, the latter advised that he and the others should escape lest Oengus and the Tuatha Dé Danann should capture them. Oengus, aware of the tragedy, arrived with the swiftness of the wind, and seeing the body, cried: "There has never been one night, since I took thee with me to the Brug na Boinne, at the

age of nine months, that I did not watch thee and carefully
keep thee against thy foes, until last night, O Diarmaid; and
alas for the treachery that Fionn hath done thee, for all that
thou wast at peace with him." Then he sang a lament, and
bearing the body to his Brug, he said, "Since I cannot restore
him to life, I will send a soul into him, so that he may talk to
me each day." [11] Oengus has less power than savage medicine-
men or gods in myth, who bring the dead back to life, or than
Demeter, who gave life to Dionysos after he was dismembered
by the Titans. But the story is an almost unparalleled example
of a god's love for a mortal. Fionn himself bears witness to the
love which Oengus had for Diarmaid as a child in his Brug,
and how when spells were put upon a boar that it should have
the same length of life as he, the god conjured him never to
hunt a boar. [12]

Another interesting instance is found in the story of Fraoch,
whose mother was a goddess. When he killed a dragon, women
of the *sid* came and carried him there, curing him of his wounds;
and so, too, when he was slain at a ford by Cúchulainn, those
divine women, clad in green, came and lamented over him and
carried his body into the *sid*. Fraoch should not have gone
near water, for this was dangerous for him, and his mother's
sister, the goddess Boann, had said, "Let him not swim Black
Water, for in it he will shed his blood." [13] In another story the
goddess Morrígan helped Tulchainde, Conaire's Druid, who
wished Dil, daughter of Lugmannair, to elope with him from
the Isle of Falga — the Isle of Man regarded as the divine land.
Dil loved an ox born at the same time as herself and insisted
that Tulchainde should take it with her; and the Morrígan
was friendly to him and at his wish brought it to Mag mBreg. [14]
The Morrígan was both hostile and friendly to Cúchulainn,
thus resembling that supernatural but ambiguous personage,
the Lady of the Lake in Arthurian tradition, now helping, now
opposing.

CHAPTER VI

DIVINE ENMITY AND PUNISHMENT

THE gods were sometimes hostile to men, not always for obvious reasons, as is curiously illustrated in the *Echtra Nerai*, or *Adventures of Nera*, an introductory tale to the *Táin Bó Cúalnge*. Here the gods are regarded as demons appearing with great power on Samhain Eve (Hallowe'en). King Ailill offered a reward to anyone who on that night would tie a withe round the foot of a captive hanged the previous day; and several tried, but were afraid. Nera was bolder, but his withe kept springing off the corpse until it told him to put a peg in it, after which the dead body asked him to carry it on his back to the nearest house for a drink, because "I was thirsty when I was hanged." The house was surrounded by a fiery lake, and into it and a second, surrounded by a lake of water, they could not enter. In a third house the corpse found water and squirted it on the faces of the sleepers so that they died, after which Nera carried the dead body to the gallows. This part of the story is connected with the vampire belief. Nera returned to Ailill's fort, but found it burnt, and a heap of human heads lay near it. He followed a company leaving it and thus came to the *síd* of Cruachan, where its king sent him to a woman in one of its dwellings, bidding him bring firewood daily to the royal house. At this task he noticed a lame man carrying a blind man to a well, and daily the blind man asked, "Is it there?" to which the lame man answered, "It is indeed; let us go away." The woman told Nera that they were guardians of the king's crown in the well, and when he described his adventures and the destruction of Ailill's fort, she explained that this was merely the

glamour of an elfin host (*sluag siabhra*), but that it would hap-
pen, unless he warned his friends. When he returned, he would
find them as he left them — a clear proof that he was in a time-
less region. They must watch next Samhain Eve, unless they
first destroyed the *síd*, and as proof of his statement he must
take from the *síd* fruits of summer — wild garlic, primrose,
and golden fern. Before his people came to destroy the *síd*, he
must warn her so that she with his cattle and the child she
would bear him might not lose their lives. Nera returned and
obtained the reward, and Ailill resolved to destroy the *síd*.
Meanwhile the woman carried the firewood, pretending that
Nera was ill; and when he came to warn her, she bade him
watch the cattle, one of which was to be his son's after his
birth. The goddess Morrígan stole this cow while Nera slept
and took it to the bull of Cúalnge, by whom it had a calf.
Cúchulainn is now introduced pursuing Morrígan and restor-
ing the cow; and on its return the woman sent Nera back to
his people — a reduplication of the first sending back. The
síd-folk could not destroy Ailill's fort until next Samhain Eve
when the *síd* would be open, and Nera now told his people of
the wonderful *síd* and how its dwellers were coming to attack
the fort. Ailill bade him bring anything of his own out of the
síd, and from it he fetched the cattle, including his child's bull-
calf which now fought the famous Findbennach, or white-
horned bull. Warned to beware of its sire, the bull of Cúalnge,
Medb swore by her gods that she would not rest until her bull
fought it. Meanwhile Ailill's men destroyed the *síd*, taking
from it the crown, Loegaire's mantle, and Dunlaing's shirt;
but Nera was left in the *síd* and will not come thence till doom
— like other mortals, he has become an inhabitant of the
gods' land.[1] Here also, as in the story of Etain, mortals wage
successful war with hostile divinities. Nevertheless the deities
survive, and only the outer works of their *síd* are destroyed.

The hostility of Morrígan to the hero Cúchulainn is seen in
the *Táin Bó Regamna*, or *Cattle-Raid of Regamon*. In his sleep

he heard a great cry, and setting off with his charioteer Loeg
to discover its meaning, they came to a chariot drawn by a
one-legged horse, the chariot-pole passing through its body and
emerging from its head. On it was a red woman, clad in red,
and near it marched a giant in a red tunic, carrying a spear
and a huge forked branch, and driving a cow. Cúchulainn
maintained that all the cows in Ulster were his, but the woman
denied this, and when he asked why she spoke for the man, she
announced that his name was Uar-gaeth-sceo Luachair-sceo.
Then the giant cried out that her name was Faebor beg-beoil
cuimdiuir folt scenbgairit sceo uath. Irritated at this gibber-
ish — an instance of the well-known concealment of divine
names — the hero leaped into the chariot, placing his feet on
the woman's shoulders and his spear at her head, and demanded her true name, to which she replied that she was a
sorceress and that the cow was her reward for a poem. Cúchulainn begged to hear it, and the woman consented, provided
that he would retire from the chariot. After the poem was recited, Cúchulainn prepared to leap again into the chariot, when
woman, giant, cow, and chariot vanished; but on the branch
of a tree was a black bird — the woman changed to this form.
Now he recognized her as Badb or the Morrígan, the battle-
goddess, and she told him that for his conduct she would pur-
sue him with vengeance. She was carrying the cow from the
síd of Cruachan, that it might be covered by the bull of Cúalnge
and when their calf was a year old, Cúchulainn would die.
She would attack him when facing his opponent at the ford
during the foray of Cúalnge, and as an eel she would twine
round his feet. "I will crush thee against the stones of the
ford, and thou wilt never obtain healing from me," answered
Cúchulainn. "As a she-wolf I will bite thy right hand and
devour thee," she replied. "I shall strike thee with my lance
and put out an eye, and never wilt thou obtain healing from
me," he returned. "As a white cow with red ears I will enter
the water, followed by a hundred cows. We shall dash upon

thee. Thou wilt fall, and thy head will be taken." "I shall
throw a sling-stone at thee, and thy heel shall be broken, and
no help wilt thou get from me," cried Cúchulainn; and with
that Morrígan disappeared into the *síd* of Cruachan.[2]

In a variant of this tale (where the cow-driving incident is
perhaps the one which is mentioned in the *Echtra Nerai*) a
different reason for this hostility is given. Morrígan appeared
as a beautiful woman offering Cúchulainn her love, her treasures, and her herds, but he replied that the opportunity was
not fitting, since he was engaged in a desperate contest, and
contemptuously refused her help. She uttered threats as in
the previous version; and when he was fighting at the ford, he
was overturned by an eel which he crushed in his hand, and
again as a wolf and a heifer Morrígan was defeated. Now no
one wounded by Cúchulainn could be healed save by himself,
and Morrígan therefore appeared as a lame and blind old
woman milking a cow with three teats. Cúchulainn asked for
milk, which she gave him from each teat, and at every draught
he pronounced the blessing of "gods and not-gods"[3] upon
her. At each benediction one of her wounds was healed, and
now she revealed herself, but was told that, had he known, she
would never have had healing from him.[4] Perhaps because of
this healing, or because of a subsequent reconcilement, before
Cúchulainn went to the last fatal fight, the goddess broke his
chariot, "for she liked not his going to the battle, knowing
that he would not come again to Emain Macha."[5] The story
also shows how divinities have the gift of shape-shifting,
though it does not always avail them against the prowess of a
hero.

The idea that gods punish neglect of their worship or com-
mands, or avenge other sinful actions, is found in most reli-
gions, and some stories seem to be derived from it, as when
Welsh legend knows of Nynnyaw and Peibaw transformed to
oxen for their sins by God — a probable substitution for a
pagan divinity.[6] Instances of the destruction of corn and milk

by divinities have been cited, and these perhaps signify punishment for neglecting the gods, seeing that, in the case of the
Milesians with Dagda, this was followed by a compact made
with him — the equivalent of the fresh covenant made with
God by His careless worshippers in the Old Testament. Possibly stories like that of Aillén mac Midhna of the Tuatha Dé
Danann, coming out of the *sid* every year to burn Tara,[7] point
to the same conception. The gods even punished members of
their own group for wrongdoing, as in the case of Aoife, who
was transformed by Bodb; and Bécuma was banished from
the gods' land because of her sin with Manannan's son. She
came to earth in a self-moving boat and by spells bound Conn,
high king of Ireland, to do her will and to banish his son Art;
but while she remained in dalliance with Conn for a year, there
was neither corn nor milk in Ireland — a direct divine punishment, for it was held that an evil king's reign was marked by
famine and destruction. The Druids told Conn that nothing
would avail save the sacrifice of "the son of a sinless couple,"
i. e. the son of the queen of a divine land, whom Conn brought
thence. To rescue the boy his mother came with a marvellous
cow, which was accepted as a sacrifice, while the queen told
Conn that he must renounce Bécuma, else Ireland would lose
a third of its corn and milk. Later, when the *sid*-folk stole the
chess-men with which Bécuma was playing with Art, she put
spells on him not to eat until he had brought Delbchaem from
a mysterious island, intending thus to cause his death. He
sailed till he reached an Elysian island, whose fair women
taught him how to escape the dangers before him and to find
Delbchaem; but when he brought her to Tara, Bécuma in
disgust left Conn for ever.[8] Punishment of a divine being is also
seen in the story of Manannan's slaying Fer Fedail because of
his misdeed, which resulted in the drowning of Tuag.[9] Con-
chean slew Dagda's son Aed for seducing his wife, and though
Dagda did not kill him, he made him carry the corpse until
he found a stone as long as Aed to put upon his grave.[10]

PLATE VIII

Squatting God

The deity has torques on his neck and lap, and is encircled by two serpents with rams' heads. Traces of horns appear on his head. He may possibly be a form of Cernunnos (see Plate XVI), and would thus be a divinity of the under-world. From an altar found at Autun, Saône-et-Loire. For a representation on a Gaulish coin see Plate III, 3; cf. also Plates IX, XXV.

Trespass on a sacred place is implied in the story of Eochaid, who eloped with his step-mother. Oengus, in disguise, told him not to camp on his meadow; and when he persisted, the god sent plagues upon him, killing his cattle and horses, and threatening to slay his household if he would not go. Oengus then gave him a horse on which to depart with his goods, and the lake which was formed afterward from the bursting of an uncovered well produced by the micturation of this horse drowned Eochaid and all his household, save his daughter Liban. This, as well as the similar story told of Eochaid's brother Ríb, who trespassed on the ground of Oengus and Midir, has affinity with tales of the bursting of a sacred well upon the impious trespasser, as in the legend of Boann.[11]

In another story Oilill pastured his cattle on the exterior of a *sid*, the grass of which the *sid*-folk now destroyed. While Oilill watched there with Ferchess, he saw fairy cattle leaving the *sid*, followed by Eogabal, son of its King, and his daughter Aine. Eogabal was slain by Ferchess, and Aine was outraged by Oilill, but she struck his right ear, leaving no flesh on it, whence his epithet "Bare Ear." Aine promised vengeance, which was wrought thus. Eogan, Oilill's son, and Lugaid mac Con heard music proceeding from a yew formed by magic as part of the means employed for vengeance, and in it was found a little harper, who was brought by them to Oilill. Before he went away, however, he made contention between Eogan and Lugaid; the latter was slain, and this caused the battle of Mag Mucrime, where Oilill's seven sons perished.[12] In this story gods are within men's power, though the latter cannot finally escape punishment. So also is it in the tale of Macha, "sun of women-folk," daughter of Midir, or of Sainred, son of Ler, who came to the house of the rich peasant, Cronnchu, and served him, bringing him prosperity and living with him as his wife. Cronnchu went to a feast of the Ulstermen, but was bidden by Macha not to say an imprudent word or mention her name. At the horse-racing, however, he boasted that his wife was swifter than the horses, whereupon King Conchobar insisted that she should be sent for, and though she was with child, forced her to run against his chariot. She said that all who saw it would suffer for the deed, and when at the goal she gave birth to twins, she condemned every Ulsterman to undergo for five days and four nights each year all the pangs which she had felt, and to have no strength during that time. Cúchulainn alone escaped the curse.[13]

The automatic working out of punishment is seen in the tragic results of the breaking of personal tabus, e. g. in the case of Cúchulainn and Fionn.[14] This is sometimes regarded as the inevitable operation of fate or as divine vengeance for wrong done to gods, not necessarily by the victim, and it receives its most mysterious illustration in the doom of Conaire Mór in the long tale of *Da Derga's Hostel.* In some versions Conaire's origin is connected with incest — itself caused by a vengeful god — while his death at the height of his prosperity is regarded as the consequence of injury done by his ancestor to the god Midir, whose wife Etain was retaken from him by Conaire's forefather Eochaid.[15] Through a trick of Midir's, Eochaid had a child, Mess Buachalla, by his daughter Ess, and Mess Buachalla was mother of Conaire. Who, then, was Conaire's father? One account regards him as King Eterscel, while Mess Buachalla is here daughter of Ess and one of the *síde,* or of Ess and Eterscel — the latter version thus introducing the incest incident in another form. Another account tells how Eochaid married Etain, daughter of Etar, King of the cavalcade from the *síd;* and their daughter Etain became Cormac's wife, but was put away because she bore him no son. Cormac ordered his infant daughter to be slain, but she smiled so sweetly on his thralls that they took her to King Eterscel's cowherds, who guarded her in a hut with a roof-light, whence her name Mess Buachalla, or "the Cowherds' Foster-Child." Through the roof-light Eterscel's people saw her when she was grown up, and told the king of her beauty. Now it was prophesied that he would have a son by a woman of unknown race, but before he sent for her, a bird flew through the roof-light, and doffing its plumage, became a man, to whom Mess Buachalla yielded herself. Before leaving her he told how she would have a son, Conaire, by him, who must never hunt birds; and Conaire was regarded as Eterscel's child when born. At Eterscel's death the new king was to be selected by divination at the "bull-feast." A bull was killed, probably as a sacrifice, and after the diviner had eaten its flesh, he dreamed of the future king — in this case a naked man with a sling coming to Tara. Meanwhile Conaire hunted a flock of wonderful birds, which suddenly became armed men, one of them telling him that he was Nemglan, King of the birds, his father, and that he was breaking his *geasa* (tabus) in hunting his kinsmen. Conaire replied that he knew nothing of this *geis*, whereupon Nemglan bade him go naked toward Tara, where watchers would meet him. In this incident there is doubtless some dim memory of clan totem-myths.

A different account of his becoming king makes Mess Buachalla tell him for the first time who his father is, viz. Eterscel, her own father, when he had just died. His successor must fulfil certain apparently impossible conditions, but Conaire met the terms and became king. Mysterious hosts brought to him by his mother stayed with him for a time and then departed, none knew whither; they were *síde* from Bri Léith, Midir's *síd*.[16] This appears to mean that Conaire was divinely assisted to become king, so that the approaching disaster might be all the greater.

To return to the other account, Nemglan told Conaire the *geasa* which he must observe. He became king, and none ever had a more prosperous reign; plenty abounded, and murder and rapine were banished. At last, however, the vengeance of the god began to work. Through a fate which he could not resist Conaire one day settled a quarrel between two of his serfs, thus breaking one of the *geasa*, and on his return he saw the whole country in flame and smoke — a delusion of the *síde*. To avoid the fire he and his men went sunwise round Tara and counter-clockwise round Bregia. These were tabued directions; and as he went, he pursued the evil beasts of Cerna, disobeying another tabu. Then, belated, he resolved to stay in the hostel of Derga ("Red"), and three red-haired horsemen clad in red and on red steeds [17] were seen preceding him to the house of Red — another of his *geasa*. He sent messengers after them begging them to fall behind, but they only went the faster and] announced: "We ride the steeds of Donn Tetscorach (Midir's son) from the *síd*. Though we are alive, we are dead. Great are the signs. Destruction of life. Sating of ravens. Feeding of crows. Strife of slaughter. Wetting of sword-edge. Shields with broken bosses in hours after sundown. Lo, my son!" With this boding prophecy they vanished, and the gods themselves thus caused the violation of Conaire's *geasa*. After arriving at the hostel he broke yet another, for there came a hideous woman who, standing on one foot, holding up one hand, and casting an evil eye on Conaire and his men, foretold their doom. Then she begged to be taken in, appealing to Conaire's generosity, and he said, "Let her in, though it is a *geis* of mine."

At this time Ingcel, whose single eye had three pupils, invaded Ireland with Conaire's foster-brothers, and they were now on their way to attack the hostel. Ingcel is described as going toward it to spy upon the inmates, returning with ever fresh reports of the wonders and the people seen by him, some of them gigantic and monstrous, with magic weapons. When the hostel was surrounded, a terrible battle began. Conaire was parched with thirst, but no water was to be obtained, though his ally MacCecht sought it in all Ireland. Lakes and rivers had been dried up, apparently by the gods, as at the first battle of Mag-Tured, and one loch alone was reached before its water disappeared. MacCecht returned with a draught, but all too late. Conaire's host was scattered and dead, and he himself was being decapitated by two of his foes, whom Mac-Cecht slew, and then poured the water into Conaire's mouth. The head thanked him for his act, and thus perished Conaire, through no fault of his own, victim of fate and of a god's vengeance.[18] The story is as tragic as a Greek drama, if its art is less consummate.

CHAPTER VII

THE LOVES OF THE GODS

LIKE the gods of Greece and India, the deities of the Celts
had many love adventures, and the stories concerning
these generally have a romantic aspect. An early tale of this
class records that one night, as Oengus slept, he saw a beautiful maiden by his bed-side. He would have caught hold of
her, but she vanished, and until next night he was restless and
ill. Again she appeared, singing and playing on a cymbal, and
so it continued for a year till Oengus was sick of love. Fergne,
a cunning leech, diagnosed the cause of his patient's illness
and bade Boann, Oengus's mother, search all Ireland for the
maiden, but though she sought during a whole year, the girl
could not be found. Fergne therefore bade Boann summon
Dagda, Oengus's father, and he advised him to ask the help
of Bodb, King of the *síde* of Munster, famed for knowledge.
Bodb discovered the maiden, and Oengus set out to see whether
he could recognize her. By the sea they found many girls,
linked two and two by silver chains; and one, taller than the
rest, was the maiden of the vision, Caer, daughter of Ethal of
síd Uaman. Dagda, advised by Bodb, sought help from Ailill
and Medb, King and Queen of Connaught — another instance
of mortals aiding gods; but Ethal refused Ailill's request to
give up Caer, whereupon Dagda's army with Ailill's forces
destroyed his *síd* and took him prisoner. Still he refused, because he had no power over his daughter, for every second
year she and her maidens took the form of birds at Loch Bél
Draccan (the "Lake of the Dragons' Mouths"); and thither
Dagda bade Oengus go. At this loch, says incidental refer-

ence to the story, the maidens were wont to remain all the year of their transformation, Caer as the most lovely of all birds, wearing a golden necklace, from which hung an hundred and fifty chains, each with a golden ball.[1] When Oengus saw the birds, he called to Caer. "Who calls me?" she cried. "It is Oengus that calls thee; come to him that he may bathe with thee." The bird-maiden came, and Oengus also took the form of a bird. Together they plunged three times in the lake, and then flew to Brug na Boinne, singing so sweetly that everyone fell asleep for three days and nights. Caer now became Oengus's wife.[2]

In this story the god Bodb is famed for knowledge, and in the incidental reference cited he is said for a whole year to have kept off by his magic power the harper Cliach, who sought his daughter's hand.[3] Possibly the shape-shifting of Caer and her maidens was the result of a curse or spell, as in other instances, unless — being goddesses — the power was in their own hands. The myth uses the folk-tale formula of the Swan-Maiden, though its main incident is lacking, viz. her capture by obtaining the bird-dress, which she has doffed.

In the story of Oengus's disinheriting Elcmar, he later appears as a suitor for Etain, daughter of Ailill, who refused her to him; but Midir was more successful, whence there was enmity between him and Oengus. The long tale which follows is extant in several manuscripts and is here pieced together mainly from the versions in the Egerton Manuscript and the *Leabhar na hUidre*. Besides Etain, Midir had another consort, Fuamnach, who was jealous of her. With the help of a Druid's spells and by her own sorceries she changed Etain into an insect and by a magic wind blew her about for seven years; but Oengus found her in this state and made for her a *grianan*, or bower filled with shrubs and flowers, on which she fed and thrived. Perhaps by night she was able to resume her true form, for Oengus slept with her; and when Fuamnach heard of this, she caused Midir to send for Oengus, so that a recon-

ciliation might be effected. Meanwhile, however, Fuamnach
went to the *grianan* and again by a magic wind ejected Etain,
who was blown upon the breeze until she fell through the roof
of Etair's house into his wife's golden cup. She swallowed the
insect and later gave birth to the divinity as an infant called
Etain, who, more than a thousand years before, had been born
as a goddess. When she now grew up, as she and her maidens
were bathing, a warrior appeared, singing about Etain, and
then vanished, this being Midir, or possibly Oengus, who had
discovered Fuamnach's treachery and struck off her head.
Here, however, is interpolated a verse telling how not Oengus
but Manannan slew or burned her, as well as her grandson,
Siugmall.[4]

The next section of the story exists in two forms and relates
how Etain was married by Eochaid Airem, King of Ireland.
His brother, Ailill Anglonnach, fell in love with her, and when
at last he disclosed this to Etain, she, after much persuasion,
arranged a meeting-place with him. At the appointed time
however, Ailill did not come, being hindered by sleep; but one
in his likeness appeared to Etain on successive occasions and
at last announced himself to be Midir, who had thus dealt with
Ailill, and told her how she was his consort, parted from him
by magic. Nevertheless, she refused to go with him; but
when she told Ailill, he was cured of his love. The Egerton
version then relates how Midir, appearing in hideous form,
carried off Etain and her handmaid Cróchan to his *síd* of Bri
Léith, near the rising of the sun, first staying on the way at the
síd of his divine relative Sínech; and when Cróchan complained of wasting time there, Midir said that this *síd* would
now bear her name.

In the version given by the *Leabhar na hUidre* the incident of
Midir's disclosing himself is more mythical in character. He
invited Etain to the gods' land, "the Great Plain," or Mag
Mór — a marvellous land, wherein is music. Its people are
graceful, and nothing is called "mine" or "thine." The plains

of Ireland are fair, but fairer is this plain, its ale more intoxicating than that of Erin! There is choice of mead and wine, and conception is without sin or crime (hence Segda in the story of Bécuma was "son of a sinless couple"). Its people are invisible: they see but are not seen, and none ever grows old. The magic food of the gods' land will be Etain's — unsalted pork, new milk, and mead. Midir now met Eochaid and proposed a game of chess with him, allowing him to win, whereupon Eochaid demanded that Midir and his folk should perform four tasks — clear the plains of Meath, remove rushes, cut down the forest of Breag, and build a causeway across the moor of Lamrach. In the *Dindsenchas*, a topographical treatise, these tasks are an *eric*, or fine, on Midir for taking Eochaid's wife, and in performing them the divine folk taught a new custom to the men of Erin, viz. placing the yoke over the oxen's shoulders instead of on their foreheads, whence Eochaid's cognomen, Airem ("Ploughman").[5] In a second game Midir won and asked that he might hold Etain and kiss her. Eochaid would not consent until a month had passed, and then Midir arrived in splendour for his reward, surrounded by armies. Etain blushed when she heard his demand, but he reminded her that by no will of hers had he won her. "Take me then," said she, "if Eochaid is willing to give me up." "For that I am not willing," cried Eochaid, "but he may cast his arms around thee." So Midir took her and then rose with her through the roof, and the assembly saw the pair as two swans winging their way to the *sid*.

The Egerton version ends by telling, how through the divination of a Druid, Eochaid discovered Midir's *sid*, destroyed it, and recovered Etain. The version in the *Leabhar na hUidre* is defective after narrating how Eochaid and his men dug up several *sid* one after another; but the *Dindsenchas* relates that Ess, Etain's daughter, brought tribute of cattle and was fostered by Midir for nine years, during which Eochaid besieged the *sid*, thwarted by his power. Midir brought out sixty women in Etain's form, among them Ess, Eochaid's daughter; but Eochaid mistook her for Etain and by her had a daughter Mess Buachalla, mother of Conaire. Recognizing his mistake, he went to Midir, who restored Etain to him; and in revenge Siugmall, Midir's grandson, afterwards killed Eochaid.[6]

Although folk-tale formulae are found in this story, it is based on myths of divine love and magic power and of a goddess's rebirth as a mortal. Midir's poetic description of the gods' land is archaic and may only later have been connected with the underground *síd*. Curious, too, is the idea, which we have noted above, of the subjection of gods to mortals — performing tasks and permitting their abode to be spoiled or a consort taken from them — but it may reflect the belief in magic power to which even divinities must yield. Nevertheless, the deities get their own back: Etain's recapture is preceded by the incest incident; Midir is slain; and his descendant, Conaire, dies because the god causes him to break his tabus, as already described.

The story of the birth of the hero Cúchulainn is based on the love of a god, Lug, for a mortal, Dechtere, sister of Conchobar, King of Ulster. It is told in two versions, one found in two recensions, the *Leabhar na hUidre* and the Egerton Manuscript; the other is also given in the Egerton Manuscript. We follow the latter (*c*), noting the chief points of difference between it and the others (*a* and *b*). Dechtere, with fifty maidens, left Conchobar's house for three years, at last returning in the form of birds which devoured everything, so that Conchobar organized a hunt which continued unsuccessfully till nightfall. The other version begins with the devastation wrought by nine flocks of mysterious birds, joined two and two by silver chains, the leading pair in each group being many-coloured; but these birds are not Dechtere and her companions, for she accompanies Conchobar in his chariot on the hunt. The next incident is obscurely told in version *c*, but comparing it with the other, it is evident that the hunters en-

tered a small house where were a man and a woman, and that
it was suddenly enlarged, beautified, and filled with all desirable things, for it was one of the gods' magic dwellings, which
they could produce on earth by glamour. The man was Lug,
the woman Dechtere, though this was known only to Bricriu.
Conchobar believed that they were his vassals and demanded
his right of sleeping with the woman, who escaped by saying
she was *enceinte;* and in the morning an infant was discovered,
the child of Dechtere by Lug, though it had the appearance of
Conchobar. The child was called Setanta, but afterward was
known as Cúchulainn.

In version *b* the host told his guests that his wife was in
childbed. Dechtere assisted her and took the child to foster
him; and at the same time the host's mare gave birth to two
foals — a common folk-tale coincidence. In the morning all
had vanished, and Conchobar's party returned home with the
child, which died soon after. When the funeral was over, Dechtere in drinking swallowed a mysterious tiny animal, and that
night Lug appeared, telling her that she was with child by him,
for it was he who had carried her off with her companions as
birds — an incident lacking in this version. His was the child
whom she had fostered, and now he himself had entered her
as the little animal. Her child, when born, would be called
Setanta. Here Setanta is at once Lug's son and his rebirth;
but the two ideas are not exclusive if we take into account
ancient ideas. In early Indian belief the father became an
embryo and was reincarnated in his first-born son, whence
funeral rites were performed for the father in the fifth month
of pregnancy, and he was remarried after the birth.[7] Probably
for a similar reason, preserved in Celtic myth after it was no
longer believed of mortals, a god who had a child by a mortal
was thought to be reborn while still existing separately himself; and this explains why the Ulstermen sought a wife for
Cúchulainn so that "his rebirth might be of himself." In
various texts Cúchulainn is called son of Lug.

When Dechtere was found to be with child, it was thought that Conchobar himself was the father, for she slept by him — a glimpse of primitive manners in early Ireland. Elsewhere Cúchulainn calls Conchobar his father,[8] and this may represent another form of the story, with Conchobar as Cúchulainn's parent by his sister Dechtere. Dechtere was meanwhile affianced to Sualtam, but ashamed of her condition, she vomited up the animal and again became a virgin; yet the child whom she bore to Sualtam was the offspring of the three years' absence — Setanta or Cúchulainn. On the whole this is a much distorted myth, but two things emerge from it — Lug's amour with Dechtere and his fatherhood of Setanta.[9]

Another tale, with Christian interpolations, tells how Connla, son of Conn, who reigned from 122 to 157 A. D., one day saw a strange woman who announced that she was from *Tír na mBeó* ("the Land of the Living"), where was no death, but perpetual feasting, and her people dwelt in a great *síd*, whence they were called *áes síde*, or "people of the *síd*." The goddess was invisible to all but Connla, whence Conn asked him with whom he spoke, to which she replied that she was one who looked for neither death nor old age and that she loved Connla and desired him to come to Mag Mell ("the Pleasant Plain"), where reigned a victorious king. Conn bade his Druid use powerful magic against her and her *brichta ban*, or "spells of women," against which at a later time St. Patrick made his prayer. The Druid pronounced an incantation to hinder Connla from seeing, and all others from hearing, the goddess, who withdrew after giving an apple to Connla. He would eat nothing but this, nor did it ever grow less; and in a month the love-lorn Connla saw her reappear in a boat of glass, calling him to come, for "the ever-living ones" invited him, so that he might escape death. Conn again called his Druid, whereupon the goddess sang that the Druids would soon pass away before a righteous one, St. Patrick — a Christian interpolation, *post eventum;* and Conn then spoke to his son, but the goddess sang that once on the waves Connla's grief at leaving his friends would be forgotten, and the land of joy would soon be reached, where there were none but women. Connla sprang into the boat, which sped across the sea into the unknown, whence he has never returned.[10] In this tale the land of women is obviously but a part of the divine land, since that is ruled by a king; and there is also confusion between the idea of an overseas region of the immortals — Mag Mell — and that of the subterranean *síd*. Connla's adventure is mentioned in the *Cóir Anmann*, or *Fitness of Names*, where another account is given, viz. that he was slain by enemies.[11] A parallel myth, perhaps of Celtic origin, is found in one of the *Lais* of Marie de France concerning the knight Lanval, with whom a fairy fell in love. When she declared herself, he sprang on horseback behind her and went away to Avalon, a beautiful island, the Elysium of the Brythonic Celts.[12]

The Land of Ever-Living Women recurs in some tales of the *imm-rama*, or romantic voyage, type, e. g. in *The Voyage of Maelduin*, an old pagan story reconstructed in Christian times. Maelduin and his companions went on a quest for his father's murderers and met with the strangest adventures, one of which describes their arrival at an island where they saw seventeen girls preparing a bath. A warrior appeared who, on bathing, proved to be a woman and sent one of the girls to bid the men enter her house. There a splendid repast was given them, and the woman, Queen of the isle, desired each to take the girl who best pleased him, reserving herself for Maelduin. In the morning she begged all to remain. Their age would not increase; they would be immortal; and perpetual feasting and excessive love without toil would be theirs. She had been wife of the King of the island, the girls were her daughters, and now she reigned alone, so that she must leave them each day to judge cases for the people of the isle. The voyagers remained three months, when all but Maelduin grew home-sick; yet he consented to go with them, and all entered their boat in the Queen's absence. Suddenly she appeared and threw out a rope which Maelduin seized, with the result that they were drawn back to the shore, where they remained three months longer, escaping then once more. This time one of Maelduin's men caught the rope thrown by the Queen, but the others severed his hand, and seeing this, she wept bitterly at their going.[13] These women were not mortals but goddesses, eager for the love of men.

Another myth tells of a goddess's love for Cúchulainn. A flock of beautiful birds appeared in Ulster, and caused all the women to long for them. Cúchulainn, in distributing his catch among them, omitted his mistress Ethne, and to appease her he promised that the two most beautiful birds which next appeared would be hers. Soon after, two birds linked together flew over the lake, singing a song which made everyone but Cúchulainn sleep. He pursued, but failing to catch them, he rested, angry in soul, against a stone, and while sleeping saw two women approaching, one in a green mantle, and the other in a purple, each armed with a horse-whip with which they attacked him. When he was all but dead, his friends found him, and on his awaking, he remained ill for a year. Then appeared a stranger who sang of the healing which could be given him by Aed Abrat's daughters, Liban and Fand, wife of Manannan. Fand desired his love, would he but come to her wondrous land; and had he been her friend, none of the things seen by him in vision would have happened. The stranger, Oengus, son of Aed Abrat, disappeared, and after the Ulstermen had persuaded Cúchulainn to tell his vision, he was advised to return to the pillar-stone. There he found Liban, who told him that Manannan had abandoned Fand, and she brought him a message from her own husband, Labraid, that he would give him Fand in return for one day's service against his enemies.[14] Labraid dwelt in Mag Mell, and there Cúchulainn would recover his strength; but the hero desired his charioteer Loeg first to go and report upon this land.

PLATE IX

A and B

Altar from Saintes

A. The obverse shows a seated god and goddess. The god is squatting (cf. Plates III, 3, VIII, XXV), and holds a torque in his hand. The goddess has a cornucopia (cf. Plates XIV, XV), and a small female figure stands beside her.

B. On the reverse is a squatting god with a purse in his right hand; to the left is a god with a hammer (see Plates XIII, XIV, XXVI), and to the right is a goddess. Three bulls' heads are shown below (cf. Plates II, 4-5, 9, III, 5, XIX, 1, 6, XX, B, XXI). From an altar found at Saintes, Charente-Inférieure, France.

At this point we hear of Loeg's visit and return, and next follows a long passage that has nothing to do with the story, which then continues as if from another version in which Liban's visit had not occurred. Cúchulainn was still ill and sent Loeg to tell Emer, his wife, how women of the *side* had destroyed his strength; but when she reproached him for his weakness, he arose and went to the enclosure (the pillar-stone of the first part). There Liban appeared, singing of Labraid's prowess and of his need for Cúchulainn, and striving to lead the hero to the dwelling of the *side* or to Labraid's home on a lake where troops of women came and went. Cúchulainn refused to go at a woman's call, whereupon Liban proposed that Loeg should bring tidings of Labraid's land. The two visits of Loeg are thus the same, but differently described: In the first Liban took Loeg by the shoulder, for he could not go in safety, unless under the protection of a woman. In a bronze boat they reached an island in a lake, and in a palace Loeg saw thrice fifty women who welcomed him. While he spoke with Fand, Labraid arrived, gloomy because of the approaching contest, but Liban cheered him by announcing that Loeg was there, and that Cúchulainn would come. Now Loeg returned to tell of all he had seen.

The other version describes how Loeg passed with Liban to the plain of Fidga, where dwelt Aed Abrat and his daughters. There Fand bade him at once bring Cúchulainn, for on that day the strife would begin; and Loeg returned, urging Cúchulainn to go and recounting what he had beheld. In one house were thrice fifty men; at the eastern gate were three purple trees with birds singing; in the forecourt was a silver tree with musical branches; from sixty other trees dropped food to nourish three hundred; and there was, too, a vat of unfailing ale. He described Fand's marvellous beauty and still urged Cúchulainn with accounts of the attractiveness of the land, without any lie or injustice, and of the glory of its warriors and its women. Cúchulainn at last went there and by his might quelled the enemies of the god. Fand and Liban now sang in praise of him, and he remained for a month with Fand, after which he bade her farewell. She appointed a tryst with him in Erin, but Emer heard of it and with fifty women came to attack Fand. Cúchulainn, however, bade Fand have no fear, and addressing Emer he told her how the goddess was more worthy of his love. Emer reproached him, and when she added, "If only I could find favour in thy sight," Cúchulainn's love for her returned: "Thou shalt find favour so long as I am in life." Then began a noble contest between Fand and Emer as to which of them should sacrifice herself for the other, and Fand sang a beautiful lament. At this moment Manannan became aware of Fand's predicament and arrived to rescue her, unseen by all save her and Loeg. Fand again sang, describing the coming of "the horseman of the crested sea-waves," and told of her former love for the god and the splendour of their espousals. Now, deserted by Cúchulainn, she would return to Manannan; but still her heart yearned for the hero, as she told Manannan when he asked her whether she would depart with him or no. Yet one thing weighed with her: Manannan had no consort worthy of him, while Cúchulainn already had Emer. So she departed; and when the hero knew it, he bounded thrice in air and gave three leaps southward, and abode for a long time fasting in the mountains. Emer went to Conchobar, who sent his Druids to bind Cúchulainn; and when the hero would have slain them, they chanted spells and fettered him, giving him a draught of oblivion so that he remembered Fand no more. Emer also shared in this potion and forgot her jealousy; "and Manannan shook his mantle between Cúchulainn and Fand, so that they should never meet again." [15] In this story Emer addresses Loeg as one who often searches the síd, while he speaks of the divine land as well-known to him and seems to see Manannan when he is invisible to the others.

Manannan himself was an ardent lover, and what St. Patrick called "a complicated bit of romance," was told to him

by Caoilte. Aillén, of the Tuatha Dé Danann, became en-
amoured of Manannan's wife, while his sister Aine, daughter of
Eogabal, loved Manannan and was dearer to him than all
mankind. Aine asked the cause of her brother's sadness, and
he told her that he loved the goddess Uchtdelbh ("Shapely
Bosom"). Aine accordingly bade him come with her where
the divine pair were, and taking her seat by Manannan, she
gave him passionate kisses. Meanwhile Uchtdelbh, seeing
Aillén, loved him; and Manannan gave her to him, himself
taking Aine.[16] On another occasion Manannan desired Tuag,
a maiden guarded by hosts of the King of Erin's daughters;
and since no man might see her, Manannan sent a divine
Druid, Fer Fídail, son of Eogabal, in the form of a woman to
gain access to Tuag. He remained with her three nights and
then, singing a sleep-strain over her, he carried her to the
shore and left her slumbering while he looked for a boat wherein
to carry her asleep to the Land of Ever-Living Women, or, in
another version, to go to take counsel of Manannan. But a
wave came and drowned her, the wave in one version being
Manannan the sea-god himself — a primitive piece of personalization of nature. For his misdeed Fer Fídail was slain by
Manannan, and probably the cause of offence was that he had
loved Tuag,[17] this explaining why she was drowned by the
disappointed god.

A parallel myth, connected with other personages, tells how
Clidna the Shapely went from the Hill of the Two Wheels, in
the Pleasant Plain of the Land of Promise, with Iuchna Curly-
Locks to go to Oengus Mac Ind Oc. But Iuchna practised
guile upon her so that she slept in the boat of bronze through
his music; and then he turned the boat's head, altering its
course till it reached the place called Clidna. At that time
occurred one of the three great seabursts which spread through
all the world. It caught up the boat, and Clidna was drowned;
whence this seaburst was called Clidna's Wave.[18] The
others were Tuag's and Rudraige's, or Ladru's and Baile's.

The story of Crimthann Nia Náir shows that one who sojourns in the divine land or tastes its food may not be able to return to earth with impunity, for he has become a member of the other-world state and is no longer fit for earth. This is found in other Irish tales and in stories of fairyland or the world of the dead elsewhere.[19] Crimthann was son of Lugaid Red Stripes, of whom one of those occasional stories of incest, not uncommon in primitive society, is told, proving that it had at one time been common in Celtic custom, perhaps in the royal house. Lugaid's mother was Clothru, a sister of Medb and Ethne. Clothru and Ethne are both said to have been wives of Conchobar after Medb left him for Ailill; and their brothers, Bres, Nár, and Lothar, were called the Three Finns, or White Ones, of Emuin. Once Clothru bewailed her childless condition to them, and as a result of her entreaties she had a son Lugaid by all three.[20] Clothru again bore a child to Lugaid, Crimthann Nia Náir, or "Nár's Man," the hero of this story and afterward supreme king, who fared on what is called "a splendid adventure" with a goddess or witch called Nár. He went to a land overseas, where he remained with her for a month and a half; and at his departure he obtained many love-tokens — a chariot and a golden draught-board, a sword richly ornamented, a spear whose wounds were always mortal, a sling which never missed its aim, two dogs worth a hundred female slaves, and a beautiful mantle. Soon after his return, however, he fell from his horse and died [21] — an incident perhaps to be explained in terms of the myths of Loegaire Liban and Oisin, who, in order to return to the divine land, were warned not to dismount from their horses.[22] On the other hand, Cúchulainn was able to return to Ireland from Elysium without hurt, and so also was Aedh, son of the King of Leinster, who was enticed into the *síd* by Bodb Dearg's daughters. For three years the folk of the *síd* cared for him while his father mourned, not knowing whither the divine people had taken him — into the sky or down under the earth. He and fifty other youths escaped, however, and Aedh met St. Patrick, who restored him to his father and said that he would eventually die as God willed, i. e. the Tuatha Dé Danann would have no further power over him.[23]

Sometimes mortals, or gods later envisaged as mortals, abducted daughters of gods. Garman took Bodb's daughter Mesca from the *sid;* but she died of shame, and the plain where her grave was dug was named after her, Mag Mesca.[24] Men of the *sid,* divine or semi-divine beings, but regarded as attendants on men, also had love-affairs with goddesses. Cliach, from *sid* Baine, was harper to the King of the three Rosses and made music at the *sid* of Femen to attract Conchenn, Bodb's daughter. For a year Bodb's magic prevented the lover from approaching nearer, so that he "could do nothing to the girls" in the *sid;* but he harped until earth opened, and a dragon issued forth, when he died in terror. This dragon will arise at the end of the world and afflict Ireland in vengeance for St. John Baptist — perhaps an altered fragment of an old cosmogonic myth.[25] Another story has some resemblance to this. Liath, a young Prince of the *side,* loved Midir's daughter Bri, who went with her attendants to meet him as he approached. But the slingers on Midir's *sid* kept him back, and their sling-stones were like "a swarm of bees on a day of beauty." Liath's servant was slain, and because Liath could not reach her, Bri turned back to the *sid* and died of a broken heart.[26]

Besides these, a large number of Irish and Welsh tales illustrate the *amours* of the gods, as may be seen elsewhere in this volume.

CHAPTER VIII

THE MYTHS OF THE BRITISH CELTS

THE surviving myths of the British Celts (Brythons), as distinguished from the Irish Celts (Goidels), exist in the form of romantic tales in the *Mabinogion* and similar Welsh stories and in the Arthurian and Taliesin literature, or are referred to in the *Triads* and Welsh poems. Have the divinities who there figure as kings and queens, heroes and heroines, magicians and fairies, retained any of their original traits and functions? The question is less easily answered than in the case of Irish divinities subjected to the same romantic and euhemerizing processes. With religious and social changes it was forgotten that the gods were gods, and they became more or less human, for the mediaeval story-teller was "pillaging an antiquity of which he does not fully possess the secret." The composition of the stories of the *Mabinogion*, like those of the great Irish manuscripts, dates from the tenth and eleventh centuries, yet in both cases materials and personages are of far older date, the supernatural element is strong, and there is a mythical substratum surviving all changes. Further, the Welsh tales belong to a systematized method of treating ancient traditions, and were the literary stock-in-trade of the *Mabinog*, or aspirant to the position of a qualified bard. This process was still further carried out in Ireland, where myths were recast into a chronological as well as a romantic mould, the *file*, or man of letters, being estimated according to the number of his stories and his power of harmonizing and synchronizing them. In Welsh literature the euhemerizing, historical process is seen at work less in the legends than in the historians Nennius and Geoffrey of Monmouth, with whom some gods became kings having a definite date, as in the Irish annals.

Certain personages and incidents of Welsh story resemble those of Irish tradition. Was there, then, once a common mythology among the ancestors of Goidel and Brython, to which new local myths later accrued? Or did Irish and Welsh myths mingle because Goidels existed either as a primitive population in Wales, conquered by Brythons, or as a later Irish immigration? Probably we are right in assuming that the *Mabinogion* literature contains the *débris* of Brythonic myths, influenced more or less from Goidelic sources, as the occasional presence of Irish names and episodes suggests. The Arthurian and Taliesin cycles are purely Brythonic. What is certain is that the dim divinities of the *Mabinogion* are local in character and belong to specific districts in Wales, gods of tribes settled there. Celtic divinities were apt to be local, though some had a wider repute. Few of the many British divinities mentioned in inscriptions are known to Welsh story. Nodons is Nudd or Lludd; Maponos is Mabon; the Belenos and Taranos of Continental inscriptions may be respectively Beli or Belinus and Taran of Welsh story, while the latter suggests the British idol called Heithiurun in the *Dindsenchas*.[1]

The *Mabinogi* of Pwyll, Prince of Dyfed,[2] begins by telling why he was called *Pen Annwfn*, or "Head of Annwfn" (Elysium). One day he observed a strange pack following a deer, but when he drove them off and urged on his own hounds, a horesman appeared, rebuking him for interfering with his sport. Pwyll apologized, and presently he and the stranger, Arawn, King of Annwfn, agreed to exchange their forms and kingdoms for a year: Pwyll would have Arawn's beautiful wife and would fight Arawn's rival, Havgan, giving him but one blow, which would slay him, for a second would resuscitate him. All this happened satisfactorily; never had Pwyll's kingdom been so well ruled, and complete friendship was effected between the monarchs. As in Irish myth, this is the theme of a mortal helping a deity in the Other-World. Yet Pwyll was once himself a god, as his title *Pen Annwfn* denotes, and was later euhemerized into a king, or confused with an actual monarch called Pwyll, while Annwfn here becomes a mere kingdom on earth.

One day Pwyll sat on a mound which had the property of causing him who was seated on it to receive a blow or see a prodigy. A beautiful woman rode toward him and his men, who pursued, but could not take her. This happened again on the morrow, but on the third day, when Pwyll himself pursued, she stood still at his bidding. She was Rhiannon, daughter of Heveidd Hên, and wished to marry him instead of Gwawl, whom she detested; and in a year he must come to her father's court for her. When Pwyll arrived, a stranger, who in reality was Gwawl, appeared demanding a boon of him, and on his promising it, asked for Rhiannon. She solved the difficulty by agreeing to be Gwawl's wife in a year, but bade Pwyll appear then as a beggar, carrying a certain magic bag, which, in the sequel, could not be filled with food. Gwawl was enraged, but was told by the beggar that unless a man of lands and riches stamped down the contents, it never could be filled. Gwawl did so and was immediately imprisoned in the bag, which was kicked about the hall by Pwyll's followers until, to escape death, he renounced his claim to Rhiannon.

The magic mound is here the equivalent of the *síd*, and such hills are favourite places for the appearance of immortals or fairies in Celtic story. Rhiannon, who suddenly appeared on the hill, was a goddess, like Fand or Connla's lover, and the theme is that of the Fairy Bride.

The story now tells how Rhiannon, whose child disappeared at birth, was accused of slaying it and was forced to sit at the horse-block of the palace, to tell her story to each new comer, and to offer to carry him inside. Meanwhile Teyrnon, Lord of Gwent-is-coed, had a mare whose foals disappeared on May-

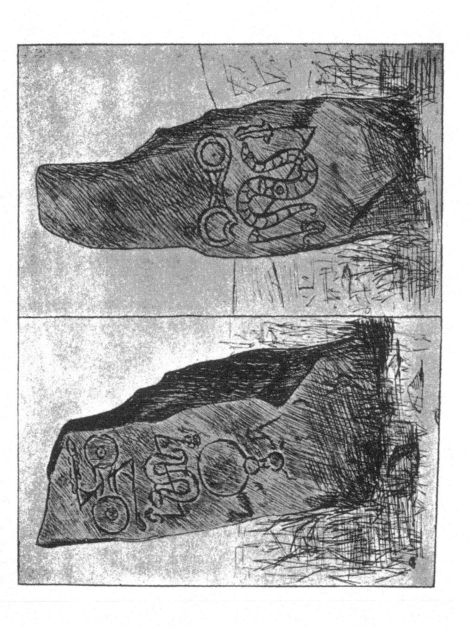

PLATE X

Incised Stones from Scotland

1. Incised stone, locally known as "the Picardy Stone," with double disc and Z-rod symbol, serpent and Z-symbol, and mirror with double-disc handle. From Insch, Aberdeenshire.

2. Incised stone with double disc and serpent and Z-rod symbols. From Newton, Aberdeenshire. Cf. Plate XVII.

Eve, and this May-Eve he saw a huge claw clutching the new-born colt. He severed it with his sword, and the intruder vanished; but at the door-way was a new-born infant, which Teyrnon nurtured. Like Cúchulainn and other heroes, it had a rapid growth and was called Gwri Golden-Hair. Noticing Gwri's likeness to Pwyll, Teyrnon carried the boy to him, and Rhiannon was reinstated, exclaiming that her anguish (*pryderi*) was past; whence Gwri was called Pryderi and succeeded Pwyll as King.

Folk-tale formulae abound in this section — that of the Abandoned Wife, found also in the *Mabinogi* of Branwen; and that of an animal born the same night as the hero; while the claw incident occurs in tales of Fionn. The importance of the story is in Pryderi's birth. The fact that Teyrnon's foal disappeared on the same night as Pryderi, who was found at Teyrnon's door, and the meanings of the names Teyrnon = Tigernonos ("Great King") or Tigernos ("Chief"), and Rhiannon = Rigantona ("Great Queen"), may point to a myth in which they were Pryderi's parents.[3] Manawyddan, who becomes Rhiannon's husband and rescues both her and Pryderi from the vengeance of Gwawl, may have been his father in another myth, for a poem associates him with Pryderi in Caer Sidi, a part of Annwfn. In the story, however, Pwyll, an original lord of Elysium, is Pryderi's parent. Does this point to a number of goddesses, bearing the name Rigantona, consorts of different gods, and later fused into one as Rhiannon? In another *Mabinogi*, Pryderi is despoiled of swine sent him by Arawn, or of which, according to a *Triad*, he was swineherd, Pwyll having brought them from Annwfn and given them to Pryderi's foster-father. Pwyll and Pryderi are thus associated with Elysium and with animals brought thence. A Taliesin poem tells of the magic cauldron of Pen Annwfn, viz. Pwyll. Round it was a ridge of pearls; it would not boil a coward's food; voices issued from it; it was warmed by the breath of nine maidens; and it formed part of the

"Spoils of Annwfn" which Arthur and others made a long journey overseas to obtain. Gweir was imprisoned in Caer Sidi through the spite (or messenger?) of Pwyll and Pryderi, associated as lords and defenders of Annwfn.[4] Arawn, Lord of Annwfn, was defeated by Amæthon, son of Dôn, at the mythic battle of Cath Godeu.[5]

The *Mabinogi* of Math, son of Mathonwy,[6] tells of Gil-væthwy's love for Goewin, Math's "foot-holder." To help him his brother Gwydion resolved to cause war and told Math that swine, unknown before, had been sent to Pryderi in Dyfed by Arawn. He and Gilvæthwy, disguised as bards, set off to the court of Pryderi, who praised Gwydion for his songs, where-upon the latter asked for the swine, but was told that they must breed double their number ere they left the country. Gwydion now obtained them in exchange for twelve stallions and twelve greyhounds magically formed by him from fungus; but these soon turned again to their original shape, and Pryd-eri invaded Math's territory, only to be defeated and slain in single combat by Gwydion's enchantments. Gilvæthwy outraged Goewin during the battle, and when Math discovered this, he transformed the brothers first into a couple of deer, then into swine, and finally into wolves. In these forms they had animal progeny, afterward changed to human shape by Math. Math now found a new "foot-holder" in Arianrhod, Gwydion's sister, but she proved no virgin, and when Math caused her to pass under his magic rod, she bore twins, one of whom was taken by Math and called Dylan. When Gwydion brought the other, who had grown rapidly, to Arianrhod's castle, she refused to give him a name. Disguised as a shoe-maker, Gwydion then arrived with the boy and made shoes for Arianrhod which did not fit. She went on board Gwyd-ion's ship, produced by magic, and saw the boy shoot a bird. Not recognizing him, she cried, "With a sure hand (*llaw gyffes*) *lleu* shoots the bird," whereupon Gwydion revealed himself and said that she had named the boy, Lleu Llaw

Gyffes. Now she refused to arm him, but once more disguised, Gwydion with Lleu caused an enchanted fleet to appear; and she armed both, only to be taunted with the stratagem. Again she said that Lleu would never have a wife of the people of this earth, but Math and Gwydion made him a bride out of flowers and called her Blodeuwedd. She was unfaithful to Lleu, however, and advised by her lover, Gronw Pebyr, she discovered that a javelin wrought for a year during Mass on Sundays would kill him when standing with one foot on a buck and the other on a bath curiously prepared by the bank of a river. Gronw made the javelin, and when Lleu, prevailed on by Blodeuwedd, showed her the fatal position, he was struck by Gronw and flew off as an eagle. Soon after, Gwydion found a pig eating worms which fell from a wasted eagle on a tree; and as he sang three verses, at each the eagle came nearer. When he struck it with a magic rod, it became Lleu, who now turned Blodeuwedd into an owl; while Gronw had to submit to a blow from a javelin which penetrated the flat stone placed by him against his body and killed him. Lleu now recovered his lands and ruled them happily.

These personages are associated with a dim figure called Dôn, who is probably not male, but female, and is mother of Gwydion, Gilvæthwy, Govannon, Amæthon, and Arianrhod, who was herself mother of Dylan and Lleu. Math is Dôn's brother. Superficially this group is equivalent to the Tuatha Dé Danann, and Dôn is parallel to Danu, while Govannon (*gôf*, "smith") is the equivalent of Goibniu, the Irish smith-god. Lleu, the reading of whose name as Llew ("Lion") may be abandoned, has been equated with Lug, and both names are said to mean "light." "Light," however, has no sense in the name-giving incident, and possibly, as Loth suggests,[7] there is a connexion with Irish *lu*, "little." The other names of the group have no parallels among the Tuatha Dé Danann. Mythological traits are the magic powers of Math and Gwydion, their shape-shifting, and the introduction of the swine.

Math Hên, or "the Ancient," is an old Welsh "high god," remembered for magic, which he taught to Gwydion; for the fact that the winds brought to him the least whisper of a conversation, wherever it might be held; and for his pre-eminent goodness to the suffering and his justice without vengeance upon the wrongdoer. The last trait shows a high ideal of divinity, and the second a conception of omniscience.

As a magician Gwydion is also prominent, and by magic he governed Gwynedd. He was the cleverest of men and possessed terrible strength, while his prophetic powers are emphasized in a *Triad*, and he had supreme gifts as story-teller and bard. His successful raid on Pryderi's pigs which came from Annwfn suggests that, like Cúchulainn, he is the culture hero bringing domestic animals from the god's land to earth, and perhaps for this reason a *Triad* calls him one of the three cowherds of Britain, guarding thousands of kine. Irish myth also frequently speaks of cattle brought from the *síd*. Gwydion's name reflects his character as an inspired bard, if it is from a root *vet*, giving words meaning "saying" or "poetry," cognate terms being Irish *fáith*, "prophet" or "poet," and Latin *vates*.[8] Gwydion would thus be equivalent to Ogma and Ogmios, gods of eloquence and letters, and a late manuscript says he first taught reading and knowledge of books to the Gaels of Anglesey and Ireland. He is not straightforward, however, when he pretends that his sister Arianrhod is a virgin, for she is his mistress and mother of his sons, an incest incident with parallels in Irish story.

Arianrhod consented to the fraud and as a further pretence to chastity disowned Lleu; yet a *Triad* calls her one of the three blessed or white ladies of Britain. Was she worshipped as a virgin goddess, while myth gave her a different character? Celtic goddesses, like the *Matres*, were connected with fertility, and goddesses of fertility or earth are apt to possess a double character, like the great Phrygian Mother, who was also regarded as a virgin.[9] Arianrhod, like Aphrodite, was lovely;

"beauty-famed beyond summer's dawn," sang a poet.[10]   Her name means "silver wheel."

Much that is said of Lleu is insignificant for mythology, though Rhŷs has built a large structure of sun, dawn, and darkness upon it. The greater part of it is a well-known folk-tale formula attached to his name — that of the Unfaithful Wife. It is doubtful whether Lleu really equals Lug merely because their uncles are respectively Govannon and Gavida (Goibniu), both meaning "smith"; for while Gavida nurtured Lug, and Lug slew Balor, Lleu was not brought up by Govannon, and the latter incident has no equivalent in his story. Moreover, Lug is prominent in connexion with the great Celtic festival, Lugnasad (celebrated on the first of August), but Lleu is not. Thus his mythological significance is lost to us.

Math caused Dylan to be baptized, and then this precocious baby made for the sea, where he swam like a fish; no billow broke under him, and he was called "son of the wave." The blow which caused his death came from Govannon — one of the three nefarious blows of Britain — but is otherwise unexplained. The waves lamented his death, and ever, as they press toward the land, they seek to avenge it.[11] Perhaps Dylan was once a sea-god, regarded as identical with the waves, like Manannan. Tradition speaks of the noise of the waters pouring into the Conway as his dying groans, and, again like Manannan, son of Ler (the sea), he is called Dylan Eil Ton or Mor ("Son of the Wave" or "Sea").[12] "As soon as he entered the sea, he took its nature."

Govannon's functions as a smith-god are illustrated from a reference in *Kulhwch and Olwen*, where his help must be gained by Kulhwch to attend at the end of the furrows to cleanse the iron,[13] though the meaning of this is obscure. In a Taliesin poem he and Math are associated as artificers.[14] Amæthon's name suggests that his functions were connected with agricul-ture (*amaeth*, "ploughman" or "labourer"), and this is illustrated by the fact that no husbandmen can till or dress a certain field for Kulhwch, "so wild is it, save Amæthon, son of Dôn; he will not follow thee of his own free will, and thou canst not force him."[15] He also brought animals from the gods' land — a roebuck, whelp, and lapwing belonging to Arawn — and this led to the battle of Godeu, in which, aided by Gwydion, he fought Arawn. Gwydion changed trees and sedges into combatants, as he had transformed fungus into hounds and horses. On either side fought personages who could not be vanquished until their names were discovered, but Gwydion affected the course of the battle by finding the name of Arawn's mysterious helper, Bran — a mythic instance of the power of the hidden name, once it becomes known to another.[16]

Whether as a survival from myth or from later folk-belief, the stars are associated with some of these divinities. The constellation of Cassiopeia is called "Dôn's Court"; Arianrhod is connected with the constellation Corona Borealis; and the Milky Way is termed "Gwydion's Castle," because he followed it in chasing Blodeuwedd across the sky — an obviously primitive myth.[17]

The *Mabinogion* of Branwen and of Manawyddan are connected and concern the families of Pwyll and Llyr.[18] The Llyr group consists of his sons, Bran and Manawyddan; their sister, Branwen; and their half-brother, Nissyen and Evnissyen. As Bran sat on a rock at Harlech, vessels arrived bearing Matholwych, King of Ireland, as a suitor for Branwen. He was accepted, and a feast was made for him in tents, for no house could hold Bran. But Evnissyen the mischief-maker mutilated Matholwych's steeds, and the king indignantly left, returning only when Bran gave him gifts, including a cauldron which restored life to the dead, though they remained dumb. This cauldron was obtained from two mysterious beings who came out of a lake in Ireland, the man bearing the cauldron, and the woman about to give birth to an armed warrior; but they and their descendants were so troublesome that they were imprisoned in a white-hot iron house, whence the pair escaped to Britain with their cauldron — an incident probably borrowed from the Ulster tale of the *Mesca Ulad.* Matholwych returned to Ireland with Branwen, and there, after two years, in retaliation for Evnissyen's conduct, she was placed in the kitchen, where the butcher struck her every morning. She accordingly sent a starling to Bran with a message, whereupon he waded over to Ireland, his men following in ships and crossing the Shannon on his body. The Irish came to terms and built Bran a vast house, in which they concealed warriors in sacks; but Evnissyen discovered this and crushed them one by one. Peace was now concluded, but Evnissyen again caused trouble by throwing Branwen's child into the fire. In the fight which followed the Irish were winning because they restored their dead in the cauldron; but Evnissyen smashed it, though he died in the effort. Bran was slain, and seven only of his people escaped, including Pryderi, Manawyddan, and Taliesin. Bran bade them cut off his head and bury it at London, looking toward France; and they reached Anglesey with Branwen, who died there of a broken heart. Meanwhile Caswallawn, son of Beli, had usurped the kingdom, Bran's son also dying of sorrow. As Bran had advised, his head-bearers remained at Harlech for seven years, feasting and listening to the birds of Rhiannon singing far overhead; and at Gwales for eighty years, the head entertaining them in a house with a forbidden door. The years passed as a day, until one of the men opened the door, when their evils were remembered, and they went to London to bury the head.

Manawyddan having lamented that he was landless, Pryderi gave him land in Dyfed and his mother Rhiannon as wife. All three, with Kicva, Pryderi's wife, were seated on a knoll when a thunder-clap was heard; and as the cloud which accompanied it cleared away, they found the country desolate, without creature or habitation. Lack of food impelled them to seek a living as saddlers, shield-makers, and shoe-makers successively, but they were always expelled by the regular craftsmen. One day they pursued a boar to a strange castle, and Pryderi entered, but trying to lift a golden cup, his hands stuck fast to it, nor could he move his feet. Manawyddan told Rhiannon of Pryderi's disappearance, and when she sought him, she met the same fate, until at another clap of thunder the castle disappeared. Manawyddan and Kicva, as shoe-makers, were again foiled by envious cobblers, and he now sowed three fields, but an army of mice ate the grain. One of these he caught and was about to hang, in spite of the entreaties of Kicva, of a clerk, and of a priest, when a bishop appeared, and Manawyddan bargained to give up the mouse if the bishop released Pryderi and Rhiannon, removed the enchantment from Dyved, and told him who and what the mouse was. The bishop was Llwyd, a friend of Gwawl, whom Pryderi's father, Pwyll, had insulted. All had happened in revenge for that: the mouse was Llwyd's wife, the other mice the ladies of the court. Everything was now restored; Pryderi and Rhiannon reappeared; and Llwyd agreed to seek no further revenge.

While the framework of *Branwen* is connected with Scandinavian and German sagas, whether borrowed by Welshmen from their Norse allies in the ninth and tenth centuries, as Nutt supposed,[19] or by Norsemen from Wales, its personages are Celtic, and it contains many native elements. Llyr Half-Speech and Manawyddan are the equivalents of the Irish sea-gods Ler and Manannan, the latter of whom is also associated with Elysium. It is uncertain whether these two were common to Goidels and Brythons, or were borrowed by the latter; but at all events they have a definite position in Welsh tradition, which knows of two other Llyrs — Llyr Marini and Llyr, father of Cordelia in Geoffrey's *History* — Shakespeare's Lear.[20] These are probably varying presentments of a sea-god. Llyr is sometimes confused with Lludd

Llaw Ereint, or "Silver-Hand." A *Triad* represents Gweir, Mabon, and Llyr as three notable prisoners of Britain; but in *Kulhwch* these are Greit, Mabon, and Lludd, father of Cordelia.[21] Are Llyr and Lludd identical, and is an Irish Alloit, sometimes called father of Manannan, the equivalent of Lludd? All this is uncertain. Rhŷs and Loth are tempted to correct Lludd into Nudd, an earlier Nodens Lāmargentios ("Nudd Silver-Hand") having been changed to Lodens (Lludd) Lāmargentios by alliteration, and to equate him with the Irish Nuada Argetlâm ("Silver-Hand"); but the possibility of such an alliterative change has been denied. Nuada is identified with the British god Nodons; but though Llyr was a sea-god, there is no proof that Nuada or Nodons was such, though some symbols in the remains of the temple of Nodons on the Severn have been thought to suggest this.[22] These, however, are not decisive, and it is equally possible that the god was equated with Mars rather than with Neptune.

Manawyddan, whose name is derived from Welsh *Manaw*, the Isle of Man, is much more humanized in Welsh story than the divine Manannan of the *Voyage of Bran;* yet he has magic powers and great superiority as a craftsman. He is associated with Arthur in a poem and is praised for his wise counsels, while Pryderi was instructed by him in various crafts and aided by him, just as the Irish Diarmaid was nurtured and taught by Manannan. Rhiannon may have been introduced accidentally into the story — "a mere invention of the narrator in order to give sequence to the narrative";[23] but possibly she is Manawyddan's real consort, not one given him by her son. If so, Pryderi would be Manawyddan's son, not Pwyll's, and his deliverance of Rhiannon and Pryderi from his magician foe would be significant.[24] Rhiannon appears magically, like Irish goddesses of Elysium, and she may thus have been associated with Manawyddan in Elysium, who with Pryderi is Lord of Annwfn in a Taliesin poem —

"Complete is my chair in Caer Sidi;
Plague and age hurt not him who is in it,
They know Manawyddan and Pryderi;
Three organs round a fire sing before it,
And about its points are ocean's streams.
And the abundant well above it —
Sweeter than white wine the drink of it." [25]

Rhiannon's magic birds, whose song brought joy and oblivion for seven years, like that of Ler's bird-children,[26] and awoke the dead and made the living sleep,[27] have an Elysian note and confirm the supposition that she is an Elysian goddess. Beyond that we need not go, and there is nothing to connect her with the dawn or the moon.

Branwen or Bronwen ("White Bosom") has no definite traits. Her marriage to Matholwych and her subsequent sufferings recall the stories of Gudrun, Kriemhild, and Signy; but whether she ever was connected as a goddess of fertility with her brother's cauldron of regeneration must remain an ingenious conjecture, not supported by the *Mabinogi*. As a sea-god's daughter, she may be "the Venus of the northern sea," as Elton supposed,[28] while the *Black Book of Caermarthen* calls the sea "the fountain of Venus," [29] though this is, perhaps, nothing more than a Classical recollection. Later romance knew her as Brangwaine, the confidante of Tristram and Yseult, giving the knight the love-potion which bound him in illicit amour with Yseult.

Bran is a more obviously mythological figure, and his gigantic size is an earlier or later method of indicating his divinity. His buried head protected the land from invasion — a mythical expression of actual custom — for bodies and heads of warriors had apotropaic virtues and were sometimes exhibited or buried in the direction whence danger was expected.[30] Hence the image of a divine head might have greater powers, and this may explain the existence of Celtic images of a god's head, often in triple form. These figures, found in Gaul, were believed by Rhŷs to be images of Cernunnos, a god of the Celtic underworld, which he regarded as a dark region, contrary to all that we can gather of it, while Bran was the Brythonic equivalent of Cernunnos and was slain by a sun-hero, his wading to Ireland representing his crossing the waters to Hades, like Yama, there to reign as lord of the dead.[31] The heads, however, can be explained only conjecturally as heads of Cernunnos. The exigencies of the story demanded that Ireland should be brought in, and as Bran had to reach it somehow, it was easiest to make the gigantic god wade there; if the parallel with Yama were true, Bran should have died before crossing the water of death. Yama's realm was not "dark," but a heavenly region of light, like the Celtic other-world, even if the latter, unlike the former, was subterranean. Far from being "dark," Bran is bright and cheerful and has Elysian traits. Eighty years are as a day, and men think only of feasting and happiness in the presence of his head, which is as agreeable to them as he himself was in life; it produces an Elysium on earth, which is lost through opening a door, exactly as others lose it and become decrepit through contact with earth. Thus if Bran, sitting on the rock at Harlech or existing as a talking head afterward solemnly buried, like Orpheus's singing head interred in a sacred place, is the equivalent of the squatting Gaulish god Cernunnos, perhaps also represented as a single or triple head, this can only be because both were lords of a bright other-world, whether the region of the dead or a divine land. Bran is certainly not a dark god of blight, but rather the reverse, since his cauldron resuscitates the dead. In crossing to Ireland he carried his musicians on his back, and this may point to his being a divinity of musicians and bards. If so, he, as the *Urdawl Ben* ("Noble Head"), may be compared to the *Uthr Ben* ("Wonderful Head") of a Taliesin poem, which boasted of being a bard, harper, and piper, and equal to seven score professionals.[32] Arthur disinterred Bran's head, not wishing to owe the defence of Britain to it.

Bran was euhemerized into a British king who was confused

with Brennus, leader of the Gauls in the sack of Rome, 390
B. C., and was transformed into a conqueror of Gaul and
Rome.[33] He also figures as a saint, Bran the Blessed, if that
was not already a pagan epithet; and remaining at Rome
seven years as hostage with his son Caradawc, he brought
Christianity thence to the Cymry. Caradawc is here the historic Caratacus, who was carried prisoner to Rome, but there
is confusion with a Caradawc ("Great Arms," or "Prince of
Combat"), son of Llyr Marini, about whom a saga may have
existed. In any case Bran was regarded as head of one of the
three saintly families of Britain.[34]

In the *Mabinogi* of Branwen, Caswallawn, clothed in a
mantle of invisibility, destroyed the heroes of Britain and
usurped the kingdom, leaving Manawyddan landless; and
though his sister was married to Llyr, he was hostile to Llyr's
descendants. Caswallawn, Lludd, Llevelys, and Nynnyaw
were sons of Beli, although Geoffrey makes his Lear long pre-
cede Beli or Heli as king, while he also introduces a Belinus
and confuses Caswallawn with Cassivellaunus, Caesar's foe.[35]
Beli and Belinus may represent the god Belenos, who was
equated with Apollo; and Beli is victorious champion of the
land and the preserver of its qualities in a Taliesin poem, in
which the singer implores him [36] — perhaps a reminiscence of
earlier divine traits. A *Triad* calls Beli father of Arianrhod,
and Rhŷs, assuming that this is Arianrhod, the daughter of
Dôn, makes Dôn consort of Beli, equates Dôn with Danu, and,
without the slightest evidence, assigns to Danu as consort the
shadowy figure Bile, father of Mile, invented by Irish annalists. Beli and Bile are then equated with the Celtic Dispater,
the divine ancestor of the Celtic race, whom he assumes to
have been a "dark" god, ruling a "dark" underworld.[37] All
this is modern mythologizing.

Caswallawn is confused in the *Triads* with Cassivellaunus, a
warrior who may have been named after him; and he is called
"war-king," an epithet which may recall his divine functions,

PLATE XI

GAULS AND ROMANS IN COMBAT

Bas-relief from a sarcophagus found near Rome.

those of a god invisibly leading armies to battle and embodied in chiefs who bore his name. Yet the epithet might be that of actual warriors, just as the German Emperor calls himself the "war-lord."

Lludd, as King, rebuilt London or Caer Ludd, and was buried at Ludgate Hill, which thus preserves his name and points to an earlier cult of Lludd at this place.[38] He is also said to have been enclosed in a narrow prison — an unexplained reference to some tale now lost. In the story of *Lludd and Llevelys* [39] his country of Britain was subjected to three plagues — the Coranians who heard every whisper, like Math Hên; a shriek on May-Eve caused by a foreign dragon attacking the dragon of the land and producing wide-spread desolation; and the mysterious disappearance of a year's supply of food. Llevelys bade Lludd bruise certain insects in water and throw the mixture over his assembled people and the Coranians; the latter alone would be poisoned by it. The dragons were to be made drunk with mead and then buried. The third plague was caused by a magician who lulled every one to sleep and then carried off the provisions; but Lludd was to keep awake by plunging into cold water and then to capture the giant, who would become his vassal. This last plague recalls "the hand of glory," the hand of a new-born infant or a criminal, which, anointed with grease and ignited, rendered a robber invisible and caused every one to sleep in whatever house the thief entered. Treasure was also discovered by its means, and as Dousterswivel in Scott's *Antiquary* said, "he who seeksh for treasuresh shall never find none at all," to which the Antiquary replied, "I dare take my corporal oath of that conclusion." Whether this episode of the story is based on such a folk-belief is not clear. As a whole nation suffers from the plagues, and as two of them affect fertility and plenty, the origin of the tale may be found in the mythical contest of divine powers with hostile potencies of blight, as at Mag-Tured.[40] In a *Triad* the plague of the Coranians is called that of March Malaen from beyond the

sea;[41] and March suggests the Fomorian Morc, who taxed
the Nemedians in two-thirds of their children, corn, and milk
on November-Eve.[42] The Welsh plagues, however, occur at Beltane, i. e. at the beginning of summer, rather than winter, as
might be expected. Lludd is praised for generosity in giving
meat and drink — the attribute of a kindly god. The Coranians are connected with Welsh còr ("dwarf") and are still
known as mischievous fairies.

In connexion with such dwarfs it is interesting to note that a
dwarf fairy-folk is described by Giraldus Cambrensis (1147–
1223). Two of them took the priest Elidurus, when a boy,
through subterranean passages to a delightful region, whose
people lived on milk and saffron, swore no oaths, and contemned
human ambition and inconstancy. Elidurus frequently visited
them, but being persuaded by his mother to steal their gold, he
was pursued and the gold was taken from him, after which he
never again found the way to fairy-land.[43] Save for their size,
these fairies recall the Tuatha Dé Danann, dwelling in the sid.

Gwyn, son of Nudd, is connected both with Annwfn and also
in later belief with fairy-land.[44] He was a great magician and a
mighty warrior — "the hope of armies" — while his horse was
also "the torment of battle";[45] without him and a certain
steed named Du, the monster boar, the Twrch Trwyth, could
not be caught by Kulhwch. Gwyn abducted Creidylad (Cordelia), daughter of Lludd, who was affianced to Gwythur; but
in the fight which followed Gwyn was victor and forced one of
his foes to eat his dead father's heart so that he became mad.
Arthur interfered, however, and ordered that Creidylad should
remain with her father, while Gwyn and Gwythur must fight
for her every day until doom, when she would be given to the
victor.[46] This story is illustrated by folk-survivals. On May-
day in the Isle of Man a girl representing the May Queen was
attended by a captain and several others; and there was also a
Queen of Winter with her company. The two bands met in
mock battle, and if the May Queen was captured, her men had

to ransom her.[47] Ritual combats between representatives of summer and winter occur among the folk everywhere and in origin symbolized the defeat of winter, as well as actually aided the gods of light and growth. The story of Creidylad is perhaps the *débris* of an old myth explaining the reason of such a contest when its real purpose was forgotten.

Another group of divine personages is found in the *Hanes Taliesin*, which was written in the sixteenth or seventeenth century, although references to incidents in it occur in far earlier poems in the *Book of Taliesin* and presuppose its existence in some form when they were composed. It contains mythical elements which introduce old divinities, a culture hero or god, Taliesin, and the conceptions of inspiration, rebirth, and shape-shifting, the last being expressed in the folk-tale formula of the Transformation Combat, as it already is in one of the poems.[48] Taliesin is unknown to the *Mabinogion*, save as a bearer of Bran's head, and this suggests his local character, while the saga was probably developed in a district to the south of the estuary of the Dyfi.[49] Before story or poem was written, three facts concerning his mythic history must have been remembered — his inspiration, his shape-shifting powers, and his being the rebirth of Gwion. Whether or not there was an actual poet called Taliesin living in the sixth or, as his latest translator and commentator, Mr. J. G. Evans, thinks, in the thirteenth century, it is certain that his poems contain many mythical references which must once have been told of a mythical being doubtless bearing the same name as himself.

Tegid the Bald lived in Lake Tegid (Bala) with his wife Cerridwen, their beautiful daughter Creirwy, and their sons Morvran and Avagddu, the latter the most ill-favoured of men, although Morvran ("Sea-Crow") is elsewhere said to have been also of repellent aspect. Cerridwen wished to compensate Avagddu by giving him knowledge, so that he might have entry among men of standing; and with the aid of the books of Ffergll (Vergil) she prepared a cauldron of inspiration

and science to boil for a year. While she went to gather herbs
of virtue, she set the blind Mordu to kindle the fire and Gwion
to stir the pot; but three drops from it fell on his finger, which
he put in his mouth, and he found himself master of knowledge,
which taught him to flee from Cerridwen's rage. Here follows
the incident of the Transformation Combat, with the goddess
as a hen finally swallowing Gwion as a grain.[50] She later gave
birth to him, and wrapping him up in a hide, placed him in the
sea. At Gwydno's weir the value of a hundred pounds was
found every first of May, and Elphin was to obtain whatever was
discovered on the next occasion, which proved to be the child.
When the package was opened, Gwydno exclaimed, "Here is
a fine or radiant brow" or "fine profit" (tal iessin), whence
Elphin named the child Taliesin, and the infant sang and
showed how deep was his knowledge. He was nurtured by
Elphin and became one of the greatest of bards. Now Elphin
had boasted at court that he had a more virtuous wife and a
better bard than any there, whence he was imprisoned until
his claim was verified. Rhun was sent to seduce his wife, but
Taliesin put a servant in her place, and she fell victim to Rhun,
who cut off her finger with her mistress's ring. When Elphin
was confronted with it, he showed an ingenuity equal to that
of Sherlock Holmes in proving that the finger was not his
wife's — the ring was too tight, the finger-nail was uncut, and on
her finger some flour had remained from her baking. Now his wife
never baked; she cut her finger-nails weekly; and the ring was
loose even on her thumb. Taliesin next came forward and by
his spells made the other bards utter nonsense. He sang of his
origin — "the region of the summer stars" — his existence in
long past ages, from that of Lucifer's fall to the days of the
Patriarchs, and his life at the Nativity and Crucifixion of
Christ, and referred to his birth from Cerridwen. Then the
castle shook; Elphin was summoned; and as Taliesin sang his
chains fell from him.[51]

The latter part of the story is purely romantic, but in poems

ascribed to Taliesin and in a *Triad* his greatness as the "chief
of bards" appears —

> "With me is the splendid chair,
> The inspiration of fluent and urgent song."

He has been with the gods and ranks himself as one of them,
telling how he was created and enchanted by them before he
became immortal;[52] he has a chair not only on earth but in
the gods' land.[53] Taliesin was the ideal bard, a god of inspiration like Ogma, and, besides his reincarnation, his birth from
Cerridwen shows his divine nature. Yet, like other semi-
divine personages connected with inspiration or culture, he
obtains his powers by accident or by force. One myth, that
of the cauldron, shows the former and is parallel to the story
of Fionn and the salmon;[54] but in another, darkly referred to
in a poem, he with Arthur and many companions goes overseas
to Caer Sidi for the spoils of Annwfn, including the cauldron
of Pen Annwfn.[55] Here, whether successfully or not, the gifts
of culture and inspiration are sought by force or craft. Are
two separate myths combined in the *Hanes Taliesin*, one making
Taliesin son of a goddess with an abode in the divine land; the
other viewing him as a culture hero, stealing the gifts of the
gods' land, and therefore obnoxious to Cerridwen? And if so,
do these myths "reflect the encroachment of the cult of a god
on that of a goddess, his worshippers regarding him as her son,
her worshippers reflecting their hostility to the new god in a
myth of her enmity to him"?[56]

Taliesin was supreme in shape-shifting and rebirth. Of no
other Brythonic god or hero is the latter asserted, and several
poems obscurely enumerate various forms which he assumed
and recount his adventures in them. When, however, the poet,
speaking in his name, asserts that he has been a sword, tear,
word, book, coracle, etc., it is obvious that this is mere bardic
nonsense and not pantheism, as some have suggested. The
claims of Taliesin and of the Irish Amairgen resemble those of
the Eskimo *angakok*, who has the *entrée* of the other-world and

can transform himself at will; [57] and the gift of transformation
and rebirth is then associated with inspiration in the *Hanes
Taliesin*. Here the equation with Fionn and Oisin, already
noted by J. G. Campbell and accepted by Rhŷs, is worth ob-
serving. Fionn and Gwion obtain inspiration accidentally.
Fionn is reborn, not as Oisin, but as Mongan, and Gwion as
Taliesin. Oisin and Taliesin are both bards, and Oisin's name
is perhaps equivalent to *-essin* or *-eisin* in Taliesin. Taliesin's
shape-shifting has no parallel with Fionn or Oisin, but Oisin's
mother and, in one tradition, Fionn's also became a fawn.
Thus inspiration, rebirth, and shape-shifting are attached to
different personages in different ways, showing that mythical
elements common to the Celtic race have been employed.

Tegid is a god of the world under waters, but is not otherwise known to existing myth; though he and Cerridwen, pos-
sessor of a cauldron, are perhaps parallel to the giant pair out
of a lake with their cauldron in *Branwen*, Cerridwen being a
local goddess of inspiration, as her cauldron of knowledge shows.
The Celtic mythical cauldron, bestowing knowledge, plenty
(like Dagda's), and life (like Bran's),[58] is recognizable as a
property of the gods' land; but it was dangerous, and a bard
sings of his chair being defended from Cerridwen's cauldron.[59]
Cerridwen was regarded as a daughter of Ogyrven, from whose
cauldron came three muses, and who was perhaps an eponymous deity of the elements of language, poetry, and the letters
of the alphabet, called *ogyrvens*, as well as a god of bards.
Cerridwen is styled "the *ogyrven* of various seeds, those of
poetic harmony, the exalted spirit of the minstrel"; but
ogyrven also means "a spiritual form," "a personified idea,"
and may here be equivalent to "goddess." [60] Thus Cerridwen
was a deity of inspiration, like Brigit, though, like other Celtic
goddesses, her primary function may have been with fertility,
of which the cauldron, supplying plenty and giving life, is a
symbol. She is also called a "goddess of grain." [61]

Tegid's water-world is the land under waves of Irish myth —

PLATE XII

THREE-HEADED GOD

The statue, adorned with torques, was once horned. For another representation of this divinity, perhaps a deity of the underworld, see Plate VII. Found at Condat, France.

one aspect of Elysium, examples of which have already been considered. Another instance occurs in the *Voyage of Maelduin*, where the voyagers reach a sea, beneath which is descried a country with castles, men, and cattle; but in a tree is a great beast eating an ox, and the sight so terrifies them that they sail quickly away. In another story Murough is invited to come below the waters. He dives down and reaches the land of King Under-Waves, whom he sees sitting on a golden throne; a year spent there feasting seems but a few days. Welsh tradition has also many stories of water-worlds, as well as of fairy brides, daughters of the lord of the lake, and cattle which came thence.[62] In a Christianized Irish version of the conception a bishop from time to time visited a monastery beneath the waters of a lake, finally disappearing from his own monastery, none knew whither.[63]

CHAPTER IX

THE DIVINE LAND

ELYSIUM, called by many beautiful Celtic names, is the gods' land and is never associated with the dead. The living were occasionally invited there, however, and either remained perpetually or returned to earth, where sometimes they found themselves decrepit and aged; time had lapsed like a dream, because they were in the immortal land and had tasted its immortal food. Many tales already cited have shown different conceptions of its situation — in the *sid*, on a mysterious island, or beneath the waters; or the gods create it on earth or produce it by glamour to mortal eyes. Occasionally such conceptions are mingled. These legends have illustrated its marvellous, beauty, its supernatural fruit trees and music, its unfailing and satisfying food and drink, and the deathless glory and youth of its people.

The tales now to be summarized will throw further light upon its nature. The first of these, *The Voyage of Bran*, is an old pagan myth retold in prose and verse in the seventh or eighth century by a Christian editor, interested in the past. Bran, son of Febal, one day heard music behind him produced by a woman from unknown lands, i. e. from Elysium. Lulled by its sweetness, he slept, and on awaking found by his side a musical branch of silver with white blossoms. Taking it into his royal house, he there saw the woman, who sang of the wondrous isle whence she had brought the branch. Four feet of white bronze upheld it, and on its plains were glistening, coloured splendours. Music swelled there; wailing, treachery, harshness, grief, sorrow, sickness, age, and death were unknown. An exquisite haze hung over it, and its people listened to the sweet music, drinking wine the while; laughter pealed there and everlasting joy. Thrice fifty islands lay to the west of it, each double or triple the size of Erin. The woman then prophesied of Christ's birth, and after she had urged Bran to sail till he reached *Tír na m-Ban* ("the Land of Women"), she disappeared, the branch leaping from Bran's hand into hers.

Next day Bran sailed with twenty-seven men, and on the voyage they saw Manannan driving his chariot over the waves. The god sang to the voyagers and told how he was passing over a flowery plain, for what Bran saw as the sea was to Manannan a plain. The speckled salmon in the sea were calves and lambs, and steeds invisible to Bran were there also. People were sitting playing and drinking wine, and making love without crime. Bran's coracle was not on the waves, but on an immortal wood, yielding fruit and perfume; the folk of that land were immortal and sinless, unlike Adam's descendants, and in it rivers poured forth honey. Finally Manannan bade Bran row to *Tír na m-Ban*, which he would reach by sunset.

Bran first came to an isle of laughter; and when one of his men was sent ashore, he refused to leave the laughing folk of this Isle of Joy. At the Land of Women their Queen welcomed Bran, throwing a ball of thread which cleaved to his hand, and by which the boat was drawn ashore. All now went into a house where were twenty-seven beds, one for each; the food never grew less and for each man it had the taste which he desired. They stayed for a year, though it was in truth many years; but home-sickness at last seized one of them, Nechtan, so that he and the others begged Bran to return. The Queen said they would rue this, yet as they were bent on going, she bade them not set foot on Erin and to take with them their comrade from the Isle of Joy. When Erin was reached, Bran told his name to the men gathered on the shore; but they said, "We do not know him, though the voyage of Bran is in our ancient stories." Nechtan now leaped ashore, but when his foot touched land, he became a heap of ashes. Bran then told his wanderings and bade farewell to the crowd, returning presumably to the divine land. "From that hour his wanderings are not known." [1]

Manannan's land overseas is the subject of a conventionalized tale in the *Colloquy of the Ancients* (*Acallamh na Senórach*), which contains primitive material. One of Fionn's men, Ciabhan, embarked with two youths, Lodan and Eolus, sons of the Kings of India and of Greece; and during a storm Manannan appeared riding over the waves. "For the space of nine waves he would be submerged in the sea, but would rise on the crest of the tenth, and that without his breast or chest wetted." He rescued them on condition of fealty to himself, and drawing them on his horse, brought them to the Land of Promise. Having passed the loch of dwarfs, they came to Manannan's stone fort, where food, wine, and music delighted them; and where they saw Manannan's folk perform many tricks, which they themselves were able to imitate. In the Land of Promise were three beautiful sisters, Clidna, Aeife, and Edaein, who eloped with the visitors in two boats, Clidna going along with Ciabhan. When he reached Erin, he went ashore to hunt, and now a great wave, known ever after as Clidna's wave, rolled in and drowned her, overwhelming at the same time Manannan's men, Ildathach and his sons, both in love with Clidna and following in pursuit of her. A different account of Clidna has already been cited.[2]

In the story of Bran, the queen-goddess fell in love with him and visited him (as in the legend of Connla) to induce him to come to her. While there are hints of other inhabitants, women or goddesses alone exist on this island — an additional parallel to the story of Connla, though there the island has a king; to the incident in *Maelduin;* and to the name "Land of Ever-Living Women" in the *Dindsenchas* of Tuag Inbir.

PLATE XIII

Sucellos

This divinity, characterized by a hammer (cf. p. 9), was a ruler of the underworld (cf. the representation of Dispater with a hammer, Plate XIV). A benevolent god, his hammer is a symbol of creative force. The artistic type (for another instance of which see Plate XXVI) was influenced by that of the Alexandrian Serapis and the Classical Hades-Pluto. Cf. also Plate IX, B. The figure was found at Prémeaux, France.

Another instance occurs in a Fionn story. Fionn and his men were hunting when there met them a huge and beautiful woman, whose finger-rings were as thick as three ox-goads. She was Bebhionn from Maidens' Land in the west, where all the inhabitants were women save their father (its king) and his three sons; and for the third time she had escaped from her husband, son of the King of the adjacent Isle of Men, and had come to seek Fionn's protection. As she sat by him and Goll, however, her huge husband came, and slaying her, eluded the heroes' pursuit, vanishing overseas in a boat with two rowers.[3]

The tradition of the Isle of Women still exists in Celtic folklore. Such an island was only a part of the divine land and may have originated in myth from actual custom — women living upon or going at certain periods to small islands to perform rites generally tabu to men, a custom to which reference is made by Strabo and Pomponius Mela.[4]

That the gods could create an Elysium on earth has been found in the story of Lug and Dechtire, and another instance occurs in the tale of Cormac mac Art, King of Ireland in the third century, of whom an annalist records that he disappeared for seven months in 248 A. D., a reference to the events of this story. To Cormac appeared a young man with a branch from which hung nine apples of gold; and when this was shaken, it produced strange music, hearing which every one forgot his troubles and fell asleep. He came from a land where there was nought save truth, and where was no age, nor decay, nor gloom, nor sadness, nor envy, nor jealousy, nor weeping; and Cormac said that to possess the branch he would give whatever was asked, whereupon the stranger answered, "give me then thy wife, thy son and daughter." Cormac agreed and now told his bargain to his wife, who, like her children, was sorrowful that he should have preferred the branch to them. The stranger carried off successively, daughter, son, and wife, and all Ireland grieved, for they were much loved; but Cormac shook the branch, and the mourning ceased. In a year desire to see his wife and children came to the King. He set off, and as he went, a magic mist surrounded him, and he saw a house in the midst of a wonderful plain. After witnessing many marvels, he reached another house where a huge and beautiful man and woman offered him hospitality. Cormac bathed, the hot stones going into the bath-water of themselves, and the man brought in a boar, while Cormac prepared the fire and set on a quarter of the beast. His host proposed that he should tell a tale, at the end of which, if it were true, the meat would be cooked, but Cormac asked him to begin first. "Well, then," said the host, "the pig is one of seven, and with them I could feed the whole world. When one is eaten, I place its bones in the sty, and next day it is alive again." This tale proved true, because the meat was already cooked. When a second quarter was placed on the fire, the host told of his corn which grew and gathered itself, and never grew less; and thus a second quarter was cooked. A third quarter was set on, and now the woman described the milk of her seven cows which filled seven tubs and would satisfy the whole world. Her tale also proved true, and now Cormac realized that he was in presence of Manannan and his wife, because none possessed such pigs as he, and he had brought his wife and her cows from the Land of Promise. Cormac then told how he had lost his wife and children — a true story, for the fourth quarter was found cooked. Manannan bade him eat, but when he refused, for he would never dine with two persons only, the god opened a door and brought in his wife and children, and great was their mutual joy. Manannan now assumed his divine form and related how he had brought the branch because he desired Cormac to come hither, and he also explained the mystery of the wonders seen by him. When they sat down to eat, Manannan produced a table-cloth on which appeared whatever food was demanded, and a cup. If one told a lie, it would break, but if truth was then spoken, it would be restored; and to prove this, he informed Cormac that his lost wife had had a new husband, whereupon the cup broke. "My husband has lied," cried the goddess, and at her words the cup was repaired. Manannan then said that table-cloth, cup, and branch would be Cormac's and that he had wrought magic upon him in order that he might be with him that night in friendship. In the morning, after a night's sleep, Cormac and his family found themselves no longer in the divine land, but in their own palace of Tara, and beside him were the cup, branch, and table-cloth which had covered the board of the god.[5] Cormac's recognition of the god through his swine shows knowledge of the myth of the gods' food — the *Mucca Mhanannain*, "to be killed and yet to be alive for evermore." [6]

A story told of Mongan has some resemblance to that of Cormac. He commiserated a poor bardic scholar, bidding him go to the *síd* of Lethet Oidni and bring thence a precious stone of his, as well as a pound of silver for himself and a pound of gold from the stream beside the *síd*. At two *síd* on his way a noble-looking couple welcomed him as Mongan's messenger, and a similar pair received him at the *síd* of Lethet Oidni, where was a marvellous chamber. Asking for its key, he took thence the stone and silver, and from the river he took the gold, returning to Mongan, who bestowed the silver upon him.[7] Another story of Mongan relates how he, his wife, and some others, entering a mysterious house during a storm, found in it seven "conspicuous men," many marvellous quilts, wonderful jewels, and seven vats of wine. Welcome was given to them, and Mongan became intoxicated and told his wife his adventures, or "frenzy," from the telling of which he had formerly asked a respite of seven years. When they woke next morning, they found that they had been in the house a full year, though it seemed but a night.[8] In this instance, however, the house had not disappeared. Examples of beautiful places vanishing at daybreak are found in Fionn tales and also in the Grail romances. The seeker of the Grail finds himself no longer in the Grail castle in the morning, and the castle itself has become invisible. Such creations of glamour were probably suggested by dreams, whose beauty and terror alike vanish "when one awaketh."

Fruit-bearing, musical trees, in whose branches birds are constantly singing, grow in the gods' land. In the *síd* of Oengus were three trees always in fruit; and there were also two pigs, one always living, and the other always cooked and ready for eating — the equivalent of the *Mucca Mhanannain*, or "Pigs of Manannan" — and a jar of excellent beer, Goibniu's ale. None ever died there.[9] The Elysian ale is doubtless a superlative form of the Irish *cuirm* or *braccat*, made from malt, of which the Gauls had a divinity, Braciaca;[10] and it is analogous to the Vedic soma and the wine of Dionysos.[11] Within the *síd*, or the gods' land, were other domestic animals, especially cows, which were sometimes brought thence by those who left it or were stolen by heroes or by dwellers in one *síd* from those of another. Where mortals steal them, there is a reminiscence of the mythical idea that the elements of civilization were wrested from the gods by man. Cauldrons were used by the Celts for domestic and sacrificial as well as other ritual purposes, and these also gave rise to myths of wonderful divine cauldrons like Dagda's, from which "no company ever went unthankful." Their contents restored the dead or produced inspiration, and they were stolen from the gods' land, e. g. by Cúchulainn and by Arthur.[12] The cauldron rimmed with pearls which Arthur and his men sought resembles the basin with rows of carbuncles on its edge in which, according to another story, a fairy woman washed.[13]

The inspiration of wisdom was obtained in the gods' land, either by drinking from a well or by eating the salmon in it; but this knowledge was tabu even to some members of the divine land. Such a well, called Connla's Well, was in the Land under Waves, and thither Sinend, grand-daughter of

PLATE XIV

Dispater and Aeracura (?)

Dispater was the great Celtic god of the underworld (see p. 9) and is here represented holding a
hammer and a cup (for the hammer cf. the deity
Sucellos, Plates XIII, XXVI, and see Plate IX, B;
the cup suggests the magic cauldron of the Celtic
Elysium; cf. pp. 41, 95–96, 100, 109–12, 120, 151,
192, 203–04 and see Plates IX, B, XXV). If the
goddess beside him holding a cornucopia (cf. Plate
IX, A) is really Aeracura, she probably represents
an old earth goddess, later displaced by Dispater.
From an altar found at Oberseebach, Switzerland.

Ler, went from the Land of Promise to behold it. Above it grew hazels of wisdom, bearing leaves, blossoms, and nuts together; and these fell into the water, where they were eaten by salmon — the salmon of knowledge of other tales. From the well sprang seven streams of wisdom, and Sinend, seeking understanding, followed one of these, only to be pursued and overwhelmed by the fount itself. Sometimes these hazels were thought to grow at the heads of the chief rivers of Erin.[14] Such a fountain with five streams, their waters more melodious than mortal music, was seen by Cormac beside Manannan's house; above it were hazels, and in it five salmon. Nuts also formed part of the food of the gods in the story of *Diarmaid and Grainne*, and in a tale from the *Dindsenchas* they are said to be eaten by the "bright folk and fairy hosts of Erin."[15] Another secret well stood in the green of Síd Nechtain, and none could approach it without his eyes bursting save Nechtan and his cup-bearers. Boann, his wife, resolved to test its power or, in another version, to prove her chastity after adultery with Dagda, and walked round it thrice withershins; but three waves from it mutilated her, she fled, and was drowned in the pursuing waters.[16]

Goddesses sometimes took the form of birds, like the swan-maidens of universal myth and folk-tale; and they sang exquisite, sleep-compelling melodies. Sweet, unending bird-music, however, was a constant note of Elysium, just as the song of Rhiannon's birds caused oblivion and loss of all sense of time for eighty years. In the late story of Teigue's voyage to Elysium the birds which feasted on the delicious berries of its trees are said to warble "music and minstrelsy melodious and superlative," causing healthful slumber;[17] while in another story the minstrel goddess of the *síd* of Doon Buidhe visited other *síde* with the birds of the Land of Promise which sang unequalled music.[18]

The lords of the *síd* Elysium were many, but the chief were Dagda, Oengus, and Midir, as Arawn in Brythonic story was king of Annwfn. In general, however, every *sid* had its own ruler, and if this is an early tradition, it suggests a cult of a local god on a hill within which his abode was supposed to be. Manannan is chief, *par excellence*, of the island Elysium, and it was appropriate that a marine deity should rule a divine region including "thrice fifty islands." In that land he had a stone fort with a banqueting-hall. Lug, who may be a sun-god, was sometimes associated with the divine land, as the solar divinity was in Greek myth, and also with Manannan; and he with his foster-brothers, Manannan's sons, came to assist the Tuatha Dé Danann, riding Manannan's steed before "the fairy cavalcade from the Land of Promise." [19] He also appeared as owner of an Elysium created by glamour on earth's surface, where Conn the Hundred-Fighter heard a prophecy of his future career,[20] this prophetic, didactic tale doubtless having an earlier mythic prototype.

The Brythonic Elysium differed little from the Irish. One of its names, Annwfn, or "the not-world," which was *is elfydd* ("beneath the world"), was later equated with Hades or Hell, as already in the story of Gwyn. In the *Mabinogi* of Pwyll it is a region of this world, though with greater glories, and has districts whose people fight, as in Irish tales. In other *Mabinogion*, however, as in the Taliesin poems and later folk-belief, there is an over-sea Elysium called Annwfn or Caer Sidi — "its points are ocean's streams" — and a world beneath the water — "a *caer* [castle] of defence under ocean's waves." [21] Its people are skilled in magic and shape-shifting; mortals desire its "spoils" — domestic animals and a marvellous cauldron; it is a deathless land, without sickness; its waters are like wine; and with it are associated the gods. The Isle of Avalon in Arthurian tradition shows an even closer likeness to the Irish Elysium.[22]

Thus the Irish and Welsh placed Elysium in various regions — local other-worlds — in hills, on earth's surface, under or oversea; and this doubtless reflects the different environments

of the Celtic folk. With neither is it a region of the dead, nor
in any sense associated with torment or penance. This is true
also of later folk-stories of the Green Isle, now seen beneath,
now above, the waters. Its people are deathless, skilled in
magic; its waters restore life and health to mortals; there
magic apples grow; and thither mortals are lured or wander
by chance.[23] The same conception is still found in a late story
told of Dunlang O'Hartigan, who fought at Clontarf in 1014.
A fairy woman offered him two hundred years of life and
joy — "life without death, without cold, without thirst, without hunger, without decay" — if he would put off combat for
a day; but he preferred death in battle to dishonour, and
"foremost fighting, fell." [24]

The parallel between Celtic and early Greek conceptions of
Elysium [25] is wonderfully close. Both are open to favoured
human beings, who are thus made immortal without death;
both are exquisitely beautiful, but sensuous and unmoral.
In both are found islands ruled by goddesses who sometimes
love mortals; both are oversea, while a parallel to the *sid*
Elysium underground may be found in the later Greek tradition of Elysium as a region of Hades, which may have had
roots in an earlier period.[26] The main difference is the occasional Celtic view of Elysium as a place where gods are at
war. This may be due to warrior aspects of Celtic life, while
the more peaceful conception reflects settled, agricultural life;
although Norse influences have sometimes been suggested as
originating the former.[27]

CHAPTER X

MYTHICAL ANIMALS AND OTHER BEINGS

THE Celts worshipped animals or their anthropomorphic representations—the horse, swine, stag, bull, serpent, bear, and various birds. There was a horse-goddess Epona, a horse-god Rudiobus, a mule-god Mullo, a swine-god Moccus, and bear-goddesses called Artio and Andarta, dedications to or images of these occurring in France and Britain.[1] Personal names meaning "son of the bear" or "of the dog," etc., suggest myths of animal descent lost to us, though they find a partial illustration in stories like that of Oisin, son of a woman transformed to a fawn. We have seen that gods and magicians assume animal forms or force these upon others; and other stories point to the belief that domesticated animals came from the gods' land.

From these we turn to tales in which certain animals have a mythic aspect, perhaps connected with a cult of them. A divine bull or swine might readily be regarded as enormously large or strong, or possessed of magic power, or otherwise distinguished; and these are the aspects under which such animals appear in the stories now to be considered.

In the Irish tale of *Mac Dáthó's Boar* (*Scél Mucci Maic Dáthó*) Mac Dáthó, King of Leinster, had a dog famed throughout the land. It could run round Leinster in a day and was coveted both by Ailill and Medb of Connaught and by Conchobar of Ulster; but Mac Dáthó promised it to both and invited the monarchs and their retinues to a feast, hoping that he would escape in the quarrel which would certainly arise between them. The chief dish was a boar reared by Mac

1

2

PLATE XV

Epona

1. The horse-goddess Epona may have been originally a deity of a spring or river, conceived as a spirited steed. She is here represented as feeding horses (for the horse see Plates II, 1–3, III, 2, 4). From a bas-relief found at Bregenz, Tyrol.

2. The goddess is shown seated between two foals, and the cornucopia which she holds would characterize her as a divinity of plenty (cf. Plates IX, A, XIV, and p. 9). From a bronze statuette found in Wiltshire.

Dáthó's grandson, Lena, who, though buried in a trench which the boar rooted up over him, succeeded in killing the animal with his sword. For seven years the boar had been nurtured on the flesh of fifty cows; sixty oxen were required to drag its carcass; and its tail was a load for sixty men; yet Conall Cernach sucked it entire into his mouth![2] The story tells nothing more of this remarkable animal, but it may commemorate an old ritual feast upon an animal regarded as divine and endowed with mythic qualities.

The *Mirabilia* added to Nennius's *History* speak of the *Porcus Troit* or *Twrch Trwyth*, hunted by Arthur, an episode related in the tale of *Kulhwch and Olwen*. This creature, which was a transformed knight, slaughtered many of the hunters before it was overcome and three desirable possessions taken from between its ears.[3] The *Porcus Troit* resembles the Wild Boar of Gulban, a transformed child, hunted by Diarmaid when the Féinn had fled before it; and tradition tells of its great size — sixteen feet long.[4] Fionn himself chased a huge boar which terrified every one until it was slain by his grandson, Oscar. It was blue-black, with rough bristles, and no ears or tail; its teeth protruded horribly; and each flake of foam from its mouth resembled the foam of a mighty waterfall.[5] A closer analogy to Arthur's hunt occurs in a story of the *Dindsenchas* concerning a pig which wasted the land. Manannan and Mod's hounds pursued it, when it sprang into a lake where it maimed or drowned the following hounds; and then it crossed to Muic-Inis, or Pig Island, where it slew Mod with its tusk.[6] Another hunting of magic swine concerns animals from the cave of Cruachan, which is elsewhere associated with divinities. Nothing grew where they went, and they destroyed corn and milk; no one could count them accurately, and when shot at they disappeared. Medb and Ailill hunted them, and when one of them leaped into Medb's chariot, she seized its leg, but the skin broke, and the pig left it in her hand. After that no one knew whither they went, although a variant version says that now they were counted. From this cave came other destructive creatures — a great three-headed bird which wasted Erin till Amairgen killed it, and red birds which withered everything with their breath until the Ulstermen slew them.[7] It is strange why such animals should be associated with this divine cave, but probably the tradition dates from the time when it was regarded as "Ireland's gate of hell," so that any evil spirit might inhabit it.

In these stories of divinities or heroes hunting fabulous swine it is possible that the animals represent some hurtful power, dangerous to vegetation; for the swine is apt to be regarded in a sinister light and might well be the embodiment of demoniac beings. On the other hand, the animal sacrificed to a god, or of which the god is an anthropomorphic aspect, is sometimes regarded as his enemy, slain by him. Whether this conception lurks behind these tales is uncertain, as also is the question whether the magic immortal swine — the food of the gods — were originally animals sacrificed to them. Divine swine appear in a Fionn tale. The Féinn were at a banquet given by Oengus, when the deity said that the best of Fionn's hounds could not kill one of his pigs, but rather his great pig would kill them. Fionn, on the contrary, maintained that his hounds, Bran and Sgeolan, could do so. A year after, a hundred and one pigs appeared, one of them coal-black, and each tall as a deer; but the Féinn and their dogs killed them all, Bran slaying the black one, whereupon Oengus complained that they had caused the death of his sons and many of the Tuatha Dé Danann, for they were in the form of the swine. A quarrel ensued, and Fionn prepared to attack Oengus's *brug*, when the god made peace.[8] In another instance a fairy as a wild boar eluded the Féinn, but Fionn offered the choice of the women to its slayer, and by the help of a "familiar spirit" in love with him Caoilte "got the diabolical beast killed." Fionn covered the women's heads lest Caoilte should take his wife, but his ruse was unsuccessful.[9]

In still another instance Derbrenn, Oengus's first love, had six foster-children; but their mother changed them into swine, and Oengus gave charge of them to Buichet, whose wife desired the flesh of one of them. A hundred heroes and as many hounds prepared to hunt them, when they fled to Oengus for help, only to find that he could not give it until they shook the tree of Tarbga and ate the salmon of Inver Umaill. Not for a year were they able to do this, but now Medb hunted them, and all were slain save one. Other huntings of these swine, less fortunate for the hunters, are also mentioned, and in one passage Derbrenn's swine are said to have been fashioned by magic.[10] Both in Irish and in Welsh story pigs are associated with the gods' land and are brought thence by heroes or by the gods. The Tuatha Dé Danann are said to have first introduced swine into Ireland or Munster.[11]

The mythic bulls of the *Táin Bó Cúalgne* were reincarnations of divinities, whence enormous strength was theirs, and the Brown Bull was of vast size. He carried a hundred and fifty children, until one day he threw them off and killed all but fifty; a hundred warriors were protected by his shadow from the heat, or by his shelter from the cold. His melodious evening lowing was such as any one would desire to hear, and no eldritch thing dared approach him; he covered fifty heifers daily, and each next morning had a calf.[12] Two gifts given to Conn by a princess who was with the god Lug were a boar's rib and that of an ox, twenty-four feet long, forming an arch eight feet high; but nothing further is told of the animals which owned these huge bones.[13]

Cattle were a valued possession of the gods' land and, like swine, were brought thence by heroes. Man easily concluded that animals useful to him were also useful to the gods, but he regarded these as magical. The divine mother of Fraoch gave him cows from the *síd*. Flidais, "one of the tribe of the god folk," was wife of Ailill the Fair and had a cow which supplied milk to three hundred men at one night's milking;

while during the *Táin* another account speaks of Flidais having several cows which fed Ailill's army every seventh day. Flidais loved Fergus and urged him to carry her off with her cow [14] — a proof of its value, which is seen also in tales of the capture of cows along with some desirable woman, divine or human. In many Welsh instances cattle are a possession of the fairy-folk dwelling under a lake and often come to land to feed.[15] The cow of Flidais resembles the seven kine of Manannan's wife; their milk suffices the people of the entire Land of Promise or the men of the whole world, while from the wool of her seven sheep came all their clothing.[16]

Though the waves were "the Son of Ler's horses in a sea-storm," Manannan rode them on his steed Enbarr, which he gave to Lug; and this horse was "fleet as the naked cold wind of spring," while its rider was never killed off its back.[17] In Elysium "a stud of steeds with grey-speckled manes and another crimson-brown" were seen by Laeg, and similar horses were given to carry mortals back to earth, whence, if they did not dismount, they could return safely to Elysium. Such a steed was brought by Gilla Decair to Fionn and his men, and miserable-looking though it was, when placed among the Féinn's horses, it bit and tore them. Conan mounted it in order to ride it to death, but it would not move; and when thirteen others vaulted on it, the Gilla fled, followed swiftly by the horse with its riders. Carrying them over land and sea, with another hero holding its tail, it brought them to the Land of Promise, whence Fionn ultimately rescued them. This forms the first part of a late artificial tale, based upon a mythic foundation.[18] Other mythical horses came from a water-world, e. g. the steeds which Cúchulainn captured, one of these being the Grey of Macha, out of the Grey Lake. Cúchulainn slipped behind it and wrestled with it all round Erin until it was mastered; and when it was wounded at his death, it went into the lake to be healed. The other was Dubsainglend of the Marvellous Valley, which was captured in similar fashion.[19]

PLATE XVI

CERNUNNOS

This horned deity with torques on his horns is perhaps identical with the horned god shown in Plate XXV. He was doubtless a divinity of the underworld (see pp. 9, 104–05, 158, and for other deities of Elysium cf. Smertullos, Plate V; the three-headed god, Plates VII, XII, the squatting god, Plates VIII–IX; Sucellos, Plates XIII, XXVI; and Dispater, Plate XIV). From an altar found at Notre Dame, Paris.

Possibly the rushing stream was personified as a steed, and the horse-goddess Epona is occasionally connected with streams, while horses which emerge from lakes or rivers may be mythic forms of water-divinities.   In more recent folk-belief the monstrous water-horse of France and Scotland was capable of self-transformation and waylaid travellers, or, assuming human form, he made love to women, luring them to destruction. Did such demoniac horses already exist in the pagan period, or are they a legacy from Scandinavian belief, or are they earlier equine water-divinities thus distorted in Christian times? This must remain uncertain, but at all events they were amenable to the power of Christian saints, since St. Fechin of Fore, when one of his chariot-horses died on a journey, compelled a water-horse to take its place, afterward allowing it to return to the water.[20] Akin to these is the Welsh *afanc*, one of which was drawn by the oxen of Hu Gadarn from a pond, while another was slain by Peredur (Percival) after he had obtained a jewel of invisibility which hid him from the monster with its poisoned spear.[21]

Mortals as well as *síde* were transformed into deer, and fairies possessed herds of those animals, while Caoilte slew a wild three-antlered stag — "the grey one of three antlers" — which had long eluded the hunters.[22] Three-horned animals — bull or boar — are depicted on Gaulish monuments, and the third horn symbolizes divinity or divine strength, the word "horn" being often used as a synonym of might, especially divine power.   On an altar discovered at Notre Dame in Paris, the god Cernunnos ("the Horned," from *cernu-*, "horn"?) has stag's horns; and other unnamed divinities also show traces of antlers. Possibly these gods were anthropomorphic forms of stag-divinities, like other Gaulish deities with bull's horns.[23]

Serpents or dragons infesting lochs, sometimes generically called *péist* or *béist* (Latin *bestia*, "beast"), occur in Celtic and other mythologies and are reminiscent of earlier reptile forms, dwelling in watery places and regarded as embodiments of water-spirits or guardians of the waters. In later tradition such monsters were said to have been imprisoned in lochs or destroyed by Celtic saints. As has been seen, a dragon's shriek on May-Eve made the land barren till Lludd buried it and its opponent alive after stupifying them with mead. They were placed in a cistvaen at Dinas Emreis in Snowdon, and long afterward Merlin got rid of them when they hindered Vortigern's building operations. Here the dragons are embodiments of powers hostile to man and to fertility, but are conquered by gods, Lludd and Merlin.[24]

Another story of a *péist* occurs in the *Táin Bó Fráich*. Fraoch was the most beautiful of Erin's heroes, and his mother was the divine Bébind, her sister the goddess Boann. Findabair, daughter of Ailill and Medb, loved him, but before going to claim her he was advised to seek from Boann treasure of the *síd*, which she gave him in abundance, while he was made welcome at Ailill's *dún*. After staying there for some time, he desired Findabair to elope with him, only to be refused, whereupon he demanded her of Ailill, but would not give the bride-price asked. Ailill and Medb therefore plotted his death, fearing that if he took Findabair by force, the Kings who sought her would attack them. While Fraoch was swimming in the river, Ailill bade him bring a branch from a rowan-tree growing on the bank, and swimming there, he returned with it, Findabair meanwhile admiring the beauty of his body. Ailill sent him for more, but the monster guardian of the tree attacked him; and when he called for a sword, Findabair leaped into the water with it, Ailill throwing a five-pronged spear at her. Fraoch caught it and hurled it back; and though the monster all the while was biting his side, with the sword he cut off its head and brought it to land. A bath of broth was made for him, and afterward he was laid on a bed. Then was heard lamentation, and a hundred and fifty women of the *síde*, clad in crimson with green head-dresses, appeared, all of one age, shape, and loveliness, coming for Fraoch, the darling of the *side*. They bore him off, bringing him back on the morrow recovered of his wound, and Findabair was now betrothed to Fraoch on his promising to assist in the raid of Cúalnge. Thus Fraoch, a demi-god, overcame the *péist*.[25] In the ballad version from the *Dean of Lismore's Book*, Medb sent him for the berries because he scorned her love. The tree grew on an island in a loch, with the *péist* coiled round its roots. Every month it bore sweetest fruit, and one berry satisfied hunger for a long time, while its juice prolonged life for a year and healed sickness. Fraoch killed the *péist*, but died of his wounds.[26] The tree was the tree of the gods and resembles the quicken-tree of Dubhros, guarded by a one-eyed giant whom Diarmaid slew.[27] These stories recall the Greek myth of Herakles slaying the dragon guardian of the apples of the Hesperides,[28] which has a certain parallel in Babylonia. A marvellous tree with jewelled fruit was seen by Gilgamesh in a region on this side of the Waters of Death; and in the Fields of the Blessed beyond these waters he found a magic plant, the twigs of which renewed man's youth. He gathered it, but a serpent seized it and carried it off. The stories of Fraoch and Diarmaid point to myths showing that gods were jealous of men sharing their divine food; and their tree of life was guarded against mortals, though perhaps semi-divine heroes might gain access to it and obtain its benefits for human beings. The guardian *péist* recalls the dragons entwined round oaks in the grove described by Lucan.[29]

Such Celtic *péists* were slain by Fionn, and in one poem Fionn or, in another, his son, Daire, was swallowed by the monster, but hacked his way out, liberating others besides himself.[30] They also defended *dúns* in Celtic story, and in the sequel to the tale of Fraoch he and Conall reached a *dún* where his stolen cattle were. A serpent sprang into Conall's belt, but was later released by him, and "neither did harm to the other." In Cúchulainn's account of his journey to Scáth, the *dún* had seven walls, each with an iron palisade; and having destroyed these, he reached a pit guarded by serpents which he slew with his fists, as well as many toads, sharp and beaked beasts, and ugly, dragon-like monsters. Then he took a cauldron and cows from the *dún*, which must have been in the gods' land across the sea, as in other tales where such thefts are related.[31]

A curious story from the *Dindsenchas* tells how the son of the Morrígan had three hearts with "shapes of serpents through them," or "with the shape of serpents' heads." He was slain by MacCecht, and if death had not befallen him, these serpents would have grown and destroyed all other animals. The hearts were burned, and the ashes were cast into a stream, whereupon its rapids stayed, and all creatures in it died.[32] In another story Cian was born with a caul which increased with his growth, but Sgathan ripped it open, and a worm sprang from it, which was thought to have the same span of life as Cian. A wood was put round it, and the creature was fed, but it grew to a vast size and swallowed men whole. Fire was set to the wood, when it fled to a cave and made a wilderness all around; but at last Oisin killed it with Diarmaid's magic spear.[33] Serpents with rams' heads are a frequent *motif* on Gaulish monuments, either separately or as the adjuncts of a god; but their meaning is unknown, and no myth regarding them has survived.

Other parts of nature besides animals were regarded mythically. Mountains, the sea, rivers, wells, lakes, sun, moon, and earth had a personality of their own, and this conception survived when other ideas had arisen. Appeal was made to them, as the runes sung by Morrígan and Amairgen show, and they were taken as sureties, or their power was invoked to do harm, as when Aed Ruad's champion took sureties of sea, wind, sun, and firmament against him, so that the sun's heat caused Aed to bathe, and the rising sea and a great wind drowned him.[34] In another instance, a spell chanted over the sea by Dub, wife of Enna, of the *side*, caused the drowning of his other wife, Áide, and her family.[35] The personality of the sea is seen also in the story of Lindgadan and the echo heard at a cliff: enraged at some one speaking to him without being asked, he turned to the cliff to be avenged upon the speaker, when the crest of a wave dashed him against a rock.[36] So, too, the sea was obedient to man, or perhaps to a god. Tuirbe Trágmar, father of the Gobán Saer, used to hurl his axe from the Hill of the Axe in the full of the flood-tide, forbidding the sea to come beyond the axe,[37] an action akin to the Celtic ritual of "fighting the waves." The voices of the waves had a warning, prophetic, or sympathetic sound to those who could hear them aright, as many instances show.

As elsewhere, personalized parts of nature came to be regarded as animated by spirits, like man; and such spirits gradually became more or less detached from these and might be seen as divine beings appearing near them. Some of them became the greater gods, while others assumed a darker character, perhaps because they were associated with sinister aspects of nature or with the dead. The Celts knew all these, and some still linger on in folk-belief. Fairy-like or semi-divine women seen by streams or fountains, or in forests, or living in lakes or rivers, are survivals of spirits and goddesses of river, lake, or earth; and they abound in Celtic folk-story as *bonnes dames*, *dames blanches*, *fées*, or the Irish *Bé Find*. Beings like mermaids existed in early Irish belief. When Ruad's ships were stopped, he went over the side and saw "the loveliest of the world's women," three of them detaining each boat. They carried him off, and he slept with each in turn, one becoming with child by him. They set out in a bronze boat to intercept him on his return journey, but when they failed, the mother killed his child and hurled the head after him, the others crying, "It is an awful crime." [38] In another tale Rath heard the mermaids' song and saw them — "grown-up girls, the fairest of shape and make, with yellow hair and white skins above the waters. But huger than one of the hills was the hairy-clawed, bestial lower part which they had beneath." Their song lulled him to sleep, when they flocked round him and tore him limb from limb.[39] Other sea-dwellers are the *luchorpáin* — a kind of dwarf, three of whom were caught by Fergus and forced to comply with his wish and to tell him how to pass under lochs and seas. They put herbs in his ears, or one of them gave him a cloak to cover his head, and thus he went with them under the water.[40]

A curious group of beings answered Cúchulainn's cry, causing confusion to his enemies, or screamed around him when he set out or was in the thick of the fight. While he fought with Ferdia, "around him shrieked the *Bocánachs* and the *Banánachs* and the *Geniti Glinne*, and the demons of the air; for it was the custom of the Tuatha Dé Danann to raise their cries about him in every battle," and thus increase men's fear of him. Or they screamed from the rims of shields and hilts of swords and hafts of spears of the hero and of Ferdia.[41] Here they are friendly to Cúchulainn, but in the *Fled Bricrend*, or *Feast of Bricriu*, one of the tasks imposed on him, Conall, and Loegaire was to fight the *Geniti Glinne*, Cúchulainn alone succeeding and slaughtering many of them.[42] What kind of beings they were is uncertain, but if *Geniti Glinne* means "Damsels of the Glen," perhaps they were a kind of nature-spirits, this being also suggested by the "demons of the air" which were expelled by St. Patrick.[43] As nature-spirits they might be classed with the Tuatha Dé Danann, as indeed they seem to be in the passage cited above.[44] In one sentence of the *Táin Bó Cúalnge*, they are associated with Némain or Badb, who brought confusion upon Medb's host; yet on the other hand they dared not appear in the same district as the bull of Cúalnge.[45]

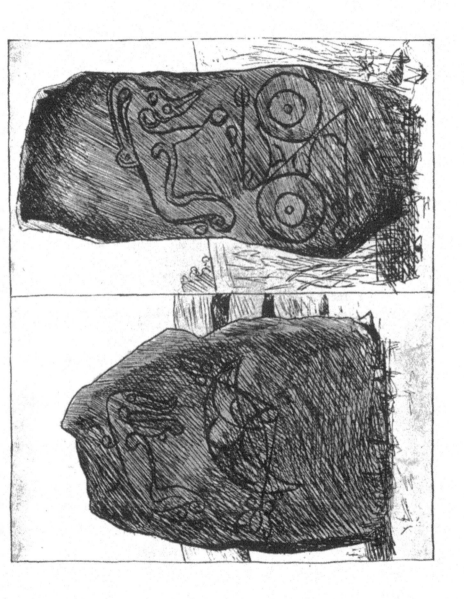

PLATE XVII

Incised Stones from Scotland

1. Incised stone with "elephant" symbol and crescent symbol with V-rod symbol. From Crichie, Aberdeenshire.

2. Incised stone with "elephant" and double disc (or "spectacles") with Z-rod symbol. See also Plate X.

CHAPTER XI

MYTHS OF ORIGINS

SAVAGE and barbaric peoples possess many grotesque myths of the origin of various parts of nature. In recently existing Celtic folk-lore and in stories preserved mainly in the *Dindsenchas* conceptions not unlike these are found and doubtless were handed down from the pre-Christian period, whether Celtic or pre-Celtic, while in certain instances a saint takes the place of an older pagan personage. In Brittany and elsewhere in France natural features — rivers, lakes, hills, rocks — are associated in their origin with giants, fairies, witches, or the devil, just as in other Celtic regions and, indeed, in all parts of the world. Many traditions, however, connect them with the giant Gargantua, who was not a creation of Rabelais' brain, but was borrowed from popular belief. He may have been an old Celtic god or hero, popular and, therefore, easily surviving in folk-memory, and may also be the Gurguntius, son of Belinus, King of Britain, mentioned by Giraldus Cambrensis. Many hills or isolated rocks or erratic boulders are described as his teeth, or as stones thrown, or vomited, or ejected by him; and rivers or lakes were formed from his blood or urine, numerous traditions regarding these being collected by Sébillot in his book on Gargantua.[1]

In Irish story similar traditions are found and are of a *naïve* character. Manannan shed "three drops of grief" for his dead son, and these became three lochs, as in the Finnish *Kalevala* a mother's tears are changed into rivers. Again, a king's daughter died of shame when her lover saw her bathing, and her foster-mother's tears made Loch Gile. In other instances lochs are formed by water pouring forth at the digging of a grave, e.g. that of Manannan, slain in battle, or that of Garman, son of Glas. Or a well is the source of a loch, because some one was drowned in it, or because its waters poured forth over intruders, or because of the breaking of a tabu connected with it, e.g. leaving its cover off. In two instances already cited the urine of a horse belonging to a god produced a loch;[2] and more curious still is the myth of the woman Odras whom the Morrígan changed into a pool of water.[3]

An interesting story tells of the magic creation of a wood. Gaible, son of Nuada, stole a bundle of twigs which Ainge, daughter of Dagda, had gathered to make a tub, for Dagda had made one which dripped during flood-tide, and she wished for a better one. Gaible threw away the bundle, and it became a wood springing up in every direction.[4] This is of a very primitive character and resembles the folk-tale incident of the Transformation Flight, in which a twig, comb, or reed thrown down by fugitives becomes a thick forest or bush impeding the pursuers.[5] Curious, too, is the story of Codal, who on a hillock fed his fosterling Ériu, from whom is named Ériu's Island (Ireland). As she grew, the hillock increased with her, and had she not complained to Codal of the sun's heat and the cold wind, it would have grown until Ireland was filled with the mountain. Another story, recalling that of the Australian Bunjel's slicing earth with a knife into creeks and valleys, tells how Fergus, with Cúchulainn's sword, the *caladbolg* out of the *síd*, sheared the tops of three mountains, which are now "Meath's three bare ones," while as a counter blow Cúchulainn did the same to three hills in Athlone.[6] In another tale Fergus, irritated against Conchobar, struck three blows on the ground and thus caused three hills to arise which will endure for ever.[7]

The first occurrence of other things is often the subject of a tradition. Many myths exist about the origin of fire, and in Irish story the first camp-fire was made by Aidne for the Mile-

sians by wringing his hands together, when flashes as large as
apples came from his knuckles, this resembling the legends of
light or fire obtained from a saint's hand. At Nemnach, near
the *síd* of Tara, rose a stream on which stood the first mill
built in Ireland, but no myth describes its origin. On the other
hand, the story of the first trap resembles that told of the
guillotine and its inventor. Coba was trapper to Erem, son
of Mile, and was the first to prepare a trap and pitfall in Erin,
but having put his leg into it to test it, his shin-bone and arms
were fractured, and he died. Brea, in the time of Partholan,
was the first man to build a house or make a cauldron — that
important vessel of Celtic myth and ritual; [8] while the first
smelting of gold was the work of Tigernmas, a mythic Irish
king. [9] The divine origin of ploughing with oxen has already
been mentioned — an interesting agricultural myth. [10] Brigit,
goddess of poetry, when her son Ruadan died at Mag-Tured,
bewailed him with the first "keening" heard in Ireland; and
she also invented a whistle for night signalling. [11] So also the
first satire, with dire effects, was spoken by Corpre, poet of
the gods. [12] Another instrument, the harp, was discovered accidentally. All was discord in the time of the Firbolgs. Canola
fled from her husband and by the shore heard a sweet murmur
as the wind played through the sinews still clinging to a whale's
skeleton. Listening, she fell asleep; and when her husband,
finding her thus, learned that the sound had lulled her, he
made a framework of wood for the sinews. On this he played,
and the pair were reconciled. [13] But the Irish could also look
back to a golden age when, in the reign of Geide the Loud-
Voiced, each one deemed the other's voice as sweet as strings of
lutes would be, because of the greatness of the peace and friendship which every one had for the other; [14] and, with the addition
of plenty and prosperity, much the same is said of Conaire's
reign, until Midir's vengeance overtook him. [15] Prosperity
was supposed to characterize every good king's reign in Ireland, perhaps pointing to earlier belief in his divinity and the

dependence of fertility on him; but the result is precisely that which everywhere marked the golden age. As elsewhere, too, gods instituted festivals, one myth telling how Lug first cele-brated that of Lugnasad, not in his own honour, but to the glory of his foster-mother.[16]

The mythic trees of Elysium were not unknown on earth, though there they were safely guarded; and another instance, besides those already described,[17] is found in the oak of Mugna. "Berries to berries the Strong Upholder [a god?] put upon it. Three fruits upon it, viz. acorn, apple, and nut; and when the first fruit fell, another used to grow." Leaves were always on this useful tree, which stood until Ninine the poet cast it down.[18] What is perhaps a debased myth of a world-tree like Yggdrasil is found in the story of the tree in Loch Guirr, seen once every seven years as the loch dried when its enchant-ment left it. A green cloth covered the tree, and a woman sat knitting under it; but once a man stole the cloth, where-upon the woman said: —

"Awake, thou silent tide;
From the Dead Woman's Land a horseman rides,
From my head the green cloth snatching."

At these words the waters pursued him and took half of his horse and the cloth from him.[19]

Few and fragmentary as these myths are, they, with the classical myths already cited,[20] prove what a rich cosmogony the ancient Celts must have had.

CHAPTER XII

THE HEROIC MYTHS

I. CÚCHULAINN AND HIS CIRCLE

THE Celts possessed many myths regarding ideal heroic figures or actual heroes who tended to become mythical. A kind of saga was formed about some of these, telling of their birth, their deeds, their *amours*, their procuring for men spoils from the gods' land, and their death or departure to Elysium; while round them were ranged other personages whose deeds are also recounted, and who may have been the subjects of separate sagas. Groups of tribes had each their hero, who occasionally attained wider popularity and was adopted by other tribes. To these heroes are ascribed magic and supernatural deeds. Some of them are of divine origin — sons of gods or reincarnations of gods — and they differ in many respects from ordinary men — in size, or appearance, or in power. In a sense they are divine and may have been at one time subjects of a cult, but in the myths they are represented as living and moving on earth, and to some of them a definite date is given. The three heroes best known, each the centre of a group, are Cúchulainn, Fionn, and Arthur. The stories concerning Cúchulainn, who is more prominent than his King, Conchobar, were current among the tribes of Ulster; those about Fionn were popular first in Leinster and Munster, then over all Ireland and the West Highlands; those about Arthur were found among the Brythons.

Cúchulainn is the chief figure about the court of Conchobar, alleged to have been King of Ulster at the beginning of the Christian era. The heroes were "champions of the Red

Branch," so called after a room in Conchobar's palace of
Emain Macha; and three are more prominent and on some
occasions rivals — Cúchulainn, Conall the Victorious, and
Loegaire the Triumphant. Others of the group are Dechtire,
Conchobar's sister, their father Cathbad the Druid, Fergus
mac Roich, Ferdia, Cúroi mac Daire, and Bricriu, while Ailill
and Medb of Connaught also enter into the saga. The stories
about these are over a hundred in number, but reference can
here be made only to those in which Cúchulainn figures
prominently.

Some of the group are descended from the Tuatha Dé
Danann, or their origin is supernatural. One story makes
Conchobar a natural son of Nessa by Cathbad. Later King
Fergus mac Roich wished to marry her, and she agreed, if he
would resign the throne for a year to Conchobar; but when
the year passed, Fergus was deposed, and the youth remained
King with many privileges. He had the *jus primae noctis* over
every girl in the province, and in whatever house he stayed
the wife was at his disposal; yet he was wisest of men, possessed
of many gifts, and a great hero.[1] In another story Nessa was
sent for water by Cathbad and brought it from the river
Conchobar, whereupon Cathbad forced her to drink it because
it contained two worms. She became pregnant after swallowing these, and at birth her child held a worm in each hand and
was named after the river. Some, however, regarded him as
son of Nessa's lover, Fachtna Fathach, King of Ulster.[2] Thus
three origins are ascribed to Conchobar — son of Cathbad,
or of Fachtna, or of a river personalized or of a river-god who
took the form of the worms. A similar origin is ascribed to
Conall. His mother Findchoém, Cathbad's daughter, being
bidden by a Druid to wash in and drink from a well over which
he sang spells, swallowed a worm and became *enceinte*, the
worm lying in the child's hand in her womb.[3]

Cúchulainn was son of the god Lug,[4] and though he was
also called son of Sualtam, Dechtire's husband, yet even here

PLATE XVIII

MENHIR OF KERNUZ

The monument shows figures of Mercury (cf. pp. 9, 158) and a child, and of a god with a club (cf. Plates IV–V). Mercury and the child have been equated with Lug and his son, Cúchulainn (see pp. 64–65, 82–84, 158–59; for Lug see also pp. 25, 28–33, 40, 122, and for Cúchulainn pp. 36, 69–71, 86–88, 128, 134, 139–59, 209, 212). The latter has also been identified with Esus, but with scant plausibility (see Plates XX, A, XXI).

his origin is semi-divine. Sualtam's mother was of the *sid*-folk; he was called Sualtam *sidech* ("of the fairy haunts") and possessed "the magic might of an elf." [5] The supernatural aspect of some of the personages is seen in Cúchulainn's feats or his "distortion"; or in Fergus, who had the strength of seven hundred men, ate seven hogs and kine at a meal, and wielded a sword as long as a rainbow, while a seventh part of him surpassed the whole of any ordinary man. [6] In one passage Conchobar is called *dia talmaide* ("a terrestrial god"), while Dechtire is termed a goddess. [7] Yet Cúchulainn was not necessarily a sun-god or sun-hero; for if he was, why does the *Táin*, in which he plays so great a part, take place in winter, while his greatest activity is from Samhain (November) until the beginning of spring. [8] Nor is every mistress of his a dawn-goddess, nor every foe a power of darkness.

The boyish deeds of Cúchulainn were described to Medb during the *Táin* by Fergus and others. Before his fifth year, when already possessed of man's strength, he heard of the "boy corps" of his uncle Conchobar and went to test them, taking his club, ball, spear, and javelin, playing with these as he went. At Emain he joined the boys at play without permission; but this was an insult, and they set upon him, throwing at him clubs, spears, and balls, all of which he fended off, besides knocking down fifty of the boys, while his "contortion" seized him — the first reference to this curious phenomenon. Conchobar now interfered, but Cúchulainn would not desist until all the boys came under his protection and guarantee. [9]

At Conchobar's court he performed extraordinary feats and expelled a band of invaders when the Ulstermen were in their yearly weakness. [10] He was first known as Setanta, and was called Cúchulainn in the following way. Culann the smith had prepared a banquet for Conchobar, who, on his way to it, saw the youth holding the field at ball against three hundred and fifty others; and though he bade him follow,

Setanta refused to come until the play was over. While the banquet was progressing, Culann let loose his great watch-dog, which had the strength of a hundred, and when Setanta reached the fort, the beast attacked him, whereupon he thrust his ball into its mouth, and seizing its hind legs, battered it against a rock. Culann complained that the safe-guard of his flocks and herds was destroyed, but the boy said that he would act as watch-dog until a whelp of its breed was ready; and Cathbad the Druid now gave him a name — Cú Chulainn, or "Culann's Dog." This adventure took place before he was seven years old.[11] Baudiš suggests that as Cúchulainn was not the hero's birth-name, a dog may have been his *manito*,[12] his name being given him in some ceremonial way at puberty, a circumstance afterward explained by the mythical story of Culann's Hound.[13]

One day Cúchulainn overheard Cathbad saying that whatever stripling assumed arms on that day would have a short life, but would be the greatest of warriors. He now demanded arms from Conchobar, but broke every set of weapons given him until he received Conchobar's own sword and shield; and he also destroyed seventeen chariots, so that nothing but Conchobar's own chariot sufficed him. Cúchulainn made the charioteer drive fast and far until they reached the *dún* of the sons of Nechtan, each of whom he fought and slew, cutting off their heads; while on his return he killed two huge stags and then captured twenty-four wild swans, fastening all these to the chariot. From afar Levarcham the prophetess saw the strange cavalcade approaching Emain and bade all be on their guard, else the warrior would slay them; but Conchobar alone knew who he was and recognized the danger from a youth whose appetite for slaughter had been whetted. A stratagem was adopted, based upon Cúchulainn's well-known modesty. A hundred and fifty women with uncovered breasts were sent to meet him,[14] and while he averted his face, he was seized and plunged into vessels of cold water. The first burst asunder; the water of the second boiled with the heat from his body; that of the third became warm; and thus his rage was calmed. Fiacha, who tells this story, now describes the hero. Besides being very handsome, with golden tresses, he had seven toes on each foot, seven fingers on each hand, and seven pupils in each eye, while on his body was a shirt of gold thread and a green mantle with silver clasps. No wonder, added Fiacha, that now at seventeen he is slaughtering so many in the *Táin Bó Cúalnge*.[15]

Cúchulainn's beauty attracted women, whence Conchobar's warriors, fearing for the virtue of their wives, sent him to woo Forgall's daughter, Emer;[16] but to hinder this, Forgall urged him to find Domnal the Warlike in Alba, hoping that he would never return. He set off with Conchobar, Loegaire, and Conall; and after Domnal had taught them extraordinary feats, he sent them to receive instruction from Scáthach, who dwelt to the east of Alba. Meanwhile Cúchulainn had refused the love of Domnal's ugly daughter, Dornolla. She vowed vengeance, and when the heroes departed, she caused a vision of Emain to rise before Cúchulainn's companions, which made them so home-sick that he had to proceed alone. Instructed by a youth, he crossed the Plain of Ill-Luck safely. On its first half men's feet stuck fast, and on the second half the grass held their feet on the points of its blades; but he must first follow the track of a wheel and then that of an apple which rolled before him. A narrow path through a glen would bring him to Scáthach's house, which was on an island approached by a narrow bridge, slippery as an eel's tail, or, in another version, high in the centre, while the other end rose up whenever anyone leaped on it, and flung him backward. This island and bridge are not mentioned in the older recensions of the story. After many attempts Cúchulainn reached the other side by his "salmon-leap." Uathach, Scáthach's daughter, fell in love with him and told him how to obtain valour from her mother. He must make his salmon-leap to the great yew-tree where Scáthach was teaching her sons, Cuare and Cet, and set his sword between her breasts. Thus he obtained from Scáthach all his wishes — acquaintance with her feats, marriage to Uathach without a dowry, and knowledge of his future, while she yielded herself to him. For a year he remained with Scáthach, learning skill in arms, and then, despite her attempts to hinder him, he assisted her in fighting the amazon Aife and her warriors. Having discovered that Aife loved above all else her charioteer and chariot-horses, he exclaimed, as he fought her, that these had perished. She looked aside, and that moment Cúchulainn overcame her and made her promise never again to oppose Scáthach. From his *amour* with Aife, a son would be born called Conlaoch, who was to wear a ring which Cúchulainn left for him and to seek his father when he was a warrior of seven years old. He must make himself known to none, turn aside for none, and refuse combat to none.

On his return to Scáthach Cúchulainn slew a hag who disputed the crossing of the bridge of leaps, and Scáthach bound him and Ferdiad, Fraoch, Náisi, and Fergus, whom she had trained, never to combat with each other. While going home to Ireland he slew the Fomorians to whom Devorgilla, daughter of the King of the Isles, was to be given in tribute — an early Celtic version of the story of Perseus and Andromeda.[17]

Though Devorgilla was awarded to Cúchulainn, he afterward gave her to Lugaid as wife, since he himself was to marry Emer; whereupon Devorgilla and her handmaid sought the hero in the form of birds, and when he wounded them, their true form appeared. Cúchulainn sucked out the sling-stone and with it some blood; and for this reason also he could not wed her, for he had drunk her blood — a mythical version of the rite of blood brotherhood. He now carried off Emer despite Forgall's opposition, and she became his wife, though not before Conchobar exercised his royal prerogative on her.[18]

The feats which Cúchulainn learned from Scáthach are no longer intelligible and are probably exaggerated or imaginary warrior exploits. Scáthach and Aife may be reminiscences of actual Celtic female warriors, though the hero's visit to Scáthach's isle is akin to his journey to Fand — it is a visit to a divine land, whose people are sometimes at war (as in the stories of Fand and Loegaire), but where wisdom, valour, and other things may be gained by mortals.

When Conlaoch came to Ireland, his father's injunctions were the cause of his slaying his own son in ignorance with his marvellous spear, the *gai bolga;* and when he recognized the ring which his son wore, great was his sorrow.[19] This is a Celtic version of the story of Suhrāb and Rustam.[20]

Cúchulainn did not at once become hero of Ulster. In the story of *Mac Dáthó's Boar*, to which reference has already been made, the hero is Conall, who never passed a day without killing a Connaughtman or slept without a Connaughtman's head under his knee. Bricriu, the provoker of strife, advised that each man should get a share of the boar according to his warlike deeds. Cet of Connaught was chief until Conall arrived and put him to shame; and then, though the boar's tail required sixty men to carry it, he sucked it into his mouth, allotting scanty portions to the men of Connaught. In the fight which ensued the latter were routed, Mac Dáthó's hound siding with the Ulstermen.[21]

The *Fled Bricrend*, or *Feast of Bricriu*, tells of a feast made for Conchobar and his men by Bricriu in a vast house built for this purpose. Bricriu prepared for himself a balcony with a window looking down on the hall, for h. knew that the Ulstermen would not allow him to enter it; yet they feared to accept the invitation lest he should provoke quarrels among them, and the dead should outnumber the living. Thereupon he asserted that if they refused, he would do still worse; and after discussion it was agreed that they should go, but that Bricriu should be guarded from entering the feast. In the sequel, however, he provoked a quarrel between Loegaire, Conall, and Cúchulainn as to which of them should receive the champion's portion; whereupon each claimed it, and a fight arose between them in the hall. This reflects actual Celtic custom, for Poseidonius speaks of festivals at which a quarter of pork was taken by the bravest; and if another claimed it, they fought until one was killed.[22] Conchobar separated the heroes, and Sencha announced that the question should be submitted to Ailill, King of Connaught. Meanwhile Bricriu stirred up strife among the heroes' wives, who had left the hall, by telling each in turn that she should have the right of first entry; and this caused a quarrel among them, every one extolling her own husband. Loegaire and Conall each made a breach in the wall so that his wife should enter first, the door having been closed; but Cúchulainn removed one side of the house, and his wife Emer had precedence. Bricriu then demanded that the damage should be repaired, but none could do this save Cúchulainn, and he only after extraordinary exertions. Conchobar now bade the heroes go to Cúroi mac Daire, whose judgements were always equitable, in order that he might settle the question.

On his way Loegaire encountered a repulsive giant with a cudgel, who beat him and made him return without horses, chariot, or charioteer; and Conall met the same fate, Cúchulainn alone being able to overcome the giant and to return in triumph with arms and horses. Bricriu thereupon announced that the champion's morsel was Cúchulainn's, but his rivals objected, saying that one of his friends of the *side* had overcome them. The Ulstermen now sought judgement from Ailill, but Cúchulainn remained behind to amuse the women with his feats until Loeg, his charioteer, reproached him with delay. By the swiftness of their chariot-horses they arrived first at Ailill's palace, where water was brought by a hundred and fifty young girls to provide baths for the heroes, and the most beautiful of these accompanied them to their couches, Cúchulainn choosing Findabair, Ailill's daughter. Ailill asked three days and nights to consider the question, and on the first night three cats — "druidic beasts" from the cave of Cruachan — arrived. Conall and Loegaire abandoned their food to them, but Cúchulainn attacked them, and at dawn the cats disappeared, after the manner of other supernatural beings, who vanish at daybreak. Ailill was in despair how to solve the problem of the championship, but Medb sneered at him, and sending for each hero, gave him a cup without the others knowing it, saying that it would assure him of the champion's morsel at Conchobar's board. Meanwhile Cúchulainn vanquished the others in the sport of wheel-throwing, while he also threw needles so that each one entered the eye of the other, forming a single line.

Medb now sent them to Ercol and Garmna to seek their judgement, and they referred them to Samera, who dispatched them to the *Geniti Glinni*. Loegaire and Conall returned without arms or garments; Cúchulainn was at first overcome, but when Loeg reproached him, his demoniac fury began, and he attacked them and filled the valley with their blood, taking their banner and going back as a conqueror to Samera, who said that he should have the champion's morsel. Returning to Ercol, the warriors were challenged to combat him and his horse. Loegaire's steed was killed by Ercol's, and he fled to Emain, saying that the others were slain by Ercol. Conall also fled, but Cúchulainn's horse, the Grey of Macha, killed Ercol's, and he then carried Ercol prisoner to Emain, where he found everyone lamenting his death. On the way Samera's daughter Buan, who had fallen in love with Cúchulainn, leaped after his chariot, and falling on a rock, was killed. A feast was prepared at Emain Macha and now each hero produced his cup in expectation of the award. Cúchulainn's cup, however, of gold and precious stones, proved the most valuable and beautiful, and all would have given him the championship, had not his rivals maintained that this was not a true judgement and threatened to attack the hero. Conchobar therefore sent them to Yellow, son of Fair, who bade them go to Terror, son of Great Fear, a giant who could assume whatever form pleased him. He proposed the "covenant of the axe," which Loegaire and Conall refused, whereas Cúchulainn accepted it, provided they would acknowledge his supremacy, the covenant being that Cúchulainn should cut off Terror's head today, while Terror cut off his tomorrow. When Cúchulainn did his part, Terror took his head and axe and plunged into his loch; but next day he appeared, and Cúchulainn placed himself in position. Three times Terror drew the axe over his neck and then bade him rise in token of his bravery; but still his rivals would not give way, so that now the Ulstermen bade them seek the judgement of Cúroi. This axe game is found in Arthurian romance in the story of *Sir Gawayne and the Green Knight*, and it is apparently based on an actual Celtic custom of a man, in token of bravery, after an entertainment, allowing someone to cut his throat with a sword.[23]

At Cúroi's castle Bláthnat, his wife, welcomed them in his absence, though he knew they would come, and she bade them take turns in guarding it. In whatever part of the world Cúroi was, he sang a spell over the castle at night, and it revolved as swiftly as a millstone, so that the entrance could not be found — an incident found elsewhere in Celtic romance. Loegaire took the first watch and saw a giant approaching from the sea, as high as heaven and bearing oak-trees in his hands, which he threw at Loegaire, missing him each time, after which the monster stretched out his hand, and squeezing him till he was half-dead, threw him outside the castle. Next night Conall met the same fate. On the night when Cúchulainn watched, the three goblins of Sescind Uairbeoil, the three herdsmen of Bregia, and the three sons of Big-Fist the Siren were to unite to take the castle, while the spirit of the lake near by would swallow it whole; but Cúchulainn slew the nine foes when they arrived, as well as two other bands of nine, making a cairn of their heads and arms. Wearied and sad, he now heard the loch roaring like the sea and saw a monster emerging from it and approaching with open jaws to gulp the castle down. With one leap he came behind it, tore out its heart, and cutting off its head, placed it on the heap. At dawn the giant arrived, and when he stretched out his hand, Cúchulainn made his salmon-leap and whirled his sword round his head, whereupon the monster vanished after having agreed to grant his three wishes — the sovereignty of Ireland's heroes, the champion's morsel, and precedence for Emer over the women of Ulster. Cúchulainn's leap had brought him outside the castle, but after several trials he sprang back into it with a sigh, and Bláthnat said, "That is a sigh of victory." When Cúroi arrived, he found the trophies outside his castle and gave judgement in Cúchulainn's favour.

Later, when all three were absent from Emain Macha, a huge boor arrived, carrying a tree, a vast beam, and an axe with a handle which required a plough-team to move it. He announced that he had sought everywhere for a man capable of fighting him and proposed the covenant of the axe. This passage repeats grotesquely the former incident, save that Fat-Neck, who struck off the boor's head, refused to fulfil his part of the covenant, as also did Loegaire and Conall on their return. Cúchulainn took his place, but the boor spared him, calling him the bravest of warriors and fulfilling for him the three wishes he had made; for he was none other than Cúroi, who had taken first the giant's, then the boor's form.[24]

The story of *The Exile of the Sons of Doel the Forgotten* (*Longes mac nDuil Dermait*) opens with a version of *Bricriu's Feast*. Cúchulainn had been cursed by Eocho Rond to have no rest until he discovered why Doel's sons left their country. With Loeg and Lugaid he captured the ship of the King of Alba's son, who gave him a charm; and thus they reached an island with a rampart of silver and a palisade of bronze, while on it was a castle where dwelt a royal pair — Riangabair and

Finnabair — with three beautiful daughters. These welcomed them, because Loeg was their son; and Riangabair told Cúchulainn that the sister of Doel's sons and her husband were in a southern isle. In the morning Cúchulainn gave a ring to Etan, one of the daughters, who had slept with him, and then sailed for the isle. Connla, husband of Achtland, Doel's daughter, had his head against a stone in the west of the isle, and his feet against another in the east — a position resembling that in which Nut is represented above the earth in Egyptian mythology.[25] Achtland was combing his hair. As the ship approached, Connla blew so violently that a wave was formed, but as no diviner had announced danger from Cúchulainn, he was allowed to land. Achtland made him a sign and then said that she knew where her brothers were and that she would go with him, for it was foretold that he would rescue them. They reached an island where two women were cutting rushes, and one of them sang of seven Kings who ruled it. Cúchulainn brained her, whereupon the other told him the names of the Kings, one of whom was Coirpre, Doel's brother. Coirpre attacked Cúchulainn, but was forced to sue for mercy and carried him into the castle, where he gave him his daughter and told him the story of Doel's sons. Next day Eocho Glas arrived to fight Coirpre, and Cúchulainn leaped on the edge of his shield, but Eocho blew him into the sea. Now he leaped on the boss of the shield, again on Eocho himself, and both times he was blown into the ocean; but at last he slew his foe with the *gai bolga*. Then came the *side* whom Eocho had outraged, among them Doel's sons, and bathed in his blood to wash away the shame. Cúchulainn returned to Riangabair's isle, where he slept with Finnabair, and finally reaching Emain Macha, he went thence to Ailill and Medb, who caused Eocho Rond to be brought. He had fought Cúchulainn because his daughter Findchoém loved him, and on her account had put *geasa* (spells) on the hero, who now, having fulfilled them, demanded and obtained her.[26]

Both these tales contain many primitive traits and mythical incidents which throw considerable light on earlier Celtic folk-belief.

Previous to Bricriu's feast must be placed a story in which Cúroi discomfited Cúchulainn. He joined the hero and others in attacking the stronghold of the god Midir in the Isle of Falga (= the Land of Promise) and led them into it when their efforts failed through the magic of its defenders, his condition being that he must have whatever jewel he chose. The invaders carried off Midir's three cows, his cauldron, and his daughter Bláthnat. To Cúchulainn's chagrin, however, Cúroi chose her and took her away by magic; and though the hero pursued him, he was bound hand and foot by Cúroi and shaved with his sword.[27] Another version of this exploit, or perhaps of an analogous feat, tells how Cúchulainn journeyed to Scáth and by aid of the King's daughter stole a cauldron, three cows, and much gold; but his coracle was wrecked, and he had to swim home with his men clinging to him.[28]

When Cúchulainn went to obtain Cúroi's judgement, he may have come to an arrangement with Bláthnat, for Keating says that, finding him alone, she told him that she loved him,[29] while a story in the *Dindsenchas* describes her as his paramour and declares that she bade him come and take his revenge. She brought it about that Cúroi was alone in his castle and as a signal she caused milk to flow down-stream to Cúchulainn, whereupon he entered and slew Cúroi, whose sword Bláthnat had taken.[30] In another version, however, the incident of the separable soul occurs. Cúroi's soul was in an apple, and this in a salmon, which appeared every seven years in a certain well, while the apple could be split only by Cúroi's sword. This knowledge was obtained by Cúroi's wife, as in parallel stories, and the sword given by her to Cúchulainn, who thus compassed her husband's death.[31] The folk-tale formula is thus complete, though doubtless Cúroi is a genuine Celtic personality, whose fame was known to Welsh bards.[32] Probably a complete saga existed about this great hero or divinity and magician, who, according to another story, with his magic wand took possession of Ireland and the great world.[33] The slaying of Cúroi should be compared with that of Lleu, brought about by Blodeuwedd's treachery, and with the killing of Searbhan by his own club, especially as Blodeuwedd's name, meaning "Flower-Face," from *blodeu* ("flowers") is akin to Bláthnat's, which is probably from *bláth* ("bloom"). In the sequel Cúroi's poet avenged his death by leaping off a cliff with Bláthnat in his arms.[34]

The greatest adventure in Cúchulainn's career occurs in the *Táin Bó Cúalnge*, or *Cattle-Raid of Cúalnge*," to which belong a number of prefatory tales, some of them already cited. Only the briefest account of this long story can be given here. Queen Medb of Connaught desired the Donn or Brown Bull of Cúalnge in Ulster, so that she might have the equivalent of her husband Ailill's bull, the Findbennach, or "White-Horned," these bulls, as narrated above,[35] being rebirths of semi-divinities. When Daire, owner of the bull, refused to give it, Medb collected an enormous force to march against Ulster at the time when the Ulstermen were in their "debility"—the result of Macha's curse.[36] Cúchulainn and Sualtam were unaffected by that curse, however, and they went against the host, in which were some heroes of Ulster, Cormac, Conall, Fiacha, and Fergus, exiled because of a quarrel with Conchobar for his treacherous murder of the sons of Usnech. As Medb set out, a beautiful girl suddenly appeared on her chariot-shaft, announcing herself as servant of Medb's people, Fedelm the prophetess (*banfaid*) from the *síd* of Cruachan (hence Medb was also of the *síde*); but she prophesied disaster because of Cúchulainn, whom she saw in a vision.

Cúchulainn, having entered a forest, stood on one leg, and using one hand and one eye, he cut down an oak sapling, which he twisted into a ring, inscribing on it his name, and placing it over a pillar-stone. This was a *geis* (tabu) to the host not to

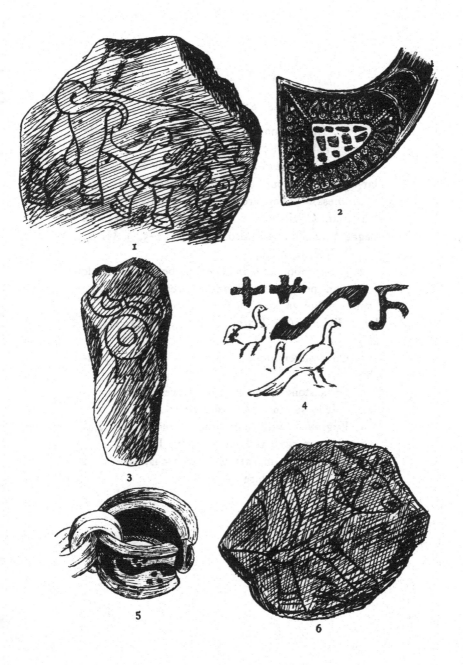

1   2

3   4

5   6

PLATE XIX

Bulls and S-Symbols

1, 6. Bulls, conventionally treated, with the characteristic Celtic spiral ornament. From stones found at Burghhead near Forres, Elginshire. Similar figures exist on stones at Inverness and Ulbster (Caithness). They are believed to date from the Christian Celtic period, but perhaps represent a pagan tradition. Cf. also Plates II, 4–5, 9, III, 5, IX, B, XX, B, XXI.

2–5. S-symbol, also believed to be of the Celtic Christian period, but doubtless derived from the same symbol as used on Gaulish coins and carried by a divinity (see Plates II, 2, 4, 7–9, 11, III, 3, IV).

2. On a silver brooch found at Croy, Inverness-shire.

3. On a stone found at Kintradwell, Sutherland-shire. It exists on a few other stones.

4. Engraved with numerous other figures and symbols on a cave at East Wemyss, Fife.

5. On a silver ring attached to a chain found at Parkhill, Aberdeenshire.

advance until they had done the same; and meanwhile he kept tryst with Conchobar's daughter Fedelm or with her handmaid. Again entering a wood, he cut down the fork of a tree, placed on it four heads of the enemy slain by him, and set it in a ford to prevent the chariots from passing until it was drawn out. Now he slew hundreds of the host, but a treaty was made that every day a warrior should meet him in single combat, while he allowed the army to proceed. These combats, described with great spirit, as well as other daring deeds of Cúchulainn's, occupy the greater part of the *Táin*, but none of them is so full of interest and pathos as the long episode of the fight with Ferdia, his former fellow-pupil with Scáthach, whom at last to his sorrow he slew.

One incident tells of the warning given by the goddess Morrígan, in the form of a bird, to the bull to beware of Medb's men, so that with fifty heifers he fled to the Heifer's Glen, but was ultimately taken and brought to Medb's host; and another passage describes Cúchulainn's rejection of Morrígan's advances, and her wounding and later healing by him.[37] There is also the incident of Medb's sending her women to bid him smear a false beard on himself when her warrior, Loch, refused to fight this beardless youth, whereupon he said a spell over some grass and clapped it to his chin, so that all thought he had a beard. The help given to Cúchulainn by Lug has already been described;[38] and the Tuatha Dé Danann likewise aided him by throwing healing herbs and plants into the streams in which his wounds were washed. Interesting is the long account of his *riastrad*, or "distortion," before wreaking his fury on the men of Connaught for slaying the "boy corps" of Emain. He grew to an immense size and quivered in every limb, while his feet, shins, and knees were reversed in his body. This was the permanent condition of Levarcham and Dornolla, already mentioned, and implied swiftness and strength, since Levarcham traversed all Ireland every day. Of Cúchulainn's eyes, one sank in his head so that a heron could not have reached it, while the other protruded from its socket as large as the rim of a cauldron. His mouth reached his ears, and fire streamed from it, mounting above his head in showers, while a great jet of blood higher and more rigid than a ship's mast shot upward from his scalp, within which his hair retreated, and formed a mist all about. This distortion frequently came upon Cúchulainn, like the terrific heat sometimes given off by his body, enough to melt deep snow for thirty feet around.

During the progress of the *Táin* Ailill sent messengers to Cúchulainn, offering him his daughter Findabair if he would keep away from the host. Finally his fool, taking Ailill's shape, approached the hero with Findabair, but Cúchulainn detected the transformation and slew him, besides thrusting a stone through Findabair's mantle and tunic. She had been offered to Ferdia and others if they conquered Cúchulainn; but later she died of shame because of the slaughter of warriors in the fight between the chiefs to whom she had been promised and her lover Reochaid and his men. In the version given in the *Book of Lecan*, however, she remained with Cúchulainn when peace was concluded. This is the same Findabair who is the heroine of the story of Fraoch cited above, and whose favours Cúchulainn had already gained.[39]

Meanwhile the Ulstermen had recovered from their debility and gathered for the battle with the enemy, while the goddess Morrígan uttered a song of slaughter between the armies. Medb's forces were defeated, but she sent the bull by a circuitous way to Cruachan; and seeing the trackless land before him, he uttered three terrible bellowings, at which the Findbennach came hurrying toward him. Bricriu saw the wild combat between the maddened animals, but as they struggled he was trampled into the earth by their hoofs. All over Ireland they drove, fighting as they went; and next day the Brown Bull was seen coming to Cúalnge with the Findbennach in a mangled heap on his horns. Women and children wept as they beheld him, but these he slew; and then, turning his back against a hill, his heart was rent with his mighty exertions. Thus ended the *Táin*.[40]

Cúchulainn was now seventeen years old, and to the few years which ensued before his death probably belong his *amour* with the goddess Fand and that with Bláthnat, since Cúroi intended to oppose him during the *Táin*, but was sent back by Medb.

The slaying of Cúroi, of Cairbre Niaper in fair fight at Ros na Rígh, and of Calatin, as well as his twenty-seven sons and his sister's son, during the *Táin*, led to the hero's death. Calatin's wife bore posthumously three monstrous sons and three daughters who were nurtured by Medb and studied magic arts in order to compass Cúchulainn's death. Joining at last with Lugaid, Cúroi's son, and Erc, Cairbre's son, they marched toward Ulster while its men were in their debility. Mighty efforts were made to restrain Cúchulainn from a combat which all knew would be fatal to him, and he was at last concealed in the Glen of the Deaf; but Calatin's daughters discovered this and created a phantasmal army out of puff-balls and withered leaves, as Lug's witches transformed into soldiers trees, sods, and stones, and Gwydion trees and sedges.[41] This army and other eldritch things filled the glen with strange noises, and Cúchulainn thought that enemies were harassing Ulster, though Cathbad told him that this was merely magic illusion. Then one of the weird daughters took the form of Niamh, daughter of Celtchar, and speaking in her name, bade Cúchulainn attack the foes who were overwhelming Ulster. Neither the protestations of the real Niamh, nor of Dechtire, nor of Conchobar, nor the assurances of Cathbad that the hosts were illusions could withhold him. On his way to Emain he saw Badb's daughter washing blood from a warrior's gear — the "Washer at the Ford," a prophecy of his own death — but he was resolute and cheerful in face of the desperate fight to which he bound himself. During the night Morrígan broke his chariot, hoping thus to stay him from the combat, but next morning he bade it be yoked with the Grey of Macha, though the horse reproached him. On his way three crones, cooking dog's flesh with poisons and spells, called him, but since one of his *geasa* was not to approach a cooking-hearth nor to eat the flesh of his namesake (*cú*, "dog"), he would have passed on, had not the crones reproached him. So he turned aside, took the flesh with his left hand, and ate it, placing his hand under his thigh, whereupon strength departed from thigh and hand. In the fight he slew many foes, until Lugaid possessed himself of Cúchulainn's spear and wounded first the Grey of Macha, which plunged into the loch for healing; and then Cúchulainn, who begged permission to crawl to the loch for water. He set himself against a pillar-stone, and there the faithful horse returned and killed many of his foes with teeth and hoofs; but at last Lugaid struck off Cúchulainn's head, though as the hero's sword fell from his grasp, it lopped off his enemy's hand. Meanwhile Conall was met by the horse, and together they sought and found Cúchulainn's body, the Grey placing its head on its master's breast. Conall pursued Lugaid, for Cúchulainn and he had vowed that whoever survived must avenge the others; and his own horse aided him, biting a piece from Lugaid's side, while Conall cut off his head, thus taking vengeance for the hero's death.[42]

Lugaid, Cúroi's son, was called *Mac na Tri Con*, or "Son of the Three Dogs," viz. Cúroi, Cúchulainn, and Conall — *con* being the genitive of *cú* ("dog")— because it was believed that his mother Bláthnat, Cúroi's wife, had loved these two as well as her husband.[43] Thus Lugaid killed one reputed father of his and was himself slain by another. A tenth century poem calls the three flags of his grave Murder, Disgrace, and Treachery.[44] He was probably not Cúchulainn's friend Lugaid Red-Stripes, who, however, was also a son of three fathers, Bres, Nár, and Lothar, by their sister Clothru.

In his old age Conall retired to the Court of Medb, who

induced him to slay Ailill; but for this the three Reds, or Wolves, killed him and cut off his head in revenge for the death of Cúroi at the hands of Cúchulainn.[45]

Conchobar met his fate in a curious way. Among the trophies in Emain Macha was a sling-ball made of the brain of Mesgegra, King of Leinster, slain by Conall. One day Cet, whom Conall killed at the feast on Mac Dáthó's Boar, stole this ball, which was mixed with earth, and thus hardened, and later induced the women of Connaught to get Conchobar to show himself to them, whereupon Cet flung the ball into his forehead, whence it could not be removed lest he should die. Years after, an earthquake occurred, and when his Druid told him that this signified our Lord's crucifixion, Conchobar, who now believed in God, felt such emotion at not being able to avenge Christ that the ball started from his head, and he died.[46]

M. d'Arbois maintained that the saga of Cúchulainn was known in Gaul. Cúchulainn's name Setanta is akin to that of the Setantii, Celtic tribes living in the district between the Ribble and Morecambe Bay, and this, according to Rhŷs,[47] suggests a British ancestry for the Irish hero. D'Arbois, on the other hand, regards this folk, as well as the Brigantes, as of Belgic Gaulish provenance, while the latter had colonies in Ireland. They had a well-known god, Esus, whom d'Arbois identifies with Cúchulainn; whence the story is of Gaulish origin, perhaps taught by the Druids; and it was ultimately carried to Ulster, where it was received with enthusiasm.[48] The identification rests on certain figured monuments, in the persons, names, or episodes of which M. d'Arbois sees those of the saga. On one altar Esus is cutting down a tree, while on the same altar is figured a bull on which are perched three birds, this animal being entitled *Tarvos Trigaranos* — "the bull with three cranes" (*garanus*), unless the cranes are a rebus for the three horns (*karenos*) of divine animals. On another altar from Trèves a god is cutting down a tree, and in its branches are a bull's head and two birds — a possible combination of the incidents on the other altar. M. d'Arbois regards this as illustrating the *Táin*. Esus, the woodman, is Cúchulainn; his action depicts what the hero did — cutting down trees to bar the way of Medb's host; "Esus" is derived from words meaning "anger," "rapid motion," such as Cúchulainn often displayed. The bull is the Brown Bull; the birds are the forms in which Morrígan and her sisters appeared,[49] though these bird-forms were those of the crow, not the crane; the personal name Donnotaurus is found in Gaul and is the equivalent of the *Donn Tarb* — the "Brown Bull." [50] Again, Diodorus says that the Dioscuri, i. e. Castor and Pollux, were the gods most worshipped by the Celts in the west of Gaul,[51] and M. d'Arbois finds these in Cúchulainn and Conall Cernach, the former being foster-brother of the latter, having been suckled by Findchoém, Conall's mother. He bases this identification on an altar found at Paris, on the four sides of which are represented the Roman Castor and Pollux and two Gaulish divinities — Smertullos attacking a serpent with a club, and an unnamed horned god, perhaps the god Cernunnos (*cernu-*, "horn"). Smertullos is, therefore, the native equivalent of Pollux, Cernunnos of Castor; and at the same time Smertullos is Cúchulainn, and Cernunnos is Conall Cernach. In the *Táin* Cúchulainn vanquished Morrígan as an eel — the serpent of the monument — and, again, to hide his youthfulness, he smeared (*smérthain*, hence Smertullos) his chin with a false beard. As for Conall Cernach, whose epithet means "victorious," M. d'Arbois connects it also with the hypothetical *cernu-* ("horn"), though Conall is never said to be horned.[52]

Lug, Cúchulainn's father, was a widely worshipped Celtic god, his equivalent in Gaul being a hypothetical Lugus, whose name appears in place-names there. As Lug was called *samildánach* ("skilled in many arts"),[53] Lugus may be the Gaulish god equated by Cæsar with Mercury, whom he calls "inventor of all arts" and associates with the *simulacra*, or

PLATE XX

A and B

Altar from Notre Dame

A. The god Esus (cf. p. 9) was perhaps a deity of vegetation, and human victims offered to him were hanged on trees. He has been identified, though with slight probability, with Cúchulainn (cf. Plate XVIII). He is here shown cutting down a tree, the branches of which are carried over to the next side of the altar.

B. The next side of the same altar, dedicated by sailors and found at Notre Dame, Paris. Under the branches of the tree which Esus is felling stands a bull with three cranes perched on his back — Tarvos Trigaranos (see p. 9). For the bull see also Plates II, 4-5, 9, III, 5, IX, B, XIX, 1, 6. The subjects of these two sides of the altar recur in an altar from Trèves (Plate XXI).

standing-stones, of Gaul. Now on one of these at Kervadel four bas-reliefs were sculptured in Gallo-Roman times, one of them depicting the god Mercury together with a smaller childish figure; and M. d'Arbois assumes that this represents the god Lug with his son Cúchulainn.[54]

Tempting as these identifications are, it must be confessed that they rest upon comparatively slender evidence and on what may be merely apparent coincidences, while they are of an extremely speculative character.

CHAPTER XIII

THE HEROIC MYTHS

(Continued)

II. FIONN AND THE FÉINN

THE annalists gave a historic aspect and a specific date and ancestry to Fionn and his men, the Féinn, but they exist and are immortal because they sprang from the heroic ideals of the folk; if they were once men, it was in a period of which no written record remains. Their main story possesses a framework and certain outstanding facts, but whatever far distant actuality the epos has is thickly overlaid with fancy, so that we are in a world of exaggerated action, of magic, whenever we approach any story dealing with the Féinn. The annalistic scheme added nothing to the epos; rather is it as if to the vague personalities of folk-tale had been given a date, names, and a line of long descent, which may delight prosaic minds, though it spoils the folk-tale for the imaginative.

Traces of the annalistic scheme occur in the chronological poem of Gilla Caemhain (ob. 1072) and in the *Annals* of Tighernach (ob. 1088), which regarded the Féinn as a hireling militia defending Ireland, consisting of seven legions or *Fianna* (also *Féinn*, literally "troops"), each of three thousand men with a commander. The Féinn of Leinster and Meath comprised those of our epos — the *clanna* Baoisgne, its later chiefs being Cumhal, Goll (of the *clanna* Morna), and Fionn. We are told of their arms, dress, and privileges, and of the conditions of admission to their ranks — some almost superhuman;[1] and we learn that their exactions became so heavy that king and people rose against them and routed them at Cnucha, where Cumhal, father of Fionn, fell. Later his opponent Goll became head of the Féinn, and then Fionn himself; but as a result of their new pretensions the Féinn were finally destroyed at Gabhra.

Many Féinn stories are coloured by this scheme, which was applied to them at an early period; yet alongside the oldest references to it we find stories or allusions which show that the imaginative aspect was as strong then as it was later, and that at an early date there was much Fionn literature so well known that mere reference to its persons or incidents sufficed.[2]

A recent writer suggests that Fionn was originally a hero of the subject race of the Galióin in North Leinster,[3] who are constantly associated with Firbolgs and Fir Domnann. These appear to be remnants of a pre-Celtic population in Ireland,[4] and are usually despised for evil qualities, though they have strong magical powers, just as conquerors often consider aboriginal races to be superior magicians, if inferior human beings. These races furnished military service for the Celtic kings of their district down to the rise of the dominant "Milesian" monarchs in the fifth century; and of these *Fianna*, Fionn (whose name means "white" and has nothing to do with *fianna* or *féinn*), whether he really existed or not, was regarded as chief. Mac Firbis, a seventeenth century author, quotes an earlier writer who says that Fionn was of the sept of the Uí Tarsig, part of the tribe of the Galióin. Cumhal, his father, of the *clanna* Baoisgne, is represented in the *Boyish Deeds of Fionn (Macgnimartha Finn)*[5] — a story copied from the tenth century Psalter of Cashel into a later manuscript — as striving at Cnucha with Uirgreann and the *clanna* Luagni, aided by the *clanna* Morna, both subject tribes, for the chief Fiannship (*Fiannuigeacht*). Only in later accounts of the battle is Conn, the High King (*Ardrí*), introduced, and though the annalistic conception colours the introduction to this otherwise mythical tale, it appears to be based on recollections of clan feuds, especially as Fionn himself was later slain by members of the *clanna* Uirgreann. With growing popularity, he became a Leinster Irish hero, fighting against other Irish tribes, mainly those of Ulster; but it was not until the middle Irish period that the Fionn story, which had now spread through a great part of Ireland among the Celtic folk, with many local developments, was adopted by the literary class of the dominant tribes, as at an earlier period they had taken over the Cúchulainn saga from the Ulstermen. They were rewriting Irish history in the light of contemporary events and of their own ambitions; and accordingly they transfigured and remoulded the legend of Fionn, which afforded them an ever-growing literary structure. The forced service of the *Fianna* became that of a highly developed militia under imaginary high kings, whence the rise of tales in which Fionn is brought into relation with these rulers — Conn, Cormac, Art, and Cairbre — in the second and third centuries. The *Fianna* became defenders of Ireland against foreign invasion; they battled with Norsemen; they even went outside Ireland and conquered European or Asiatic kings.

In origin Fionn was the ideal hero of a subject, non-Celtic race, as Cumhal had been, and they were located at Almha — the Hill of Allen. They tended, however, to become historic figures, associated primarily with the forced service of such a race, then with the later mythic national militia; but despite this, a mythic aspect was theirs from first to last, while the cycle of legends was constantly being augmented. To Oisin, son of Fionn, are ascribed many poems about the Féinn: hence he must have been regarded traditionally as the poet of the band, rather than his father, who studied the art and ate the salmon of knowledge. Few excelled in bravery Oisin's son, Oscar. Caoilte mac Ronan, Fionn's nephew, was famed for fleetness; at full speed he appeared as three persons and could overtake the swift March wind, though it could not outstrip him. Diarmaid uí Duibhne, who "never knew weariness of foot, nor shortness of breath, nor, whether in going out or in coming in, ever flagged," possessed a "beauty-spot" (*ball-seirc*); and no woman who saw it could resist "the lightsome countenance" of "yellow-haired Diarmaid of the women." Goll of *clanna* Morna, Fionn's enemy, and then his friend, but with whom a feud arose which ended in his death, was probably the ideal warrior, prodigiously strong, noble, and brave, of a separate saga. Conan Maol was also of *clanna* Morna, and his father aided in slaying Cumhal at Cnucha, for which Fionn afterward put an *eric*, or fine, upon him. Although of the Féinn, he was continually rejoicing at their misfortunes in foul-mouthed language; and this Celtic Thersites, "wrecker and great disturber of the Féinn," was constantly in trouble through his boldness and reckless bravery — "claw for claw, and devil take the shortest nails, as Conan said to the devil." In later accounts he appears rather as a comic character. MacLugach of the Terrible Hand is also prominent; so, too, is Fergus True-Lips, the wise seer, interpreter of dreams, and poet. Others come and go, but round these circles all the breathless interest of this heroic epos. Their occupations were fighting on a vast scale, the records of which, like those of the Cúchulainn saga, are often tiresome and ghastly; mighty huntings, watched from some hill-top by Fionn, and described with zest and not a little romantic beauty as the hunt wends by forests, glens, watercourses, or smiling valleys; lastly, love-making, for these warriors could woo tenderly and with compelling power. Their vast strength and size — one of their skulls held a man seated — tend to remove them from the puny race of mere human beings; yet though of divine descent, they were not immortal, so that Caoilte says of a goddess: "She is of the Tuatha Dé Danann, who are unfading and whose duration is perennial; I am of the sons of Milesius, that are perishable and fade away."[6]

While the Cúchulainn legend had a definite number of tales and, after a certain date, remained complete, the Fionn cycle received continual additions. New stories were written, new incidents invented or borrowed from existing folk-tale or saga, until comparatively recent times. Again, unlike the Cúchulainn saga, the Fionn cycle contains numerous poems; while the former has fewer folk-tale versions of its literary stories than the latter.

The interest of Fionn's ancestral line begins with Cumhal. *The Boyish Deeds* shows him engaging in a clan feud with the *clanna* Luagni, assisted by the *clanna* of which Morna was chief. Morna's son Aodh took a leading part in the battle and was prominent afterward under the name Goll ("One-Eyed"), because he lost an eye there; Cumhal fell at his stroke.[7] A different account of the battle is given in the *Leabhar na hUidhre*. In this, Tadg, a Druid, succeeded to Almha, the castle of his father Nuada, who also was a Druid; and Tadg's daughter Muirne was sought in marriage by Cumhal, but refused, because Tadg foresaw that he would lose Almha through him. Cumhal then abducted her, whereupon Tadg complained to the High King, Conn, who ordered Cumhal to give her up or leave the country. He refused, however, and collecting an army, fought Conn's men, including Uirgreann, Morna, and Goll, the latter of whom slew him, whence there was feud between Cumhal's descendants and Goll.[8]

Although Tadg and Nuada are called Druids, Nuada is elsewhere one of the Tuatha Dé Danann, and he is probably the god Nuada who fought at Mag-Tured;[9] while Tadg is also said to be from the *síd* of Almha, which is thus regarded both as a divine dwelling and as a fort. Hence Fionn is affiliated to the gods, and another tradition makes his mother's father Bracan, a warrior of the Tuatha Dé Danann.[10] Cumhal has been identified with a god Camulos, known from inscriptions in Gaul and Scotland, whose name is also found in Camulodunum (? Colchester). As Camulos was equated with Mars, he was a warrior-god — a character in keeping with that of Cumhal, though if the latter was a non-Celtic hero, and if his name should be read Umall, the identification is excluded.[11]

Fionn, a posthumous child, was at first called Deimne. For safety's sake he was taken by Bodhmhall and the Liath Luchra and reared in the wilds, where, while still a child, he strangled a polecat and had other adventures.[12] At ten years old he came to a fortress on the Liffey, where the boys were playing hurley, and beat them; and when they described him as "fair" to its owner, he said that his name should be Fionn ("Fair"), but that they must kill him if he returned. Nevertheless, next day he slew seven of them and a week later drowned nine more when they challenged him at swimming.[13] While this incident resembles one in Cúchulainn's early career, in other, probably later, accounts, the match takes place in the presence of the High King, Conn, who called the boy "Fionn."[14] In the *Colloquy with the Ancients*, however, another incident is found. Goll had been made chief of the Féinn after Cumhal's death; and when ten years old, Fionn came to Conn, announcing that he wished to be reconciled with him and to enter his service. Conn now offered his rightful heritage to him who would save Tara from being burnt by Aillen mac Midhna of the Tuatha Dé Danann, who yearly made every one sleep through his fairy music and then set fire to the fortress. Fionn did not succumb to the music, because of the magic power of a weapon given him by one of his father's comrades, and he also warded off with his mantle the flame from Aillen's mouth and succeeded in beheading him, so that he was given Goll's position, while Goll made friends with him rather than go into exile.[15] In the account of Cumhal's death as given in the *Leabhar na hUidhre*, Conn advised Muirne to go to her sister Bodhmhall, at whose house Fionn was born. Later he challenged Tadg to single combat, or to fight him with many, or to pay a fine for Cumhal's death; and Tadg, appealing for a judgement, was forced to surrender Almha to Fionn. Peace was now made between Fionn and Goll.[16]

The story of Fionn's "thumb of knowledge" belongs in some versions to this period. To learn the art of poetry he went to Finnéces, who for seven years sought to capture a salmon which would impart supernatural knowledge to him — the "salmon of knowledge"— and after he had caught it, he bade Fionn cook it, forbidding him to taste it. When Finnéces inquired whether he had eaten any of it, Fionn replied, "No, but my thumb I burned, and I put it into my mouth after that"; whereupon Finnéces gave him the name Fionn, since prophecy had announced that Fionn should eat the salmon. He ate it in fact, and ever after, on placing his thumb in his mouth, knowledge of things unknown came to him.[17] This story, based on the universal idea that supernatural knowledge or acquaintance with the language of beasts comes from eating part of an animal, often a snake, is parallel to the story of Gwion's obtaining inspiration intended for Avagddu [18] and to that of the Norse Sigurd, who, roasting the heart of the dragon Fafnir, intended for the dwarf, burned his finger, placed it in his mouth, and so obtained supernatural wisdom. In German tales the animal is a *Haselwurm*, a snake found under a hazel, like the Celtic salmon which ate the nuts falling from the hazels of knowledge. As told of Fionn, the story is a folk-tale formula applied to him, but the conception ultimately rests upon the belief in beneficial results from the ritual eating of a sacred animal with knowledge superior to man's. Among American Indians, Maoris, Solomon Islanders, and others there are figured representations of a medicine-man with a reptile whose tongue is attached to his own, and it is actually believed by the American Indians that the postulant magician catches a mysterious otter, takes its tongue, and hangs it round his neck in a bag, after which he understands the language of all creatures.[19]

When Fionn sought supernatural knowledge, he chewed his thumb or laid it on his tooth, to which it had given this clairvoyant gift; or, again, the knowledge is already in his

PLATE XXI

Altar from Trèves

A deity (Esus) fells a tree in the foliage of which a bull's head appears, while three cranes perch on the branches (Tarvos Trigaranos). The bas-relief thus combines the subjects of two sides of the altar from Notre Dame (Plate XX).

thumb. Cúldub from the *síd* stole the food of the Féinn on three successive nights, but was caught by Fionn, who also followed a woman who had come from the *síd* to obtain water. She shut the door on his thumb, which he extricated with difficulty; and then, having sucked it, he found that he knew future events.[20] In another account, however, part of his knowledge came from drinking at a well owned by the Tuatha Dé Danann.[21]

Folk-tale versions of Fionn's youth resemble the literary forms, with differences in detail. Cumhal did not marry, because it was prophesied that if he did he would die in the next battle; yet having fallen in love with the king's daughter, he wedded her secretly, although a Druid had told the monarch that his daughter's son would dethrone him, wherefore he kept her concealed — a common folk-tale incident. As his death was at hand Cumhal begged his mother to rear his child, but it was thrown into a loch, from which it was rescued by its grandmother, who caused a man to make them a room in a tree and, to preserve the secret, killed him. When the boy was fifteen, she took him to a hurling-match, and the king, who was present, cried, "Who is that *fin cumhal* ('white cap')?" The woman called out, "Fin mac Cumhal will be his name," and again fled, this being followed by the thumb incident with the formula of Odysseus and the Cyclops, in which a one-eyed giant is substituted for Finnéces. Later, Fionn fought the beings who threw down a *dún* which was in course of construction and for this obtained the king's daughter, while the heroes killed by these beings were restored by him and became his followers.[22] Scots ballad and folk-tale versions contain some of these incidents, but vary much as to Cumhal. In one he goes to Scotland and defeats the Norse, and there sets up as a king; but Irish and Norse kings entice him to Ireland, persuade him to marry, and kill him in his wife's arms. His posthumous son is carried by his nurse to the wilds, and then follows the naming incident and that of the thumb of knowledge, though here Black Arcan, Cumhal's murderer, takes the place of Finnéces and is slain by Fionn on learning of his guilt from his thumb. Lastly Fionn obtains his rightful due.[23] His birth incident and subsequent history is an example of the Aryan "Expulsion and Return" formula, as Nutt pointed out, and is paralleled in other Celtic instances.

In the *Boyish Deeds of Fionn* Cruithne became Fionn's wife, but in other tales he possesses other wives or mistresses. In the *Colloquy with the Ancients* his wife Sabia, daughter of the god Bodb Dearg, died of horror at the slaughter when Fionn's men fought Goll and the *clanna* Morna.[24] An Irish ballad also makes Dearg's daughter mother of Oisin, while a second daughter offered herself to Fionn for a year to the exclusion of all others, after which she was to enjoy half of his society; but he refused, whereupon she gave him a potion which caused a frenzy.[25] Sabia, Oisin's mother, is the Saar of tradition, whom a Druid changed into a deer. Spells were laid on Fionn to marry the first female creature whom he met, and this was Saar, as a deer, though by his knowledge he recognized her as a woman transformed. He afterward found a child with deer's hair on his temple, for if Saar licked her offspring, he would have a deer's form; if not, that of a human being. She could not resist giving him one lick, however, and hair grew on his brow, whence his name Oisin, or "Little Fawn." Many ballads recount this incident, but in one the deer is Grainne, whose story will be told presently,[26] although elsewhere she is called Blai.[27] Another divine or fairy mistress of Fionn's could assume many animal shapes, and hence he renounced her. Mair, wife of Bersa, also fell in love with him and formed nine nuts with love-charms, sending them to him that he might eat them; but he refused and buried them, because they were "an enchantment for drinking love."[28] Another love-affair turned Fionn's hair grey. Cuailnge, smith to the Tuatha Dé Danann, had two daughters, Miluchradh and Aine, both of whom loved Fionn. Aine, however, said that she would never marry a man with grey hair, where-upon Miluchradh caused the gods to make a lake, on which she breathed a spell that all who bathed there should become grey. One day Fionn was drawn to this lake by a doe and was induced to jump into it to recover the ring of a woman sitting by the shore; but when he emerged, she had vanished, and he was a withered old man. The Féinn dug down toward Miluchradh's *síd*, when she appeared with a drinking-horn which restored Fionn's youth, but left his hair grey, while Conan jeered at his misfortune.[29] One poem offers a partial parallel to the incident of Cúchulainn and Conlaoch, without its tragic ending. Oisin, angry with his father, went away for a year, after which father and son met without recognition. Fionn gave Oisin a blow, and both then reviled each other until the discovery of their relationship, when the dispute was happily settled.[30]

Fionn's hounds, Bran and Sgeolan, were nephews of his own, for Illan married Fionn's wife's sister Tuirrean, whom his fairy mistress transformed into a wolf-hound which gave birth to these famous dogs. Afterward, when Illan promised to renounce Tuirrean, the fairy restored her form.[31]

Fionn's adventures are mainly of a supernatural kind — combats with gods, giants, phantoms, and other fantastic beings, apart from those in which he fought Norsemen or other foreign powers, an anachronism needing no comment. On one occasion Fionn, Oisin, and Caoilte came to a mysterious house, where a giant seized their horses and bade them enter. In the house were a three-headed hag and a headless man with an eye in his breast; and as they sang at the giant's bidding, nine bodies arose on one side and nine heads on the other, shrieking discordantly. Slaying the horses, he cooked their flesh on rowan spits, and a part, uncooked, was brought to Fionn, but was refused by him. Then a fight began, and Fionn wielded his sword until sunrise, when all three heroes fell into a swoon. When they recovered, the house had vanished, and they realized that the three "phantoms" were the three shapes out of Yew Glen, which had thus taken revenge for injury done to their sister, Culenn Wide-Maw.[32]

In *The Fairy Palace of the Quicken-Trees* (*Bruighean Caorthuinn*) Fionn defeated and killed the King of Lochlann, but spared his son Midac, bringing him up in his household. Midac requited him ill, for he chose land on either side of the Shannon's mouth, where armies could land, and then invited Fionn and his men to the palace of the quicken-trees, while Oisin, Diarmaid, and four others remained outside. Presently Midac left the palace, when all its splendour disappeared, and the Féinn were unable to move. Meanwhile an army arrived, but Diarmaid and the others repulsed it after long fighting; and he released Fionn and the rest with the blood of three kings.[33] In a folk-tale version the blood was exhausted before Conan was reached, and he said to Diarmaid, "If I were a pretty woman, you would not have left me to the last," whereupon Diarmaid tore him away, leaving his skin sticking to the seat.[34] The house created by glamour in these stories, and vanishing at dawn, has frequently been found in other tales.

The Féinn were sometimes aided by, sometimes at war with, the Tuatha Dé Danann, though in later tales these seem robbed of much of their divinity, one story regarding them almost as demoniac. Conaran, a chief of the Tuatha Dé Danann, bade his three daughters punish Fionn for his hunting. On three holly sticks they hung hasps of yarn in front of a cave and reeled them off withershins, while they sat in the cavern as hideous hags and magically bound Fionn and others who entered it. Now arrived Goll, Fionn's former enemy, and with him the hags fought; but two of them he halved by a clean sword-sweep, and the third, after being vanquished, restored the heroes. Afterward, however, when she reappeared to avenge her sisters' death, Goll slew her and then burned Conaran's *síd*, giving its wealth to Fionn, who bestowed his daughter on him.[35] Goll is here deemed a hero, as in many poems which lament his ultimate lonely death by Fionn, after a brave defence. In these Goll is superior to Fionn, and he was the popular hero of the Féinn in Donegal and Connaught, as if there had been a cycle of tales in these districts in which he was the central figure.[36]

Fionn also fought the Muireartach, a horrible one-eyed hag whose husband was the ocean-smith, while she was foster-mother to the King of Lochlann. She captured from the Féinn their "cup of victory" — a clay vessel the contents of which made them victorious — but after a battle in which the King of Lochlann was slain, the cup was recovered. The hag returned, however, and killed some of the Féinn, but Fionn caused the ground to be cut from under her and then slew her.[37] This hag, whose name perhaps means "the eastern sea," has been regarded as an embodiment of the tempestuous waters; and in one version the ocean-smith says that she cannot die until she is drowned in "deep, smooth sea"— as if this were a description of the storm lulled to rest. When she is let down into the ground, the suggestion is that of water confined in a hollow space;[38] and if so, the story is a romantic treatment of the Celtic rite of "fighting the waves" with weapons at high tides.[39]

While the King of Lochlann is associated with this hag, he and the Lochlanners are scarcely discriminated from Norsemen who came across the eastern sea, invading Ireland and capturing Fionn's magic possessions, his dogs, or his wife. Yet there is generally something supernatural about them; hence, probably before Norsemen came to Ireland, Lochlann was a supernatural region with superhuman people. Rhŷs equates it with the Welsh Llychlyn — "a mysterious country in the lochs or the sea" — whence Fionn's strife would be with supernatural beings connected with the sea, an interpretation agreeing with the explanation of the Muireartach.

Once Fionn, having made friends with the giant Seachran, was taken with him to the castle of his mother and brother, who hated him. While dancing, Seachran was seized by a hairy claw from the roof, but escaped, throwing his mother into the cauldron destined for him. He and Fionn fled, pursued by the brother, who slew Seachran, but was killed by Fionn, who learned from his thumb that a ring guarded by warriors would heal him who drank thrice above it. Diarmaid obtained the ring, but was pursued by the warriors, whom Seachran's wife slew, after which the giant was restored to life.[40]

Other stories record the chase of enchanted or monstrous animals. Oisin slew a huge boar of the breed of Balor's swine, which supplied a week's eating for men and hounds; but meanwhile Donn, one of the *side*, carried off a hundred maidens from Aodh's *sid*. Aodh's wife, secretly in love with Donn, changed them into hinds, and when he would not return her love, transformed him into a stag. In this guise he boasted that the Féinn could not take him, but after a mighty encounter, Oisin, with Bran and Sgeolan, slew him.[41] In another tale a vast boar, off whom weapons only glanced, killed many hounds; but at last it was brought to bay by Bran, when "a churl of the hill" appeared and carried it away, inviting the Féinn to follow. They reached a *sid* where the churl changed the boar into a handsome youth, his son; and in the *sid* were many splendours, fair women, and noble youths. The churl was Eanna, King of the *sid*, his wife Manannan's daughter. Fionn offered to wed their daughter, Sgáthach, for a year; and Eanna agreed to give her, saying that the chase had been arranged in order to bring Fionn to the *sid*. Presents were then given to him and his men, but at night Sgáthach played a sleep-strain on the harp which lulled to slumber Fionn and the others, who in the morning found themselves far from the *sid*, but with the presents beside them, while it proved that the night had not yet arrived, an incident which should be compared with a similar one in the story of Nera.[42] This overcoming of the Féinn by glamour and enchantment is a common episode in these stories.

Allusion has already been made [43] to the *Tale of the Gilla Dacker and his Horse* (*Tóruighecht in Ghilla Dhecair*). After the horse had disappeared with fifteen of the Féinn, Fionn and his men sought them overseas and reached a cliff up which Diarmaid alone was able to ascend by the magic staves of Manannan. He came to a magic well of whose waters he drank, whereupon a wizard appeared, fought with him, and then vanished into the well. This occurred on several days, but at last Diarmaid clasped him in his arms, and together they leaped into the well. There he found himself in a spacious country where he conquered many opposing hosts; but a giant advised him to come to a finer land, *Tír fó Thiunn*, or "Land under Waves," a form of the gods' realm, and there he was nobly entertained, the wizard being its King, with whom the giant and his people were at feud, as in other tales of Elysium its dwellers fight each other. Meanwhile Fionn and his men met the King of Sorcha and helped him in battle with other monarchs, among them the King of Greece, whose daughter Taise, in love with Fionn, adored him still more when he slew her brother! She stole away to him, but was intercepted by one of the King's captains; and soon after this, Fionn and the King of Sorcha saw a host approaching them, among whom was Diarmaid. He informed Fionn that the Gilla was Abartach, son of Alchad, King of the Land of Promise, and from him Conan and the others were rescued. Goll and Oscar now brought Taise from Greece to Fionn, and indemnity was levied on Abartach, Conan choosing that it should consist of fourteen women, including Abartach's wife; but Abartach disappeared magically, and Conan was balked of his prize. [44] This story, the romantic incidents of which are treated prosaically, jumbles together myth and later history, and while never quite forgetting that *Tír fó Thiunn*, Sorcha, and the Land of Promise are part of the gods' realm, does its best to do so.

Several other instances of aid given by the Féinn to the

folk of Elysium occur in the *Colloquy with the Ancients*. The Féinn pursued a hind into a *síd* whose people were Donn and other children of Midir. When their uncle Bodb Dearg was lord of the Tuatha Dé Danann, he required hostages from Midir's children, but these they refused, and to prevent Bodb's vengeance on Midir, they sought a secluded *síd*. Here, however, the Tuatha Dé Danann came yearly and slew their men until only twenty-eight were left, when, to obtain Fionn's help, one of their women as a fawn had lured him to the *síd*, as the boar led Pryderi into the enchanted castle.[45] The Féinn assisted Midir's sons in next day's fight against a host of the gods, including Bodb, Dagda, Oengus, Ler, and Morrígan's children, when many of the host were slain; and three other battles were fought during that year, the Féinn remaining to assist. Oscar and Diarmaid were wounded, and by Donn's advice, Fionn captured the gods' physician and caused him to heal their wounds, after which hostages were taken of the Tuatha Dé Danann, so that Midir's sons might live in peace.[46] Caoilte told this to St. Patrick centuries after, and he had scarce finished, when Donn himself appeared and did homage to the saint. The old gods were still a mysterious people to the compilers or transmitters of such tales, but they were capable of being beaten by heroes and might be on good terms with saints. Even in St. Patrick's time the *síde* or Tuatha Dé Danann were harassed by mortal foes; but old and worn as he was, Caoilte assisted them and for reward was cured of his ailments.[47] Long before, moreover, he had killed the supernatural bird of the god Ler, which wrought nightly destruction on the *síd*, and when Ler came to avenge this, he was slain by Caoilte.[48] Thus were the gods envisaged in Christian times as capable of being killed, not only by each other but by heroes.

Sometimes, however, they helped the Féinn, nor is this unnatural, considering Fionn's divine descent. Diarmaid was a pupil and *protégé* of Manannan and Oengus and was aided by the latter.[49] Oengus helped Fionn in a quarrel with Cormac mac Art, who taunted him with Conn's victory over Cumhal; whereupon Fionn and the rest forsook their strife with Oengus (the cause of this is unknown), and he guided them in a foray against Tara, aiding in the fight and alone driving the spoil.[50] Again when the Féinn were in straits, a giant-like being assisted them and proved to be a chief of the *síde*, and in a tale from the *Dindsenchas* Sideng, daughter of Mongan of the *síd*, brought Fionn a flat stone with a golden chain, by means of which he slew three adversaries.[51] Other magic things belonging to the Féinn were once the property of the gods. Manannan had a "crane-bag" made of a crane's skin, the bird being the goddess Aoife, transformed by a jealous rival; and in it he kept his treasures, though these were visible only when the tide was full. This bag became Cumhal's.[52] Manannan's magic shield has already been described, and it also was later the property of Cumhal and Fionn.[53] In the story of *The Battle of Ventry* (*Cath Finntrága*), at which the Tuatha Dé Danann helped the Féinn, weapons were sent to Fionn through Druidic sorcery from the *síd* of Tadg, son of Nuada, by Labraid Lamfhada, "the brother of thine own mother"; and these weapons shot forth balls of fire.[54] Others were forged by a smith and his two brothers, Roc and the ocean-smith, who had only one leg and one eye.[55] Whether these beings are borrowings from the Norse or supernatural creations of earlier Celtic myth is uncertain. Fionn had also a magic hood made in the Land of Promise, and of this hood it was said, "You will be hound, man, or deer, as you turn it, as you change it." [56]

We now approach the most moving episode of the whole cycle — *The Pursuit of Diarmaid and Grainne* (*Tóruigheacht Dhiarmada agus Ghráinne*), the subject of a long tale with many mythical allusions, of several ballads and folk-tales, and of numerous references in earlier Celtic literature. Only the briefest outline can be given here, but all who would know that literature at its best should read the story itself. Early

accounts tell how Fionn, seeking to wed Grainne, had to perform tasks; but when he had accomplished these and married her, she eloped with Diarmaid.[57] In the longer narrative,
when Fionn and his friends came to ask Grainne's hand, she
administered a sleeping-potion to all of them save Oisin and
Diarmaid, both of whom she asked in succession to elope with
her. They refused; but, madly in love with Diarmaid's beauty,
she put *geasa* on him to flee with her. Thus he was forced to
elope against his will, and when the disappointed suitor Fionn
discovered this, he pursued them and came upon them in a
wood, while in his sight Diarmaid kissed Grainne. At this
point the god Oengus came to carry them off unseen, and
when Diarmaid refused his help, Oengus took Grainne away,
the hero himself escaping through his own cleverness. Having
reached Oengus and Grainne, "whose heart all but fled out
of her mouth with joy at meeting Diarmaid," he received
advice from the god, who then left them. They still fled,
with Fionn on their track, while the forces sent after them
were overpowered by Diarmaid. For long he would not consent to treat Grainne as his wife, and only when he overheard
her utter a curious reproach would he do so.[58] From two
warriors, whose fathers had helped in the battle against
Cumhal, Fionn demanded as *eric*, or fine, either Diarmaid's
head or a handful of berries from the quicken-tree of Dubhros;
but when the warriors came to Diarmaid, he parleyed long with
them and at last, as they were determined to fight him, he bound
them both. Grainne, who was now with child, asked for these
wonderful berries, whereupon Diarmaid slew their giant guardian and sent the warriors with the berries to Fionn. He and
Grainne then climbed the tree; and when Fionn arrived, he
offered great rewards to the man who would bring down
Diarmaid's head. Oengus again appeared, and when nine of
the Féinn climbed the tree and were slain, he gave each one
Diarmaid's form and threw the bodies down, their true shape
returning only when their heads were cut off. Oengus now

PLATE XXII

Page of an Irish Manuscript

Rawlinson B 512, 119 *a* (in the Bodleian Library, Oxford), containing part of the story of "The Voyage of Bran, Son of Febal."

carried Grainne in his magic mantle to the Brug na Boinne, while Diarmaid alighted like a bird on the shafts of his spears far outside the ring of the Féinn and fought all who opposed him, Oscar, who had pleaded for his forgiveness, accompanying him to Oengus's *síd*. Meanwhile Fionn sought the help of his nurse from the Land of Promise, and she enveloped the Féinn in a mist, herself flying on the leaf of a water-lily, through a hole in which she dropped darts on Diarmaid. He flung his invincible spear, the *gai dearg*, through the hole and killed the witch, whereupon Oengus made peace between Fionn and Diarmaid, who was allowed to keep Grainne.

Fionn, however, still sought revenge against Diarmaid, who one night heard in his sleep the baying of a hound. He would have gone after it, for it was one of his *geasa* always to follow when he heard that sound,[59] but Grainne detained him, saying that this was the craft of the Tuatha Dé Danann, notwithstanding Oengus's friendship. Nevertheless at daylight he departed, refusing to take, despite Grainne's desire, Manannan's sword and the *gai dearg;* and at Ben Gulban Fionn told him that the wild boar of Gulban was being hunted, as always, in vain. Now Diarmaid was under *geasa* never to hunt a boar, for his father had killed Roc's son in the *síd* of Oengus, and Roc had transformed the body into a boar which would have the same length of life as Diarmaid, whom Oengus now conjured never to hunt a boar. Diarmaid, however, resolved to slay the boar of Gulban, viz. the transformed child, though he understood that he had been brought to this by Fionn's wiles; and in the great hunt which followed "the old fierce magic boar" was killed, though not before it had mortally wounded the hero. In other versions Diarmaid was unhurt, but Fionn bade him pace the boar to find out its length, whereupon a bristle entered his heel and made a deadly wound.[60] Diarmaid now lay dying, while Fionn taunted him. He begged water, for whoever drank from Fionn's hands would recover from any injury; and he recalled all he had ever done for him, while

Oscar, too, pleaded for him. Fionn went to a well and brought water in his hands, but let it slowly trickle away. Again Diarmaid besought him, and again and yet again Fionn brought water, but each time let it drop away, as inexorable with the hero as Lug was with Bran. So Diarmaid died, lamented by all. Oengus, too, mourned him, singing sadly of his death; and since he could not restore him to life, he took the body to his *síd*, where he breathed a soul into it so that Diarmaid might speak to him for a little while each day.[61] Fionn, who knew that Grainne intended her sons to avenge Diarmaid, was afterward afraid and went secretly to her, only to be greeted with evil words. As a result of his gentle, loving discourse, however, "he brought her to his own will, and he had the desire of his heart and soul of her." She became his wife and made peace between him and her sons, who were received into the Féinn.[62]

So ends this tragic tale, the cynical conclusion of which resembles a scene in *Richard III*. A ballad of the *Pursuit*, however, relates that Diarmaid's daughter Eachtach summoned her brothers and made war with Fionn, wounding him severely, so that for four years he got no healing.[63] In a Scots Gaelic folk-tale Grainne, while with Diarmaid, plotted with an old man to kill him, but was forgiven. Diarmaid was discovered by Fionn through wood-shavings floating down-stream from cups which he had made, and Fionn then raised the hunt-ing-cry which the hero must answer, his death by the boar following.[64] In the *Dindsenchas* this "shavings" incident is told of Oisin, who was captured by Fionn's enemies and hidden in a cave, his presence there being revealed in the same way to Fionn, who rescued him.[65] Ballad versions do not admit that Diarmaid ever treated Grainne as his wife, in spite of her reproaches or the spells put upon him; and it was only after his death that Fionn discovered his innocence and constancy, notwithstanding appearances.[66] In tradition the pursuit lasted many years, and sepulchral monuments in Ireland are still known as "the beds of Diarmaid and Grainne." Some incidents of the pursuit are also told separately, as when one story relates that after an old woman had betrayed the pair to Fionn, they escaped in a boat in which was a man with beautiful garments, viz. the god Oengus.[67]

Various reasons for the final quarrel between Fionn and Goll are given, but in the end Goll was driven to bay on a sea-crag with none beside him but his faithful wife, where, though overcome by hunger and thirst, he yet refused the offer of the milk of her breasts. Noble in his loneliness, he is represented in several poems as recounting his earlier deeds. Then for the last time he faced Fionn, and fighting manfully, he fell, covered with wounds.[68]

The accounts of Fionn's death vary, some placing it before, some after, the battle of Gabhra, which, in the annalistic scheme, was the result of the exactions of the Féinn. Cairbre, High King of Ireland, summoned his nobles, and they resolved on their destruction, whereupon huge forces gathered on both sides, and "the greatest battle ever fought in Ireland" followed. Few Féinn survived it, and the most mournful event was the slaying of Oisin's son Oscar by Cairbre — the subject of numerous laments, purporting to be written by Oisin,[69] full of pathos and of a wild hunger for the brave days long past. In Fionn's old age he always drank from a quaigh, for his wife Smirgat had foretold that to drink from a horn would be followed by his death; but one day he forgot this and then, through his thumb of knowledge, he learned that the end was near. Long before, Uirgreann had fallen by his hand, and now Uirgreann's sons came against him and slew him.[70] In another version, however, Goll's grandson plotted to kill him with Uirgreann's sons and others, and succeeded.[71] There is no mention of the High King here, and it suggests the long-drawn clan vendetta and nothing more. Thus perished the great hero, brave, generous, courteous, of whom many noble things are spoken in later literature, but none nobler than

Caoilte's eulogy to St. Patrick — "He was a king, a seer, a poet, a bard, a lord with a manifold and great train, our magician, our man of knowledge, our soothsayer; all whatsoever he said was sweet with him. Excessive perchance as ye deem my testimony of Fionn, nevertheless, by the King that is above me, he was three times better still." [72] Yet he had undesirable traits — craft and vindictiveness, while his final unforgiving vengeance on Diarmaid is a blot upon his character. One tradition alleged that, like Arthur, Fionn was still living secretly somewhere, within a hill or on an island, ready to come with his men in the hour of his country's need; and daring persons have penetrated to his hiding-place and have spoken to the resting hero.[73] Noteworthy in this connexion is the story which makes the seventh century King Mongan, who represents an earlier mythic Mongan, a rebirth of Fionn, this being shown by Caoilte's reappearance to prove to Mongan's poet the truth of the King's statement regarding the death of Fothad Airglech. "We were with thee, with Fionn," said Caoilte. "Hush," said Mongan, "that is not fair." "We were with Fionn then"; but the narrator adds, "Mongan, however, was Fionn, though he would not let it be said."[74] Other stories, as we have seen, make Mongan the son of Manannan.

Of the survivors of the Féinn, the main interest centres in Oisin and Caoilte, the latter of whom lingered on with some of his warriors until the coming of St. Patrick. In tales and poems of later date, notably in Michael Comyn's eighteenth century poem, Oisin went into a síd or to Tír na nÓg ("the Land of Youth"). The Colloquy with the Ancients, on the other hand, says that he went to the síd of Ucht Cleitich, where was his mother Blai, although later he is found in St. Patrick's company without any explanation of his return; and now Caoilte rejoins him.[75] This agrees with the Scots tradition that a pretty woman met Oisin in his old age and said, "Will you not go with your mother?" Thereupon she opened a door in the rock, and Oisin remained with her for centuries, although it seemed only a week; but when he wished to return to the Féinn, she told him that none of them was left.[76] In an Irish version Oisin entered a cave and there saw a woman with whom he lived for what seemed a few days, although it was really three hundred years. When he went to revisit the Féinn, he was warned not to dismount from his white steed; but in helping to raise a cart he alighted and became an old man.[77] The tales of his visit to the Land of Youth vary. Some refer it to his more youthful days, but Michael Comyn was probably on truer ground in placing it after the battle of Gabhra. In these, however, it is not his mother, but Niamh, the exquisitely beautiful daughter of the King of Tír na nÓg, who takes him there, laying upon him *geasa* whose fulfilment would give him immortal life. Crossing the sea with her, he killed a giant who had abducted the daughter of the King of Tír na m-Beo ("the Land of the Living"); and in Tír na nÓg he married Niamh, with whom he remained three centuries. In one tale he actually became King because he outraced Niamh's father, who held the throne until his son-in-law should do this; and to prevent it he had given his daughter a pig's head, but Oisin, after hearing Niamh's story, accepted her, and her true form was then restored.[78] In the poem the radiant beauty and joy of Tír na nÓg are described in traditional terms; but, in spite of these, Oisin longed for Erin, although he thought that his absence from it had been brief. Niamh sought to dissuade him from going, but in vain, and now she bade him not descend from his horse. When he reached Erin, the Féinn were forgotten; the old forts were in ruins; a new faith had arisen. In a glen men trying to lift a marble flagstone appealed to him for aid, and stooping from his horse, he raised the stone; but as he did so, his foot touched ground, whereupon his horse vanished, and he found himself a worn, blind old man. In this guise he met St. Patrick and became dependent on his bounty.[79]

These stories illustrate what is found in all Celtic tales of divine or fairy mistresses — they are the wooers, and mortals tire of them and their divine land sooner than they weary of their lovers. Mortals were apt to find that land tedious, for, as one of them said, "I had rather lead the life of the Féinn than that which I lead in the *sid*"— it is the plaint of Achilles, who would liefer serve for hire on earth than rule the dead in Hades, or of the African proverb, "One day in this world is worth a year in Srahmandazi."

The meeting of the saint with the survivors of the Féinn is an interesting if impossible situation, and it is freely developed both in the *Colloquy with the Ancients* and in many poems. While a kindly relationship between clerics and Féinn is found in the *Colloquy*, even there Caoilte and Oisin regret the past. Both here and in the poems St. Patrick shows much curiosity regarding the old days, but in some of the latter he is not too tender to Oisin's obstinate heathendom. Oisin, it is true, is "almost persuaded" at times to accept the faith, but his paganism constantly breaks forth, and he utters daring blasphemies and curses the new order and its annoyances — shaven priests instead of warriors, bell-ringing and psalm-singing instead of the music and merriment of the past. Yet in these poems there is tragic pathos and wild regret — for the Féinn and their valorous deeds, for the joys never now to be recalled, for shrunken muscles and dimmed eyes and tired feet and shaking hands, for Oisin's long silent harp, above all for his noble son Oscar.

> "Fionn wept not for his own son,
> Nor did he even weep for his brother;
> But he wept on seeing my son lie dead,
> While all the rest wept for Oscar.
>
> From that day of the battle of Gabhra
> We did not speak boldly;
> And we passed not either night or day
> That we did not breathe heavy sighs." [80]

One fine ballad tells how Oisin fought hopelessly against the new order, scorning Christian rites and beliefs, but at last craved forgiveness of God, and then, weak and weary, passed away.

> "Thus it was that death carried off
> Oisin, whose strength and vigours had been mighty;
> As it will every warrior
> Who shall come after him upon the earth." [81]

In others the Féinn are shown to be in hell, and St. Patrick rejoices in their fate. Sometimes Oisin cries on Fionn to let no devil in hell conquer him; sometimes, weak old man as he is, his cursing of St. Patrick mingles with confession of sin and prayers for Fionn's welfare and regrets that he cannot be saved.

> "Oh, how lamentable the news
> Thou relatest to me, O cleric;
> That though I am performing pious acts,
> The Féinn have not gained heaven." [82]

Tradition maintains that Oisin was baptized, and a curious story from Roscommon tells how, at St. Patrick's prayer for solace to the Féinn in hell, though they cannot be released, Oscar received a flail and a handful of sand to spread on the ground. The demons could not cross this to torment the Féinn, for if they attempted to do so, Oscar pursued them with his flail.[83]

CHAPTER XIV

THE HEROIC MYTHS

(Continued)

III. ARTHUR

NENNIUS, writing in the ninth century, is the first to mention Arthur.[1] This hero is *dux bellorum*, waging war against the Saxons along with kings who had twelve times chosen him as chief; and twelve successful battles were fought, the last at Mount Badon, where Arthur alone killed over nine hundred men. Gildas (sixth century), however, refers to this struggle without mentioning Arthur's name.[2] In one of these conflicts Arthur carried an image of the Virgin on his shoulder, or a cross made at Jerusalem; and the *Mirabilia* added by a later hand to Nennius's *History* state that Arthur and his dog Caball (or Cavall) hunted the *Porcus Troit*, the dog leaving the mark of its foot on a stone near Builth. Nennius himself gives a simple, possibly semi-historical, account of Arthur; and the *Annales Cambriae* (tenth century) say that Arthur with his nephew and enemy Medraut (Mordred) fell at Camlan.

Geoffrey of Monmouth (1100–54), who reports the Arthurian legend as it was known in South Wales, states that Uther Pendragon, King of Britain, loved Igerna, wife of Gorlois, Duke of Cornwall; but for safety Gorlois shut her up in Tintagel. Merlin now came to Uther's help and by "medicines" gave him Gorlois's form, and his confidant Ulfin that of the Duke's friend, while Merlin himself took another guise, so that Uther thus gained access to Igerna. News of Gorlois's death arrived, and the messengers marvelled to see him at

Tintagel; but Uther disclosed himself and presently married Igerna, who bore him Arthur and a daughter Anne, the former becoming king at Uther's death. His exploits against Saxons are related and how he carried his shield Pridwen, with a picture of the Virgin, and his sword Caliburnus, which was made in the Isle of Avalon. His conquests extended to Ireland, Iceland, Gothland, the Orkneys, Norway, and Gaul; his coronation and his court are described, and how he resolved to conquer Rome. On the way he slew a giant who had abducted to St. Michael's Mount Helena, niece of Duke Hoel, and had challenged Arthur to fight after his refusal to send him his beard, which was to have the chief place in a fur made by the giant from the beards of other kings. This monster was greater than the giant Ritho, whom Arthur had fought on Mount Aravius. After conquering the Romans, Arthur heard how his nephew Mordred had usurped the throne, while Queen Guanhumara (Gwenhwyfar, Guinevere) had married him. Arthur returned and vanquished Mordred, but was mortally wounded and carried to Avalon, resigning the crown to Constantine, while Guanhumara entered a nunnery.[3]

Geoffrey obtained some information from a book in the British tongue, and some from Walter, Archdeacon of Oxford; besides which he must also have incorporated floating traditions, to which William of Malmesbury (ob. 1142) refers as "idle tales." The narrative has a mythical aspect and is embellished after the manner of the time. Arthur's widespread conquests and his fights with giants resemble Fionn's, while his birth of a father who changed his form recalls that of Mongan, son of Manannan, who did the same,[4] whence Uther may be a Brythonic god, and Arthur a semi-divine hero like Mongan or Cúchulainn. Fionn, who in one account was a reincarnation of Mongan, was betrayed by his wife Grainne and his nephew Diarmaid,[5] Arthur by his wife and nephew; and as Mongan went to Elysium, so Arthur went to Avalon. Geoffrey, as well as all existing native Welsh story, knows nothing of the Grail or of the Round Table, which first appears in Wace's *Brut*, completed in 1155.

Three questions now arise. Was there a historic Arthur on whom myths of a fabulous personage were fathered? Is Geoffrey in part rationalizing and amplifying in chivalric fashion an existing mythic story of Arthur? Does he omit some existing traditions of Arthur? These questions are probably to be answered in the affirmative. If the name "Arthur" is from Latin *Artorius*,[6] it must have been introduced into Britain in Roman times; and hence the mythic Arthur need not have been so called unless the whole myth post-dates the possibly historic sixth century Arthur. If, moreover, the Latin derivation is correct, the supposed source in a hypothetical Celtic *artor* ("ploughman" or "one who harnesses for the plough") falls to the ground. Had the mythic personality a name resembling Artorius? That is possible, and there was a Celtic god Artaios, who was equated with Mercury in Gaul. Artaios may be akin to Artio, the name of a bear-goddess, from *artos* ("bear"), although Rhys connects it with words associated with ploughing, e. g. Welsh *âr* ("ploughland").[7] Artaios would then be equivalent to *Mercurius cultor;* but the connexion of Artaios and Arthur is problematical.

In any case the story of Arthur is largely mythic, like that of Cúchulainn or of Fionn. Nennius appears to know a more or less historic Arthur; but if there was a mythic Arthur-saga in his time, why does he not allude to it? Did the "ancient traditions" to which he had access not know this mythic hero, or was he not interested in this aspect of his "magnanimous Arthur?" Still more curious is it that neither Gildas nor Bede refers to Arthur. Geoffrey's narrative became popular and is the basis of Wace's *Brut*, where the Round Table appears as made by Arthur to prevent quarrels about precedence, and it is said that the Britons had many tales about it. Layamon (*c.* 1200), on the other hand, states that it was made by a cunning workman and seated sixteen hundred,

PLATE XXIII

ARTIO

The bear-goddess (see p. 124) feeds a bear. The inscription states that "Licinia Sabinilla (dedicated this) to the goddess Artio," and the box pedestal has a slit through which to drop offerings of coins. Found at Berne ("Bear-City"), which still preserves a trace of the ancient Celtic cult in its famous den of bears. Cf. Plate II, 10.

while in the Romances it was made by Merlin. Layamon also declares that three ladies prophesied at Arthur's birth regarding his future greatness — the three *Matres* or *Fées* of Celtic belief, found also in other mythologies. Yet before Geoffrey's time Arthur was known in Brittany, whither Britons had fled from the Saxons; and there the Normans learned of the saga, which they carried to Italy before 1100 A. D., so that Alanus ab Insulis (ob. *c.* 1200) says that in his time resentment would have been aroused in Brittany by the denial of Arthur's expected return.

Among the Welsh romantic tales about Arthur the chief is that of *Kulhwch and Olwen*,[8] where he and his warriors, some of whom have magic powers, aid Kulhwch in different quests. The story, which antedates Geoffrey, and proves that an Arthurian legend existed before his time, is based on the folk-tale formula of a woman's hatred to her step-son. She bade Kulhwch seek as his wife Olwen, daughter of Yspaddaden Penkawr, whose eyelids, like Balor's, must be raised by his servitors, though he is not said to possess an evil eye. The quest was difficult, and when Kulhwch found Yspaddaden's castle, he learned that many suitors for Olwen had been slain, for Yspaddaden would die when she married — a variant of the theme of the separable soul.[9] Yspaddaden set Kulhwch many tasks, some of them connected with each other, and in many of these his cousin Arthur assisted him. Among them is the capture of the *Twrch Trwyth* (Nennius's *Porcus Troit*), on account of the scissors, comb, and razors between its ears, which Yspaddaden desired. This boar was a knight transformed by God for his sins, and to capture it the aid of Mabon, son of Modron, must be obtained. First, however, his prison must be found, for he had been stolen on the third night after his birth, and none knew where he was. With the help of various animals his place of bondage was discovered, and he was released by Arthur, whose aid, with that of others, Yspaddaden had said that Kulhwch would never obtain. Arthur now collected an army for the chase of the boar, and this pursuit recalls many stories of Fionn. A great combat with it took place, and after Arthur had fought it for nine days and nights without being able to kill it, he sent to it and its pigs Gwrhyr Gwalstawt in the form of a bird to invite one of them to speak with him. The invitation was refused, however, and accordingly Arthur, with his dog Cavall and a host of heroes, hunted the boar from place to place. Many were slain, but at last the boar was seized, and the razor and scissors were taken. Nevertheless, before the comb could be obtained, the boar fled to Kernyu (Cornwall), where it was captured; although all that had happened previously was merely a game compared with the taking of the comb. The boar was now chased into the sea, and Arthur went north to obtain the blood of the sorceress Gorddu on the confines of hell, another of the things required by Yspaddaden. Arthur slew Gorddu, and Kaw of Prydein (Pictland) collected her blood, which, with the other marvellous objects, was taken to Yspaddaden, who was now slain.

In this story Kulhwch comes to Arthur's court, which is attended by many warriors and supernatural personages, some of whose names (e. g. Conchobar, Cúroi) recur in the Romances or are taken from other parts of Brythonic as well as Irish traditions. The gate was shut while feasting went on, save to a king's son or to the master of an art — an incident recalling the approach of Lug, "master of many arts," to the abode of the Tuatha Dé Danann before the battle of Mag-Tured [10] — all others being entertained outside with food, music, and a bedfellow. Among the personages of this tale who recur in the Romances are Kei, Bedwyr (Bedivere), Gwalchmei (Gawain), and Gwenhwyfar; characters from the Mabinogion or other tales are Manawyddan, Morvran, Teyrnon, Taliesin, and Creidylad, daughter of Lludd. Mabon, son of Modron, is the Maponos of British and Gaulish inscriptions, where he is equated with Apollo; and his mother's name

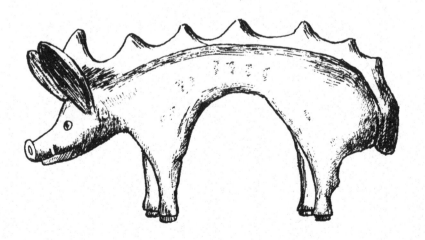

PLATE XXIV

Boars

The boar appears as a worshipful animal on Gaulish coins (see Plate III, 1, 3, 6), and there was a Gallic boar-deity, Moccus (p. 124). It also plays a *rôle* in Irish saga (pp. 124–27, 172) and in the Welsh story of the *Twrch Trwyth* (or *Porcus Troit*) (pp. 108, 125, 187–88). Bronze figures found at Hounslow, Middlesex.

is equivalent to that of the goddesses called *Matronae* (akin to the *Matres*), whose designation appears in that of the Marne. *Mabon* means "a youth," and *Maponos* "the great (*or* divine) youth," whence he must have been a youthful god. His immortality is suggested by the fact that he had been in prison so long that animals which had attained fabulous ages had no knowledge of him, and only a salmon, older than any of them, knew where his prison was. It carried Kei and Gwrhyr thither on its shoulders, and when Arthur attacked the stronghold, it supported Kei and Bedwyr, who made a breach in the wall and released the captive. Mabon rode a horse swifter than the waves, and he is called "the swift" in the *Stanzas of the Graves*. The chase of the boar could not take place without him, and he followed it into the Bristol Channel, where he took the razor from it. Reference is made to Mabon's imprisonment in a *Triad;* and he and Gweir, whose prison is mentioned in a Taliesin poem about Arthur and his men, with Llyr Lledyeith, were the three notable prisoners. Yet there was one still more notable — Arthur, who was three nights in prison in Caer Oeth and Anoeth, three nights in prison by Gwenn Pendragon, and three nights in an enchanted prison under Llech Echymeint; but Goreu, his cousin, delivered him.[11]

Other mythical or magic-wielding personages in *Kulhwch* are the following. Gwrhyr, who could speak with birds and animals, transformed himself into a bird in order to speak to the boar; and Menw also took that shape and sought to remove one of the boar's treasures, when it hurt him with its venom. He could also make Arthur and his men invisible, though they could see other men. Morvran, son of Tegid Voel, seemed a demon, covered with hair like a stag; none struck him at the battle of Camlan on account of his ugliness, just as none struck Sandde Bryd-angel because of his beauty. Sgilti Light-Foot could march on the ends of tree-branches, and so light was he that the grass never bent under him. Drem saw the

gnat rise with the sun from Kelliwic in Cornwall to Pen
Blathaon in Scotland. Under Gwadyn Ossol's feet the highest
mountain became a plain, and Sol could hold himself all day
on one foot. Gwadyn Odyeith made as many sparks from the
sole of his foot as when white-hot iron strikes a solid object;
he cleared the way of all obstacles before Arthur and his men.
Gwevyl, when sad, let one of his lips fall to his stomach,
while the other made a hood over his head; and Ychdryt
Varyvdraws projected his beard above the beams of Arthur's
hall. Yskyrdaw and Yseudydd, servants of Gwenhwyfar, had
feet as rapid as their thoughts; and Klust, interred a hundred
cubits underground, could hear the ant leave its nest fifty
miles away. Medyr could pass through the legs of a wren in
the twinkling of an eye from Cornwall to Esgeir Oervel in
Ireland; Gwiawn could remove with one stroke a speck from
the eye of a midge without injuring it; Ol found the track of
swine stolen seven years before his birth. Many of these
invaluable personages have parallels in Celtic as well as other
folk-tales, and are the clever companions of the hero, who
execute tasks impossible to himself.[12]

In the *Dream of Rhonabwy* the hero had a vision of the
knightly court of Arthur, different from that in *Kulhwch*,
and found himself transported thither. Arthur had mighty
armies, and he and others were of gigantic size, while his
mantle rendered the wearer invisible. The story describes
Arthur's game at chess with Owein, and how Owein's crows
were first ill-treated and then killed their tormentors. These
crows are frequently mentioned in Welsh poetry, and Arthur
is said to have feared them and their master. In this tale we
also hear of Iddawc (mentioned in the *Triads*), whose horse,
on exhaling its breath, blows far off those whom he pursues,
and as it respires, it draws them to him. He was an interme-
diary between Arthur and Mordred at Camlan, sent with
gracious words from Arthur, reminding Mordred how he had
nurtured him and desiring to make peace; but Iddawc altered

these messages to threats and thus caused the battle. Arthur's court appears again in *The Lady of the Fountain*, a Welsh tale which is the equivalent of Chrétien's *Yvain* (twelfth century), but here again the conception of it is far more knightly and romantic than in *Kulhwch*. The supernatural in this story, whether Celtic or not, is found, e. g., in the one-eyed black giant with one foot and an iron club, who guards a forest in which wild animals feed. He tells Kynon to throw a bowlful of water on a slab by a fountain, when a storm will burst, followed by the music of birds, and a black-armoured knight will appear and fight with Kynon. In these two tales the following personages known to Welsh literature and the Romances appear — Mordred, Caradawc, Llyr, Nudd, Mabon, Peredur, Llacheu, Kei, Gwalchmei, Owein, March son of Meirchion (Mark, King of Cornwall), and Gwchyvar.

In the early Welsh poems there are many references to Arthur and his circle, as when, in the *Black Book of Caermarthen* (twelfth century), one poem, telling of Arthur's expedition to the north, mentions Kei, whose sword was unerring in his hand, Bedwyr the Accomplished, Mabon, Manawyddan, "deep was his counsel," and Llacheu, Arthur's son. Kei pierced nine witches, probably the nine witches of Gloucester mentioned in *Peredur*, while Arthur fought with a witch and clove the Paluc Cat. A *Triad* declares that this creature was born of a pig hunted by Arthur, because it was prophesied that the isle would suffer from its litter; and although Coll, its guardian, threw the cat into the Menai Strait, Paluc's children found it and nourished it until it became one of the three plagues of Mon (Anglesey). This demon cat, which should be compared with those fought by Cúchulainn, recurs in *Merlin*, but is then located on the continent. In this poem Arthur is also said to have distributed gifts.[13] Llacheu figures in another poem, which tells of his death, as "marvellous in song," and he is mentioned there with Bran, Gwyn, and Creidylad.[14] The *Stanzas of the Graves* refer to the graves of

Gwythur, March, and Arthur, the latter's being *anoeth bid* ("the object of a difficult search"); and Arthur's horse Cavall, not his dog Cavall or Caball (as in Nennius and *Kulhwch*, where Bedwyr held it in leash), is mentioned in another poem.

Arthur's expedition to Annwfn in *Kulhwch*, where Annwfn is equivalent to hell, lying to the north, is paralleled by another in a Taliesin poem to which reference has already been made.[15] Arthur and others went in his ship Prydwn (Prytwenn in *Kulhwch*, where it goes a long distance in the twinkling of an eye [16]) over seas to Caer Sidi for the "spoils of Annwfn," including the magic cauldron of Penn Annwfn, and apparently to release Gweir, who had been lured there through the messenger of Pwyll and Pryderi. While Annwfn was spoiled, Gweir "grievously sang, and thenceforth till doom he remains a bard"; but the expedition was fatal to many who went on it, for "thrice Prydwn's freight" voyaged to Caer Sidi, but only seven returned.[17] This recalls Cúchulainn's similar journey to Scáth for its cauldron and cows;[18] and there is also a parallel in *Kulhwch*, where one of the treasures desired of the hero by Yspaddaden is the cauldron of Diwrnach the Irishman, who refused it when Arthur sent for it. Arthur then sailed for Ireland in his ship, and Bedwyr seized the cauldron, placing it on the shoulders of Arthur's cauldron-bearer, who brought it away full of money.[19] Another treasure which Kulhwch had to obtain, but of which there is no further mention, is the basket of Gwyddneu, from which the whole world might eat according to their desire, this basket resembling Dagda's cauldron.[20]

The Guinevere incident in Geoffrey is differently rendered in Welsh tradition. A *Triad* says that the blow given her by Gwenhwyfach (her sister in *Kulhwch*) caused the battle of Camlan,[21] and another *Triad* speaks of Medraut's drawing her from her royal seat at Kelliwic and giving her a blow, while he is also said to have outraged her. Medraut at the same time consumed all the food and drink, but Arthur retaliated by doing likewise at Medraut's court and leaving neither man nor beast alive. Medraut resembled Hir Erwn and Hir Atrym in *Kulhwch*, who wherever they went ate all provided for them and left the land bare;[22] although another view of him is found in a *Triad* which speaks of the blow given him by Arthur as "an evil blow" and of himself as gentle, kindly, and fair. Guinevere seems to have had an ill character in Welsh tradition, a spiteful couplet speaking of her as "bad when young, worse later." [23] Her name means "white phantom or *fée*," from *gwen* ("white") and *hwyvar*, a word cognate with Irish *siabur*, *siabhra* ("phantom," "fairy"), the corresponding Irish name being Finnabair;[24] and this seems to point to her divine aspect, just as Etain was called *bé find* ("white woman") by Midir. A *Triad* speaks of three Guineveres, all wives of Arthur, with different fathers; but Celtic myth loved triple forms, and the different Guineveres, Llyrs, Manawyddans, etc., may have been local forms of the same divinity.

The departure of the wounded Arthur to Avalon, though mentioned by Geoffrey, does not occur in native Welsh story; yet in other sources which refer to it there is probably to be found a Brythonic tradition on the subject. In the *Vita Merlini* attributed to Geoffrey, Avalon appears as *Insula Pomorum*, or "Isle of Apples," where the labour of cultivating the soil is unnecessary, so abundant is nature. Grapes and corn grow plentifully, and nine sisters, of whom Morgen is chief, and who can take the form of birds, bear rule there. These nine recall the nine maidens whose breath boiled the cauldron of Annwfn, and the bird sisters perhaps recur in the *Perceval* story where Perceval, attacked by black birds, kills one which turns to a beautiful woman whom the others bear away to Avalon.[25] In another description the island lacks no good thing and is unvisited by enemies. Peace, concord, and eternal spring and flowers are there; its people are youthful; there is no old age, disease, or grief; all is happiness, and all things are in common. A *regia virgo* rules it, more beautiful than the lovely maidens who serve her; she healed Arthur when he was brought to the court of King Avallo and now they live together.[26] Her name is Morgen, though elsewhere Morgen is Arthur's sister, and Giraldus Cambrensis calls her *dea phantastica;* while William of Malmesbury speaks of Avalloc (Avallo) as dwelling at Avalon with his daughters. How close is the resemblance of this island to the Irish Elysium must at once be seen. It is mainly a land of women; there is no toil, but plenty; no sickness nor death, but immortal youth; and the divine women there can take the form of birds like Fand, Liban, and others. They who visit Arthur find the place full of all delights, says the *Vita Merlini;* and if Arthur went to Avalon to his sister, he resembles Oisin who, in one account, went with his mother to Elysium.[27] In the Didot *Perceval* Arthur declares that he will return, so that Britons expect him and have sometimes heard him hunting in the forest;[28] and Layamon, who lived in a district where Brythonic tradition must have abounded, says also that Arthur, when wounded, announced his departure to the fairest of all maidens, Argante, Queen in Avalon, who would heal him, but that he would return. A boat appeared, in which were two women, who placed him in it; and now he dwells in Avalon with the fairest of elves, the *fées* or goddesses of other traditions, while Britons await his coming.[29] In Malory the boat is full of queens, among them Morgen, Arthur's sister, and Nimue, the Lady of the Lake, "always friendly to Arthur." From her had come the sword Excalibur, and her home was in a wonderful palace within a rock in a lake — an Elysium water-world. All this points to the interest taken in a hero by other-world beings.

The identification of Glastonbury with Avalon may be due to two influences. Glastonbury and its Tor were surrounded by marshes, which would cause it to be considered as an island; and probably, too, the Tor was a divine abode analogous to the *sid*, as the legend of Gwyn suggests. Some local myth would lead this "island" to be regarded as Elysium, while in Arthur's case it came to be called Avalon either because a local lord of Elysium was named Avallo, or because magic trees with apples (*avall*, "apple-tree"), like those of the Irish Elysium, were supposed to grow there. Glastonbury as a *sid* Elysium is supported by another early Arthur tradition; and one form of this had been transferred to Italy by the Normans, for Gervase of Tilbury speaks of a groom finding himself in a castle on Etna, wherein Arthur lay in bed, suffering from Mordred's wounds, which broke out afresh each year.[30] More usually, however, the legend is that of Arthur and his knights waiting, like Fionn, in an enchanted sleep within a hill for the time when their services will be required, this story being attached to the Eildon Hills and other places.[31]

Welsh literature shows that at a period contemporary with Geoffrey, and in manuscripts perhaps going back to an earlier period, there was an Arthurian tradition in Wales which differed considerably from that of the historian and was much fuller. Arthur became a figure to whom floating myths and traditions might be attached and, like Fionn, he was a slayer of witches, monsters, and serpents, so that in the Life of St. Carannog a huge reptile which devastated the land was hunted and destroyed by him. It is certain that, before the great French poems of the Arthurian cycle were written, Arthur was popular both in Britain and in Brittany.[32]

The outburst of Arthurian romance proper, that of the Anglo-Norman writers, belongs to the end of the twelfth and the beginning of the thirteenth century, opening with the *Lais* of Marie de France and the *Tristan, Erec, Chevalier de la Charette*, and *Conte del Graal* of Chrestien de Troyes. Whence was its subject-matter drawn? Some hold that beyond the scanty facts related of the historic Arthur, all was taken from Armorican sources, popularized by *conteurs* there. These traditions, according to Zimmer, were originally Welsh, but were brought to Armorica by immigrants from

Britain; but others, e. g. Gaston Paris and A. Nutt, find the sources in Welsh tradition and native Celtic tales, learned by Normans after the Conquest of England and passed thence to France, either directly or *via* Anglo-Norman poems. This is supported by the identity of episodes in the Romances with those of Irish sagas; and Miss Weston has adduced new evidence which indicates that in Wauchier's *Perceval*, the *Elucidation*, and the English *Gawain* poems "we have a precious survival of the earliest collected form of Arthurian romantic tradition."[33] Wauchier de Denain refers to a certain Bleheris, of Welsh birth, whose patron was the Count of Poitiers, and to him he attributes the source of his narrative. Bleheris is probably the Blihis to whom the *Elucidation* refers as source of the Grail story, the Bledhericus described by Giraldus as *famosus ille fabulator*, and the Breri mentioned by an Anglo-Norman poet named Thomas, who wrote on Tristan about 1170.[34] Arthurian romance is thus traced directly to Welsh sources through this writer, who certainly flourished not later than the beginning of the twelfth century.

Arthur and Arthur's court are a centre toward which or from which stories converge or issue, whence other personages are apt to be regarded as more interesting than he or to have a larger number of deeds attributed to them. Conchobar's court, with its heroes, where boys are brought up and go forth armed to their first adventures, suggests the primitive Celtic Arthurian court, unaltered by mediæval chivalric ideas.[35] In the Cúchulainn stories it is not so much Conchobar who is the chief figure as Cúchulainn, though he is always in the background, and in this Arthur in relation to Gawain, Perceval, and others corresponds to him. Arthur has little to do with the Grail, and new important personages, not necessarily of the early Celtic group, tend to be introduced.

Gawain was Arthur's nephew as Cúchulainn was Conchobar's, and the earlier presentation of him is more just than the later. "He never returned from a mission without having

fulfilled it; he was the best of walkers and the best of horsemen," says *Kulhwch;* and according to the *Triads*, he had a
golden tongue and was one of the best knights of Arthur's
court for guests and strangers.[36] He had a valuable steed
Gringalet as Cúchulainn had two. His sword *Escalibur*
(Latin *Caliburnus*), made in Avalon, was given him by Arthur,
its first owner; and its Welsh name, *Caledvwlch*, seems identical
with that of Cúchulainn's *caladbolg*, which was forged in the
síd. One incident of Gawain's legend is his visit to an island
castle where are many knights and maidens, who can never
speak to each other, ruled by a mysterious lady allied with its
magician chief, the captor of these knights and maidens; and
he who goes there must remain always. Gawain reached it,
guided by the lady, who met him at a fountain,[37] a visit which
suggests those of Bran, Connla, and Cúchulainn to Elysium
(*not* the region of the dead) at the invitation of a goddess
connected with its lord. Gawain was given up as dead, and
this legend persisted, though he returned to Arthur. Probably, like Connla, he remained in Elysium, so that mediæval
tradition regarded him as living in fairy-land. In a second
incident the other-world momentarily appears. Guinevere
was abducted by Meléagant (Melwas) to a castle on an island
whence no traveller returned. It was approached by a sword-
bridge and an under-water bridge, Lancelot crossing by the
former, Gawain choosing the latter; and although in Chrestien's *Le Chevalier de la Charette* Lancelot rescues Guinevere,
evidence exists which points to Gawain as the real hero of the
adventure.[38] A sword-bridge is otherwise unknown to Celtic
myth; a realm reached by descending into water is known;
and Gawain himself came to a palace under water, where
he met with strange adventures.[39] Possibly Gawain, like his
brother Mordred, was lover of Guinevere, a situation to
which Lancelot succeeded when he was later evolved. The
question also arises whether Gawain and Mordred were
Arthur's sons by his sister, wife of King Loth, as Malory

asserts of Mordred.[40] This is not impossible, just as one tradition made Cúchulainn son of Conchobar by his sister Dechtire. Gawain, in Miss Weston's opinion, is the earliest hero of the Grail, his position as such being emphasized by Wauchier, drawing on a version by Bleheris. Perceval next became the hero of the Quest, then Lancelot, and finally Galahad, who achieved it.

Among those who are known to Welsh literature and who appear in the Romances is Kei. His counsel was not to open the gate to Kulhwch, but Arthur said that courtesy must be shown; and he was one of those whose help Kulhwch demanded on entering. He passed for offspring of Kynyr Keinvarvawc, who told his wife that if her son took after him, his heart and hands would always be cold, and he would be obstinate; when he carried a burden, none would perceive him from behind or before, and none would support fire and water as long as he. Kei could breathe for nine days and nine nights under water and could remain that time without sleeping, while nothing could heal a blow of his sword. When he pleased, he could become as high as the highest tree; and when heavy rain fell, all that he held in his hand was dry above and below to the distance of a handbreadth, so great was his natural heat, which also served as fuel to his companions when they suffered most from cold.[41] These characteristics recall those of Celtic saints, who remained dry in wet weather and could produce light from their hands, and also Cúchulainn's "distortion" and heat. Kei took an important part with Bedwyr in seeking Olwen for Kulhwch, Bedwyr seizing one of the poisoned javelins thrown at them by Yspaddaden; and he was also active in questing for the treasures and reached the castle of Gwrnach Gawr, where, as at the stronghold of Arthur and the Tuatha Dé Danann, none could enter but the master of an art. Kei proclaimed himself the best sword-polisher in the world and gained entrance by saying that he had a companion whom the porter would recognize because his spear-head would detach itself from the shaft, draw blood from the wind, and resume its place on the shaft. This was Bedwyr. Kei then killed Gwrnach with his own sword and carried it off, since the boar could be killed by it alone.[42] Kei and Bedwyr discovered and aided in releasing Mabon, and obtained the leash made from the beard of Dillus Varvawc while he was living, which alone could hold the Little Dog of Greit; but Arthur sang a teasing verse about this and irritated Kei so much that peace between them was restored with difficulty. At the hunt of the boar Bedwyr held Arthur's dog Cavall in leash.[43]

In *Kulhwch*, as in the *Black Book of Caermarthen*, Kei is not only a mighty warrior, fighting against a hundred, but also a great drinker, and his valour as well as his nobility and wisdom is sung in later poetry. In a curious dialogue between Arthur and Guinevere after her abduction she told him that Kei could vanquish a hundred, including Arthur, while she described Arthur as small compared with Kei the tall. Possibly Kei rather than Melwas was here Guinevere's ravisher.[44] In Geoffrey, Kei is Arthur's sewer and received a province from him, while Bedwyr is butler and Duke of Normandy, and both assist Arthur in his adventures and are mentioned together.[45] Kei is also sewer in the Welsh romances which show traces of Continental influence — *Peredur, Olwen and Lunet* — where, as in the Anglo-French romances, his boastful, quarrelsome nature appears. He is always ready to fight, yet always overthrown; and he is to the Arthur saga what Conan and Bricriu are to those of Fionn and Cúchulainn. Reference is made in *Kulhwch* to his death at the hands of Gwddawc, a deed revenged by Arthur, but in the Welsh *Saint Graal* Kei slew Arthur's son, Llacheu, and made war on Arthur.

Of Bedwyr *Kulhwch* says that he never hesitated to take part in any mission on which Kei was sent; none equalled him in running save Drych; though he had but one hand, three combatants did not make blood flow more quickly than he; and his lance, which produced one wound in entering, caused nine in retiring — i. e. it was studded with points turned back so that they caught the flesh on being withdrawn.[46] In like manner Cúchulainn's *gai bolga* inflicted thirty wounds when pulled out, and reference is frequently made to pointed spears of similar character. Bedwyr is praised in Welsh poetry and is the Sir Bedevere of the Romances. In Geoffrey he reconnoitred the hill where the giant was supposed to live and comforted the nurse of the dead woman abducted by him, and he is also said to have been slain by the Romans.[47]

Nennius relates that Vortigern's attempts to build a city mysteriously failed until his wise men said that he must obtain a child without a father and sprinkle the foundation with his blood — an instance of the well-known Foundation Sacrifice. This victim is at last found because a companion is heard taunting him, as they play at ball, that he is "a boy without a father." His mother alleged that he had no mortal sire, and the child exposed the wise men's ignorance, by telling what would be discovered beneath the foundation — a pool, two vases, with a tent, and in it two serpents. One of these expelled the other, and all this is explained as symbolic of the world, Vortigern's kingdom, the Britons, and the Saxon invaders. Giving his name as Ambrose (Embreis *gwledig*, or "prince") and saying that a Roman consul was his father, the boy obtained the place as a site for a citadel of his own, Dinas Emrys.[48] Ambrosius Aurelianus the *gwledig* was a real person who fought the Saxons in the fifth century,[49] and to his history these myths have been attached. In Geoffrey this boy is Merlin or Ambrosius Merlin, whose mother said that often a beautiful youth appeared, kissed her, and vanished, although afterward he sometimes spoke with her invisibly and finally as a man slept with her, leaving her with child. One of Vortigern's wise men explained him as an *incubus* (the Celtic *dusius*). Merlin told how two dragons were asleep in two hollow stones, and when dug up, they fought, the red dragon finally being worsted; and he now uttered many tedious prophecies, in-

cluding that of the coming of Ambrosius as king. At a later
time he advised Ambrosius, who wished to erect a memorial
for native heroes, to send for the "Giants' Dance" to Ireland,
whither African giants had carried it; and by Merlin's ingenuity the stones, which had healing and magic virtues, were
removed to Stonehenge. Geoffrey then recounts how Merlin
transformed Uther so that he might gain access to Igerna.[50]

In Welsh literature Merlin or Myrddin is connected with
the Britons of the north. Whether this Merlin is the same as
Geoffrey's is uncertain, the former being called Merlin the
Wild or Caledonius, but at all events the two are combined
in later literature. He is a bard and prophet who fled frenzied
to the Caledonian Forest after learning of his sister's son's
death; and there he prophesied to his pig under an apple-tree
and had a friend Chwimbian, the Viviane of romance. The
later chroniclers and romantic accounts develop Merlin's
magic, e. g. his shape-shifting, the removal of the stones here
becoming supernatural; while his birth is ascribed to demoniac
power, and but for his baptism he would have been a kind of
Antichrist. He took the child Arthur; and when, as King,
Arthur unwittingly had an *amour* with his sister, he appeared
as a child and revealed the secret of the king's birth, after
which, as an old man, he disclosed to Arthur how he had
sinned with his sister in ignorance. In the *Triads* he and his
nine bards went into the sea in a glass house, or he took with
him the Treasures of Britain to the isle of Bardsey. In other
accounts, however, his disappearance was caused by his fairy
mistress's treachery, for she learned the secret of his magic
power and how to imprison a man in a wall-less tower; in which
she shut him up, visiting him daily, while it appeared to
others as a "smoke of mist." Another version describes him
as enclosed in a rocky grave, whence perhaps the phrase of a
Welsh poem — "the man who speaks from the grave"— and
in yet another tradition he retires from the world in an
Esplumeor, which he made himself.[51]

How much of all this is pure romance, how much is genuine Brythonic myth, is uncertain; and Merlin may be an old god degraded to a mere magician. Nennius and Geoffrey in their narratives suggest the well-known "Expulsion and Return" formula — the boy without a father, taunted when playing at ball, comes into favour because he shows why a castle cannot be built. This recalls Fionn's youth and how, overcoming the beings who destroyed a *dún*, he thus regained his heritage.[52] Merlin's father was doubtless a god, but as "the son without a father" he recalls "the son of a sinless couple" in the story of Bécuma, as well as Oengus, who was taunted with having no known father.[53] The incident of his disappearance of his own will suggests the legends of heroes sleeping in hills, just as his imprisonment by his mistress recalls that of Kronos in the British myth cited by Plutarch and the stories of mortals bound by the love of immortals to the other-world. While Merlin is connected with Arthur in Geoffrey and the Romances, he is not one of the throng around the hero in *Kulhwch*.

The debatable ground of the Grail romances cannot be discussed here in detail, especially as the episode did not enter into the earliest Perceval romances, of Welsh origin, and is lacking in the Welsh *Peredur*, written in full knowledge of the Perceval-Grail stories, and in the English *Syr Percyvelle*. Perceval probably succeeded Gawain as the hero of the Grail, to be superseded himself by Galahad. In Wauchier's continuation of Chrestien's *Perceval* Gawain rode beyond Arthur's kingdom through a waste land to a castle by the sea, where he saw a knight on a bier with a sword on his breast. A procession of clergy, singing the Vespers of the Dead, entered; and then followed a feast at which "a rich Grail" provided the food and served the guests, "upheld by none." Later Gawain saw a lance with a stream of blood flowing from it into a silver cup, and finally the King of the castle entered and bade Gawain fix the two halves of a broken sword together. Unable to do this, he failed in the Quest, but having asked about lance and sword, he learned that the lance was that by which Christ's side was pierced, while the sword was that of the Dolorous Stroke by which Logres and all the country was destroyed. Here Gawain fell asleep and next morning found himself on the shore, while the castle had vanished. Nevertheless the land was now fertile, because he had asked about the lance; had he asked about the Grail, it would have been fully restored.

In Chrestien's *Perceval* there is a procession with a sword, a lance from which a drop of blood runs down, the Grail, shining so as to put out the candles' light, and finally a maiden with a silver plate. The Grail is of gold and precious stones; but in other versions it is the dish or cup of the Last Supper, or a vessel in which Joseph received the Saviour's Blood, or a chalice, or a reliquary, or even something of no material substance, or a magic stone (Wolfram's *Parzival*). It provides food magically, with the taste which each one would desire, though sometimes it feeds those only who are not in sin. It gives perfume and light, heals the wounded, and, after the successful quest, removes barrenness from the land and cures its guardian or raises him from death. It prevents those who see it from being deceived or made to sin by devils, or it gives the seeker spiritual insight. In *Peredur* there is no Grail, but the hero sees a procession with a spear from which come three drops of blood, and a salver containing a head.

The Grail and its accompanying objects have a twofold aspect and source, pagan and Christian. The Grail and lance are associated with events of Christian history, but they have pagan Celtic parallels — the divine cauldron from which none goes unsatisfied and which restores the dead, the enchanted cup in tales of Fionn which heals or gives whatever taste is desired to him who drinks from it, and which is sometimes the object of a quest. The head in *Peredur* recalls Bran's head, the lance and sword the spear which slew him and the sword by which he was decapitated, as well as Lug's unconquerable spear, Nuada's irresistible sword, Manannan's magic sword, Tethra's talking sword. The Stone of Fal suggests the Grail as a stone, and it, like Dagda's cauldron and the spear and swords of Lug, Nuada, and Manannan, belonged to the Tuatha Dé Danann. The Grail, sword, and spear have affinity with these as much as with the Christian symbols. Yet no theory quite accounts for the assimilation of the two groups, and while the Grail has magic properties, we should remember that miraculous food-producing and healing of the sick were works of our Lord, which might easily be associated with objects connected with Him, as a result of the belief in relics. Failing the discovery of an early manuscript in which the actual sources of the Grail story may be found, much is open to conjecture.

A theory connected with the prevailing study of vegetation rituals sees in the objects and their effects survivals of Celtic ritual resembling that of Adonis or Tammuz, its aim being the preservation of the fertility of the land.[54] There is no evidence, however, that at such rituals a miraculous food-supplying vessel had any part; such vessels belong to the domain of myth, and the story of the Grail has more the appearance of being derived from a myth which was possibly based on such rituals. It is in myth that magico-miraculous powers flourish, not in ritual; and such a myth could be Christianized. When, moreover, the theory makes the further assumption that the ritual was of the nature of a "mystery," there is again no evidence for this, for vegetation rituals are open to all in the fields, even where Christianity has been adopted. The theory, however, postulates a mystery-cult, with a plain and evident meaning for the folk — associated with powers of life and generation — and with other significations for the initiate — phallic, philosophic, spiritual. The story of this pagan mystery, which expressed three planes or worlds — "the triple mysteries of a life-cult"— was gradually Christianized by those ignorant of its meaning and was finally

PLATE XXV

Horned God

The deity, wearing a torque and pressing a bag from which escapes grain on which a bull and a stag feed, is supported by figures of Apollo and Mercury (cf. pp. 8–9). He may possibly be identical with Cernunnos, a deity of the underworld (Plate XVI). His attitude suggests the squatting god of Plates III, 3, VIII, IX, and his cornucopia corresponds to the purse of the divinity of Plate IX, B, as well as to the cup held by Dispater (Plate XIV). For other gods of the underworld see Plates V, VII, XII, XIII, XXVI. From a Gallo-Roman altar found at Rheims.

worked up by Robert de Borron (twelfth century) in terms of a corresponding traditional esoteric Christian mystery. The procession with Grail, etc., was the presentation of the mystery, its meaning being divulged according to the degree of initiation; but though the quester is the initiate, yet he fails in his Quest.[55] The present writer is wholly unable to believe that such mysteries and initiations existed among the barbarous Celts or that they survived until the early middle ages, or that lance and cup have a phallic significance — "life symbols of the lowest plane" — or that there was a traditional esoteric Christianity, save in the minds of cranks of all ages. Why, again, should a mystery known only to initiates have been the subject of a story? Were initiates likely to reveal it? To regard the Grail story from a phallic, occult point of view and to interpret it by means of a mystic jargon is to degrade it. If the modern occultist possesses a divine secret, the world does not seem to be much the better for it; and such secrets are apt to be mere "gas and gaiters." The truth is that occultism renders squalid whatever it touches, be that Christianity, or Buddhism, or the romantic stories of the Grail.

In spite of the numerous and important characters who enter into the saga, Arthur is the central figure, the ideal hero of Brythonic tribes in the past, to whom leadership at home and abroad might be assigned, and whose presence in all battles might be asserted. Originating as a champion, real or mythical, of northern Brythons in southern Scotland, his legend passed with emigrants to Wales, where it became popular. Like Fionn among the Goidels, so Arthur among the Brythons was located in every district, as numerous place-names show; and if Fionn was at first a non-Celtic hero adopted by Goidels, so Arthur was a Brythonic hero adopted by Anglo-Normans as their truest romantic figure.[56]

CHAPTER XV

PAGANISM AND CHRISTIANITY

APART from the occasional Christianizing of myths or the interpolation of Christian passages in order to make the legends less objectionable, the Irish scribes frequently created new situations or invented tales in which mythical personages were brought into contact with saints and missionaries, as many examples have shown. In doing this they not only accepted the pagan stories or utilized their conceptions, but sometimes almost contrasted Christianity unfavorably with the older religion.

The idea of the immortality or rebirth of the gods survived with the tales in which it was embodied and was sometimes utilized for a definite purpose. The fable of the coming of Cessair, Noah's granddaughter, to Ireland before the flood was the invention of a Christian writer and contradicted those passages which said that no one had ever been in Ireland previous to the deluge. All her company perished save Finntain, and he was said to have survived until the sixth century of our era.[1] The reason for imagining such a long-lived personage is obvious; in no other way could Cessair's coming, or that of Partholan and of the other folk who reached Ireland, have been known. Poems were ascribed to Finntain in which he recounted the events seen in his long life until at last he accepted the new faith.[2]

Even at this early period, however, there was a story of another long-lived personage with incidents derived from pagan myths. Long life, excessive as Finntain's was, might have been suggested from Genesis, but the successive transformations of Tuan MacCairill could have their origin only in myth; and the wonder is that such a doctrine was accepted by Christian scribes. Tuan was Partholan's nephew and through centuries was the sole survivor of his race, which was tragically swept away by pestilence in one week for the sins of Partholan. Obtaining entrance to the fortress of a great warrior by the curious but infallible process of "fasting against" him, St. Finnen was told by his involuntary host that he was Tuan MacCairill and that he had been a witness of all events in Ireland since the days of Partholan. When he was old and decrepit, he found on awaking one morning that he had become a stag, full of youth and vigour; this was in the time of Nemed, and he described the coming of the Nemedians. He himself, as a stag, had been followed by innumerable stags which recognized him as their chief; but again he became old, and now after a night's sleep he awoke as a boar in youthful strength and became King of the boars. Similarly he became a vulture, then a salmon, in which form he was caught by fishers and taken to the house of King Caraill, whose wife ate him, so that from her he was reborn as a child. While in her womb he heard the conversations which went on, and knowing what was happening, he was a prophet when he grew up, and in St. Patrick's time was baptized, although he had professed knowledge of God while yet paganism alone existed in Ireland.[3]

The mythical *données* of this story are sufficiently obvious. Metamorphosis and rebirth have frequently been found in the myths already cited, and these were used by the inventors of Tuan MacCairill, the closest parallels to him being the two Swineherds and Gwion.[4]

The conversion of pagan heroes or euhemerized divinities to Christianity is sometimes related. When Oengus took Elcmar's *síd*,[5] the latter's steward continued in his office; and his wife became the mother of a daughter Ethne, afterward attendant to Manannan's daughter Curcog, who was born at the same time as she. Ethne was found to be eating none of the divine pigs nor drinking Goibniu's beer, yet she remained in health; a grave insult had been offered to her by a god, and now she could not eat, but an angel sent from God kept her alive. Meanwhile Oengus and Manannan brought cows from India, and as their milk had none of the demoniac nature of the gods' immortal food, Ethne drank it and was nourished for fifteen hundred years until St. Patrick came to Ireland. One day she went bathing with Curcog and her companions, but she returned no more to the *sid* with them, for through the power of Christianity in the land she had laid aside with her garments the charm of invisibility, the *Féth Fiada*. She could now be seen by men and could no longer perceive her divine companions or the road to the invisible *sid*. Wandering in search of 'them, she found a monk seated by a church and to him she narrated her story, whereupon he took her to St. Patrick, who baptized her. One day, as she sat by the door of the church, she heard the cries of the invisible *sid*-folk searching for her and bewailing her; she fainted and now fell into a decline, dying with her head on the Saint's breast.[6] In this tale the general Christian attitude to the gods obtrudes itself — although the conception of their immortality and invisibility is accepted, they are demons or attended by these; Ethne had a demon guardian who left her when the angel arrived and as a result of her chastity. Not unlike this story is that of Liban, daughter of Eochaid, whose family were drowned by the bursting of a well. Liban and her lapdog were preserved for a year in the water, but then she was changed into a salmon, save her head, and her dog into an otter. After three hundred years she was caught by her own wish and was baptized by St. Comgall, dying thereafter.[7]

In the Cúchulainn saga Conchobar was born at the hour of Christ's Nativity, and Cathbad sang beforehand a prophecy of the two births, telling also how Conchobar would "find his death in avenging the suffering God," though the hero did not

PLATE XXVI

Sucellos

The hammer-god, also shown on Plate XIII, here has five small mallets projecting from his great hammer. Found at Vienne, France.

pass away until he had believed in God, before the faith had yet reached Erin. He is said to have been the first pagan who went thence to heaven, though not till after his soul had journeyed to hell, whence it was carried with other souls by Christ at the Harrowing of Hades, he having died just after the Crucifixion.[8] Cúchulainn was a pagan to the last, but coincidentally with his passing thrice fifty queens who loved him saw his soul floating in his spirit-chariot over Emain Macha, singing a song of Christ's coming, the arrival of Patrick and the shaven monks, and the Day of Doom.[9] Loegaire, King of Erin, refused to accept the faith unless Patrick called up Cúchulainn in all his dignity, and next day Loegaire told how, after a piercing wind from hell preceding the hero's coming, while the air was full of birds — the sods thrown up by Cúchulainn's chariot-horses — he had appeared as of old. He was in bodily form, more than a phantom, agreeably to the Celtic conception of immortality; and he was clad as. a warrior, while his chariot was driven by Loeg and drawn by his famous steeds. Loegaire now desired that Cúchulainn should return and converse longer with him, whereupon he again appeared, performing in mid-air his supernatural feats and telling of his deeds. He besought Patrick to bring him with his faithful ones to Paradise and advised Loegaire to accept the faith. The king now asked Cúchulainn to tell of his adventures, and he did so, finishing by describing the pains of hell, still urging Loegaire to become a Christian, and again begging the saint to bring him and his to Paradise. Then heaven was declared for Cúchulainn, and Loegaire believed.[10]

Some of the Féinn stories also show this kindly attitude toward the old paganism, especially *The Colloquy with the Ancients*, which dates from the thirteenth century.[11] When Oisin had gone to the *síd*, Caoilte with eighteen others survived long enough to meet St. Patrick and his clerics. These were astonished at "the tall men with their huge wolf-dogs," but the saint sprinkled holy water upon them and dispersed into the hills the legions of demons who floated above them. At Patrick's desire Caoilte showed him a spring and told him stories of the Féinn, the saint interjecting the words, "Success and benediction, Caoilte, this is to me a lightening of spirit and mind," although he feared that it might be a destruction of devotion and prayer. During the night, however, his guardian angels bade him write down all the stories which Caoilte told; and next morning Caoilte and his friends were baptized. The hero gave Patrick a mass of gold — Fionn's last gift to him — as a fee for the rite and "for my soul's and my commander's soul's weal"; and the saint promised him eternal happiness and the benefit of his prayers.[12] The *Colloquy* describes journeys taken by Patrick and his followers with the Féinn, while Caoilte tells stories of occurrences at various spots. He also relates how Fionn, through his thumb of knowledge, understood the truth about God, asserted his belief in Him, and foretold the coming of Christian missionaries to Ireland and the celebration of Mass there, adding that for this God would not suffer him to fall into eternal woe. The Féinn likewise understood of God's existence and of His rule over all because of certain dire events which befell many revellers in one night,[13] a parallel to this being found in *The Children of Ler*, where, through their sorrows, these children are led to believe in God and in the solace which would come from Him; so that in the sequel they received baptism after they had resumed human form.[14]

Akin to these meetings of saint and heroes is one which is referred to in some verses from a fourteenth century manuscript and which concerns St. Columba and Mongan, either the pagan king of that name or his mythic prototype. Like Manannan, whose son he was, he was associated with Elysium — "the Land with Living Heart" — and from that "flock-abounding Land of Promise" he came to converse with the saint. Another poem gives Mongan's greeting to Columba on that occasion, and nothing could exceed the gracious terms in which he praises him; while a third poem tells how Mongan went to Heaven under the protection of the saint — "his head — great the profit! under Columcille's cowl." [15]

Not the least interesting aspect of the reverence with which Christian scribes and editors regarded old mythic heroes is found in the prophecies of Christianity put into their mouths. Some instances of this have been referred to, but a notable example occurs in *The Voyage of Bran*, where the goddess who visits Bran tells how "a great birth will come in after ages ": —

> "The son of a woman whose mate will not be known,
> He will seize the rule of many thousands.
>
> 'Tis He that made the Heavens,
> Happy he that has a white heart,
> He will purify hosts under pure water,
> 'Tis He that will heal your sicknesses."

So, too, Manannan speaks of the Fall and prophesies how

> "A noble salvation will come
> From the King who has created us,
> A white law will come over the seas,
> Besides being God, He will be man." [16]

By such means, which recall the noble teaching of St. Clement and Origen, did Christian Celts make gods and heroes do homage to the new faith, while yet they recounted the mythic stories about them and preserved all "the tender grace of a day that is dead." Even more remarkable is one version of a story telling how the narrative of the *Táin* was recovered. It existed only in fragments until Fergus mac Róich, a hero of the Cúchulainn group, rose from his grave and recited it, appearing not only to the poets, but to saints of Erin who had met near his tomb, while no less a person than St. Ciaran wrote the story to his dictation. Among these saints were Columba, Brendan, and Caillin, and in company with Senchan and other poets they were fasting at the grave of Fergus so that he might appear, after which the tale was written down in Ciaran's book of cow-hide. [17]

The same charitable point of view is seen in the fact that the gods and heroes still have their own mystic world in the *síd* and are seldom placed in hell. Yet there are exceptions, for Cúchulainn came from hell, as we saw, but St. Patrick transferred him to heaven. Even in hell, however, he had still been the triumphant hero, and when the demons carried off his soul to "the red charcoal," he played his sword and his *gaí bolga* on them, as Oscar did his flail,[18] so that the devils suffered, even while they crushed him into the fire.[19] Caoilte craved that his sister might be brought out of hell, and Patrick said that if this were good in God's sight, she and also his father, mother, and Fionn himself would be released.[20] In other poems, however, the Féinn are and remain in hell, as has already been seen.

Thus, while the Church set its face against the old cults, so that only slight traces of these remain, or gave a Christian aspect to popular customs by connecting them with saints' days or sacred places, it was on the whole rather proud than otherwise of the heroes of the past and preserved their memory, together with much of the gracious aspect of the ancient gods. Exceptions to this exist and were bound to exist, e. g. in many Irish and Scots Ossianic ballads; and there was, too, a tendency to confuse Elysium with hell, more especially in Welsh legend, this being inevitable where myths of Elysium were still connected with a local cult. Gwyn was lord of Annwfn, which was located on Glastonbury Tor, or king of fairy-land, and here St. Collen was invited to meet him. Seeing a wonderful castle and a host of beautiful folk, he regarded them as devils, their splendid robes as flames of fire, their food as withered leaves; and when he threw holy water over them, everything vanished.[21] Probably a cult of Gwyn existed on the hill. Gwyn was also thought to be a hunter of wicked souls, yet it is also said of him that God placed in him the force of the demons of Annwfn (here the equivalent of hell) in order to hinder them from destroying the people of this world.[22]

We owe much to the Christian scribes and poets of early mediaeval Ireland and Wales, who wrote down or re-edited the mythic tales, romantic legends, and poems of the pagan period, thus preserving them to us. These had still existed among the folk or were current in the literary class, and that they were saved from destruction is probably due to the fact that Ireland and Wales were never Romanized. Causes were at work in Gaul which killed the myths and tales so long transmitted in oral forms; and since they were never written down, they perished. Elsewhere these causes did not exist, or a type of Christianity flourished which was not altogether hostile to the stories of olden time, as when Irish paganism itself was described symbolically as desiring the dawn of a new day. The birds of Elysium were "the bird-flock of the Land of Promise," and in one story were brought into contact with St. Patrick, welcoming him, churning the water into milky whiteness, and calling, "O help of the Gaels, come, come, come, and come hither!" [23]

That is an exquisite fancy, more moving even than that which told how

> "The lonely mountains o'er
> And the resounding shore,
> A voice of weeping heard and loud lament"

— the mournful cry, "Great Pan is dead," at the moment of Christ's Nativity. Celtic paganism, Goidelic and Brythonic, surely bestowed on Christianity much of its old glamour, for nowhere is the history of the Church more romantic than in those regions where Ninian and Columba and Kentigern and Patrick lived and laboured long ago.

NOTES

INTRODUCTION

Citation by author's name or by title of a text or a volume of a series refers to the same in the various sections of the Bibliography. Where an author has written several works they are distinguished as [a], [b], etc.

1. Caesar, *De bello Gallico*, vi. 14.
2. See especially *CIL*, *CIR*.
3. 3 vols., Leipzig, 1896 ff.
4. See *infra*, pp. 157–58.
5. The exact meaning of *simulacra* in this passage is a little uncertain. Possibly they were boundary stones, like the Classical herms (cf. *Mythology of All Races*, Boston, 1916, i. 194–95); but they were probably "symbols" rather than "images" (see MacCulloch [b], pp. 284–85), and may have been standing-stones (see *infra*, pp. 158–59).
6. *De bello Gallico*, vi. 17.
7. ib. vi. 18.
8. MacCulloch [b], pp. 29 ff.
9. *Argonautica*, iv. 609 f.
10. Diodorus Siculus (first century B. C.), ii. 47.
11. *Herakles*, 1 ff.
12. Solinus, xxii. 10.
13. Giraldus Cambrensis, *Topographia Hiberniae*, ii. 34 ff.
14. *Pharsalia*, iii. 399 ff.
15. *De bello Gallico*, vi. 17.
16. Livy, V. xxxix. 3.
17. Pausanias, X. xxiii. 7.
18. Avienus (fourth century A. D.), *Ora maritima*, 644 ff.
19. *ZCP* i. 27 (1899).
20. ib.
21. Justin (probably third century A. D.), XXIV. iv. 3.
22. Diodorus Siculus, V. xxiv. 1.
23. See *infra*, p. 117.
24. Diodorus Siculus, iv. 19.
25. Propertius, V. x. 41.
26. Pliny, *Historia naturalis*, xxix. 3.
27. Lucan, *Pharsalia*, i. 455 ff.; Diodorus Siculus, v. 28.

28. Cf. *Mythology of All Races*, Boston, 1916, i. 6–8.

29. Plutarch, *De defectu oraculorum*, 18, *De facie lunae*, 26.

30. See *infra*, pp. 54, 90, 95–96, 119–20, 122, 127, 132, 192.

31. Procopius, ed. W. Dindorf, Bonn, 1833, ii. 566 f.

32. Cf. *Mythology of All Races*, Boston, 1916, i. 145–46.

33. Claudian, *In Rufinum*, i. 123.

34. Villemarque [a], i. 136; Le Braz [a], i. p. xxxix.

35. Pliny, *Historia naturalis*, iv. 13; Strabo, ii. 4 (= p. 104, ed. Casaubon).

36. *Historia naturalis*, ii. 98.

37. So called from the Greek Euhemerus (fourth century B. C.), who, in a philosophical romance, of which only scanty fragments have survived, showed how the gods had been actual men and their myths records of actual events (see E. Rohde, *Der griechische Roman und seine Vorläufer*, 2nd ed., Leipzig, 1900, pp. 236–41, and J. Geffcken, "Euhemerism," in *ERE* v. 572–73).

38. Cited as *LL* and *LU*. They have been edited at Dublin in 1880 and 1870 respectively, but neither has been completely translated.

39. See *Bibliography of Irish Philology and of Printed Irish Literature*, Dublin, 1913, pp. 80–122.

40. See Wentz, *passim*.

CHAPTER I

1. Keating, i. 141 ff. (*ITS*).

2. MS H 2, 18; text and translation in *Ériu*, viii. 1 ff. (1915).

3. Harleian MS. 5280, text and translation by W. Stokes, in *RCel* xii. 61 ff. (1891).

4. ib. xv. 69 (1894).

5. *LL* 169 *a*, 214 *b*.

6. *RCel* xv. 439 (1894).

7. Harleian MS. 5280, § 39 f.

8. ib. §§ 25 f., 165.

9. E. O'Curry, in *Atlantis*, iv. 159 (1863).

10. Harleian MS. 5280, §§ 11, 33 f.

11. ib. § 53 f.

12. The "Land of Promise" is a name for Elysium, perhaps borrowed by Christian editors from Biblical sources.

13. E. O'Curry, in *Atlantis*, iv. 159 ff. (1863).

14. Harleian MS. 5280, § 74 f.

15. ib. § 84 f.

16. ib. § 88 f.

17. ib. §§ 96, 122; see also *infra*, pp. 51, 120.

18. See *Mythology of All Races*, Boston, 1917, vi. 50.

19. Harleian MS. 5280, §§ 100, 122, *LL* 11 *a*, W. Stokes, in *RCel* xv. 541 (1894).

20. Harleian MS. 5280, §§ 102, 122, S. H. O'Grady, ii. 219.

21. Harleian MS. 5280, § 123, W. Stokes, in *RCel* xvi. 59 (1895).

22. Harleian MS. 5280, § 125 f.

23. ib. § 129 f.

24. MacNeill, i. 135 (*ITS*).

25. Harleian MS. 5280, §§ 137, 149 f.

26. *Book of Fermoy*, 24 *b*.

27. Harleian MS. 5280, § 162 f.

28. Loth, *Mabinogion*, i. 306.

29. Harleian MS. 5280, § 166 f.

30. W. Stokes, in *RCel* xv. 311 f. (1894).

31. *LL* 9 *b*.

32. There is some connexion between Manannan and Eogan, for Fand says that she dwelt in Eogan's bower.

33. Cf. *supra*, pp. 14–15, on Plutarch's myth of Elysium.

34. *LL* 275 *b*; d'Arbois, *Cours*, ii. 356 ff.

35. W. Stokes, in *RCel* xvi. 273 (1895).

36. D'Arbois, *Cours*, ii. 145.

37. W. Stokes, in *RCel* xii. 129 (1891).

38. L. C. Stern, in *Festschrift Whitley Stokes . . . gewidmet*, Leipzig, 1900, p. 17.

39. Text and translation by E. O'Curry, in *Atlantis*, iv. 159 ff. (1863).

40. Harleian MS. 5280, § 3 f.

CHAPTER II

1. *Annals of Tigernach*, ed. and tr. W. Stokes, in *RCel* xvi. 394, 404 ff. (1895).

2. *TOS* v. 234 (1860).

3. *Dindsenchas*, ed. and tr. W. Stokes, in *RCel* xv. 446 (1894).

4. *LL* 9 ff.; Keating, ii. 79 ff. (*ITS*).

5. S. H. O'Grady, ii. 260.

6. ib. ii. 171.

7. See MacNeill, i. introd., pp. xxv, xxxviii f. (*ITS*), and his articles in *New Ireland Review*, xxv–xxvi (1906).

8. *LL* 245 *b*.

9. W. Stokes, in *RCel* xvi. 35 (1895).

10. *LL* 7 *a*.

11. D. Fitzgerald, in *RCel* iv. 187 ff. (1879); cf. S. H. O'Grady, in *TOS* iii. 114 (1855).

CHAPTER III

1. E. Windisch, in *IT* i. 14; Stokes, *Tripartite Life of Saint Patrick*, p. 314.
2. Ed. and tr. W. M. Hennessy, in *RIA:TLS* i. 3 (1889).
3. O'Curry [a], i. 505.
4. *LL* 246.
5. *Book of Fermoy*, 111 f.; E. O'Curry, in *Atlantis*, iii. 385 (1862); *RIA:IMS* i. 45 f. (1870).
6. Text and translation by E. O'Curry, in *Atlantis*, iv. 113 ff. (1863).
7. L. C. Stern, in *ZCP* v. 523 (1905); Stirn, in *RCel* xxvii. 332, xxviii. 330 (1906–07).
8. A. Nutt, in *RCel* xxvii. 328 (1906).
9. *LL* 209 b; text and translation by L. Gwynn, in *Ériu*, vii. 210 f. (1914).
10. See *Mythology of All Races*, Boston, 1916, i. 5–8.
11. MacCulloch [b], p. 81.

CHAPTER IV

1. Caesar, *De bello Gallico*, vi. 14.
2. S. H. O'Grady, ii. 203.
3. E. O'Curry, in *Atlantis*, iii. 387 f. (1862).
4. S. H. O'Grady, ii. 243.
5. S. H. O'Grady, in *TOS* iii. 113 f. (1855); see *infra*, pp. 171–72.
6. For other instances see *infra*, pp. 59, 62–63, 80, 154, 184–85.
7. Skene [a], i. 532; J. G. Evans, *Llyvyr Taliesin*, p. 26.
8. Guest, iii. 356 ff.
9. E. Windisch, in *IT* III. i. 235 f.
10. W. Stokes, in *RCel* xv. 444 (1894).
11. Larminie, p. 82.
12. *Book of Fermoy*, 131 a; Nutt [c], i. 64 ff.
13. MacNeill, i. 119 (*ITS*).
14. W. Stokes, in *RCel* xv. 307 (1894).
15. W. Stokes, ib. xvi. 65 (1895).
16. ib. p. 69.
17. W. Stokes, ib. ii. 200 (1874).
18. S. H. O'Grady, ii. 311 ff.

Chapter V

1. *LU* 133 *a*, Harleian MS. 2, 16; text and translation in Nutt [c], i. 42 ff.
2. *Book of Fermoy*, 85 *a*; Nutt [c], i. 58 ff.
3. Nutt [c], ii. 24 f.
4. See *infra*, pp. 73–74.
5. Windisch, *Táin*, pp. 342, 366.
6. N. O'Kearney, in *TOS* ii. 80 (1855).
7. Windisch, *Táin*, p. 550.
8. E. Windisch, in *IT* iii. 2.
9. S. H. O'Grady, in *TOS* iii. 87 ff. (1855).
10. "The Gilla Dacker," in S. H. O'Grady, ii. 300.
11. "Diarmaid and Grainne," in *TOS* iii. 69 ff. (1855).
12. ib. p. 179.
13. *LU* 63 *b*; W. Stokes, in *RCel* xvi. 139 (1895); J. F. Campbell [c], p. xxxix.
14. W. Stokes, in *RCel* xvi. 62 (1895).

Chapter VI

1. Text and translation by K. Meyer, in *RCel* x. 212 ff. (1889); cf. W. Stokes, ib. xv. 465 (1894).
2. E. Windisch, in *IT* II. ii. 241 f.
3. For the meaning of this phrase see MacCulloch [b], p. 67, note 1.
4. *LU* 74 *a*, 77 *a*; Windisch, *Táin*, pp. 306, 312 f.
5. *LL* 119 *a*; text and translation by W. Stokes, in *RCel* iii. 175 (1877).
6. Loth, *Mabinogion*, i. 302.
7. See *infra*, p. 165.
8. Text and translation by R. I. Best, in *Ériu*, iii. 149 f. (1907).
9. See *infra*, p. 89.
10. W. Stokes, in *RCel* xvi. 42 (1895).
11. J. O'B. Crowe, in *JRHAAI* IV. i. 94 ff. (1871); W. Stokes, in *RCel* xv. 482 (1894), xvi. 152 (1895); see also *infra*, p. 121.
12. W. Stokes, in *RCel* xiii. 426 f. (1892).
13. D'Arbois, *Cours*, v. 370; W. Stokes, in *RCel* xvi. 45 (1895).
14. See *infra*, pp. 156, 179.
15. See *infra*, pp. 80–82.
16. *Book of Ballymote*, 139 *b*.
17. See *supra*, p. 70.

18. Text and translation by W. Stokes, in *RCel* xxii. 9 ff. (1901); for the relation of the different accounts of Conaire to each other, see M. Nettlau, ib. xii. 229 ff. (1891).

Chapter VII

1. *Leabhar Breac*, Dublin, 1872–76, p. 242; O'Curry [a], pp. 426, 632.
2. Text and translation from Egerton Manuscript 1782 (British Museum) by E. Müller, in *RCel* iii. 342 f. (1877).
3. O'Curry, *loc. cit.*
4. *LU* 129 b.
5. W. Stokes, in *RCel* xv. 463 (1894).
6. W. Stokes, ib. p. 291; E. Gwynn, in *RIA:TLS* vii. 3, 70 (1900). For the text and translation of the story of Etain see Leahy, i. 1 ff.; L. C. Stern, in *ZCP* v. 524 (1905); E. Müller, in *RCel* iii. 350 (1877); A. Nutt, ib. xxvii. 334 (1906).
7. *Code of Manu*, ix. 8 (tr. G. Bühler, in *Sacred Books of the East*, xxv. 329 [1886]); J. A. MacCulloch, "First-Born (Introductory and Primitive)," in *ERE* vi. 34.
8. *LU* 60 a.
9. Text and translation by L. Duvau, in *RCel* ix. 1 ff. (1888); d'Arbois, *Cours*, v. 22; E. Windisch, in *IT* i. 134 ff.
10. *LU* 120 a, text also in Windisch, *Kurzgefasste irische Grammatik*, p. 120, translation by d'Arbois, *Cours*, v. 385, where the gods' land is wrongly regarded as the realm of the dead (see MacCulloch [b], p. 374).
11. W. Stokes, in *IT* iii. 335.
12. *Lais de Marie de France*, ed. K. Warnke, pp. 86–112.
13. *LU* 25 b; text and translation by W. Stokes, in *RCel* x. 63 f. (1889); see also d'Arbois, *Cours*, v. 485.
14. See *supra*, p. 36.
15. *LU* 43 f.; E. Windisch, in *IT* i. 205 f.; text and translations in Leahy, i. 51 f., E. O'Curry, in *Atlantis*, i. 362 f., ii. 98 f. (1858–59); cf. d'Arbois, *Cours*, v. 170 f.
16. S. H. O'Grady, ii. 196.
17. Text and translations of the versions by W. Stokes, in *RCel* xvi. 151 (1895) and *FL* iii. 510 (1892).
18. W. Stokes, in *RCel* xv. 437–38 (1894).
19. For instances see M. Jastrow, *Religion of Babylonia and Assyria*, Boston, 1898, p. 550; *Homeric Hymn to Demeter*, 399; G. Maspero, *Études de mythologie égyptienne*, ii. 226, Paris, 1893; J. Muir, *Original Sanskrit Texts*, London, 1858–72, v. 320; G. Brown, *Melanesians and Polynesians*, London, 1910, p. 194; C. G. Seligmann, *Mel-*

anesians of British New Guinea, Cambridge, 1910, pp. 656, 734;
L. Spence, in *ERE* iii. 561 (Chinook) ; cf. J. A. MacCulloch, ib. iv.
653, v. 682 (1911–12); see also E. Westermarck, *Origin and Development of the Moral Ideas*, London, 1906–08.
20. W. Stokes, in *RCel* xvi. 148 (1895).
21. *LU* 51 *b*; W. Stokes, in *RCel* xv. 332, xvi. 73 (1894–95); d'Arbois, *Cours*, ii. 364.
22. See pp. 37, 181.
23. S. H. O'Grady, ii. 204, 213, 220.
24. W. Stokes, in *RCel* xv. 312 (1894).
25. W. Stokes, ib. p. 441.
26. W. Stokes, in *RCel* xvi. 78 (1895).

CHAPTER VIII

1. Holder, *s. v.*; W. Stokes, in *RCel* xv. 279 (1894).
2. Loth, *Mabinogion*, i. 81 f.; Guest, iii. 7.
3. E. Anwyl, in *ZCP* i. 288 (1899).
4. Skene [a], i. 264; J. G. Evans in his *Llyvyr Taliesin* translates the lines which Rhŷs and Skene agree as referring to an imprisonment of Gweir by Pwyll and Pryderi in Caer Sidi as follows —
"Complete was his victory at Whirlpool's Fort [Caer Sidi],
    By reason of extraordinary thought and care."
Skene's rendering is —
"Complete was the prison of Gweir in Caer Sidi,
    Through the spite of Pwyll and Pryderi."
Rhŷs renders "spite" as "messenger." The text is *Bu gweir gyvrang yng Haer sidi, drwy oi chestol bwyll a phryderi*. Evans does not regard Gweir, Pwyll, and Pryderi in the text as proper names.
5. Loth, *Mabinogion*, i. 301.
6. ib. i. 173 f.; Guest, iii. 189 f.
7. Loth, *Mabinogion*, i. 195.
8. Rhŷs [a], p. 276.
9. Cf. *Mythology of All Races*, Boston, 1916, i. 273–76.
10. Rhŷs [c], p. 157; J. G. Evans, *Llyvyr Taliesin*, p. 63.
11. Skene [a], i. 543, ii. 145.
12. ib. i. 282, 288; Rhŷs [a], p. 387.
13. Loth, *Mabinogion*, i. 301.
14. Skene [a], i. 286–87.
15. Loth, *Mabinogion*, i. 300.
16. Skene [a], i. 275, 278; *Myrvyrian Archaiology*, i. 167.
17. Guest, iii. 255.
18. Loth, *Mabinogion*, i. 119, 151 f.; Guest, iii. 81, 143 f.

19. *FLR* v. 1 f. (1878).
20. Loth, *Mabinogion*, i. 331; Geoffrey of Monmouth, *Historia Britanniae*, ii. 11.
21. Loth, *Mabinogion*, i. 327.
22. Bathurst, p. 127.
23. E. Anwyl, in *ZCP* ii. 127 (1899).
24. Nutt [c], ii. 17.
25. Skene [a], ii. 51; J. G. Evans, *Llyvyr Taliesin*, p. 54.
26. See *supra*, p. 51.
27. Loth, *Mabinogion*, i. 307.
28. Elton, p. 291.
29. Skene [a], i. 302.
30. MacCulloch [b], p. 242.
31. Rhŷs [a], p. 94 f., [c], ch. ii; cf. MacCulloch [b], p. 33. For Yama see *Mythology of All Races*, Boston, 1917, vi. 68–70, 159–60.
32. Skene [a], i. 298.
33. Geoffrey of Monmouth, *Historia Britanniae*, iii. 1 f.
34. Loth, *Mabinogion*, i. 119, 360.
35. Geoffrey of Monmouth, *Historia Britanniae*, iv. 1 f.
36. Skene [a], i. 431.
37. Rhŷs [a], p. 90, *et passim*.
38. Geoffrey of Monmouth, *Historia Britanniae*, iii. 20.
39. Loth, *Mabinogion*, i. 131 f.
40. See *supra*, pp. 24–25.
41. Loth, *Mabinogion*, i. 233.
42. Rhŷs [a], p. 609.
43. *Itinerarium Cambriae*, i. 8.
44. See *infra*, p. 194.
45. Skene [a], i. 293.
46. Loth, *Mabinogion*, i. 284, 315, 331.
47. Train, ii. 118.
48. See *supra*, p. 57.
49. E. Anwyl, in *ZCP* i. 293 (1899).
50. See *supra*, p. 57.
51. Guest, iii. 356 f.
52. Skene [a], i. 260, 274 f., 278, 281 f., 286 f.; J. G. Evans, *Llyvyr Taliesin*, pp. 10 ff., 27 ff.
53. See *supra*, p. 104; J. G. Evans, *op. cit.* p. 64 f.
54. See *infra*, p. 166.
55. Skene [a], i. 265; J. G. Evans, *op. cit.* p. 127.
56. MacCulloch [b], p. 118.
57. Cf. *Mythology of All Races*, Boston, 1916, x. 5–7.
58. See *supra*, p. 100.
59. Skene [a], i. 275.

60. Skene [a], i. 260, 498, 500, ii. 5, 234; W. O. Pughe, *Dictionary of Welsh*, London, 1803, *s. v.*
61. N. Thomas, in *RHR* xxxviii. 339 (1898).
62. J. Rhŷs, "Welsh Fairy Tales," in *Y Cymmrodor*, iv. 163 ff. (1881); cf. also Rhŷs [d], *passim*.
63. S. H. O'Grady, ii. 94 f.

Chapter IX

1. Text and translation in Nutt [c], i. 2 f.
2. S. H. O'Grady, ii. 198 f.; see also *supra*, p. 89.
3. S. H. O'Grady, ii. 238.
4. Strabo, iv. 6 (= p. 198, ed. Casaubon); Mela, iii. 6; see Mac-Culloch [b], p. 385 f.
5. E. Windisch, in *IT* iii. 183 f.; S. H. O'Grady, in *TOS* iii. 213 f. (1857).
6. E. O'Curry, in *Atlantis*, iii. 387 (1862).
7. Nutt [c], i. 52 f.
8. ib. i. 56 f.
9. *LL* 246 a.
10. Holder, *s. v.* "Braciaca."
11. Cf. *Mythology of All Races*, Boston, 1916–17, x. 46–48, i. 218 ff.
12. See pp. 95–96, 151, 192.
13. *Da Derga's Hostel*, ed. W. Stokes, in *RCel* xxii. 14 (1901).
14. W. Stokes, in *RCel* xv. 546 (1894); O'Curry [b], ii. 142 f.
15. W. Stokes, in *FL* iii. 506 (1892).
16. W. Stokes, in *RCel* xv. 315 (1894); S. H. O'Grady, ii. 519; *LL* 209 b.
17. S. H. O'Grady, ii. 390.
18. ib. ii. 253.
19. See *supra*, p. 29.
20. O'Curry [a], pp. 388, 621.
21. Skene [a], i. 285.
22. See *infra*, pp. 194–95.
23. MacDougall, p. 261.
24. Hyde [c], p. 440.
25. Cf. *Mythology of All Races*, Boston, 1916, i. 147–48.
26. Nutt [c], i. 276, 289.
27. MacCulloch [b], p. 373.

Chapter X

1. Holder, *s. v.*; cf. also MacCulloch [b], ch. xiv.
2. E. Windisch, in *IT* i. 96 f.; W. Stokes, in *RCel* xvi. 63 (1895).
3. See *infra*, pp. 187–88.
4. See *infra*, p. 177.
5. K. Meyer, in *RIA:TLS* xvi. 65 (1910).
6. W. Stokes, in *RCel* xv. 426, 474 (1894).
7. W. Stokes, ib. xiii. 449 (1892), xv. 470 (1894).
8. J. O'Daly, in *TOS* vi. 133 (1861).
9. J. F. Campbell [b], i. 53.
10. W. Stokes, in *RCel* xv. 421, 471, 473 (1894).
11. S. H. O'Grady, ii. 574.
12. *LL* 69 a; *LU* 64 b; Windisch, *Táin*, pp. 184, 188.
13. O'Curry [a], p. 388.
14. Leahy, ii. 105; W. Stokes, in *IT* iii. 295.
15. Rhys [d], *passim*.
16. J. O'Daly, in *TOS* vi. 223 (1861).
17. W. Stokes, in *RCel* xii. 104 (1891); S. H. O'Grady, ii. 199; E. O'Curry, in *Atlantis*, iv. 163 (1863).
18. S. H. O'Grady, ii. 292 f.
19. *Fled Bricrend*, ed. G. Henderson, London, 1899, p. 38 (*ITS*).
20. W. Stokes, in *RCel* xii. 347 (1891).
21. Loth, *Mabinogion*, i. 303; Guest, ii. 269 f.
22. S. H. O'Grady, ii. 123.
23. See Plates VIII, XII, XVI, XXV.
24. See *supra*, pp. 24–25, 47, 107–08.
25. Text and translation by A. O. Anderson, in *RCel* xxiv. 126 ff. (1903); Leahy, ii. 3 ff.; G. Henderson, in J. F. Campbell [c], p. 1 ff.; J. O'B. Crowe, in *RIA:IMS* i. 134 ff. (1870).
26. *Dean of Lismore's Book*, ed. and tr. T. McLauchlan, Edinburgh, 1862, p. 54 f.; G. Henderson, in J. F. Campbell [c], p. 18 f.
27. See *supra*, pp. 54–55, 66.
28. Cf. *Mythology of All Races*, Boston, 1916, i. 87–88.
29. See *supra*, p. 11.
30. N. O'Kearney, in *TOS* ii. 51, 69 (1855); for parallel instances of the "swallow" *motif* among the North American Indians see *Mythology of All Races*, Boston, 1916, x. 69, 79, 139.
31. *LU* 113; J. O'B. Crowe, in *JRHAAI* IV. i. 371 f. (1870).
32. W. Stokes, in *RCel* xv. 304 (1894); S. H. O'Grady, ii. 523.
33. S. H. O'Grady, in *TOS* iii. 125 (1855).
34. W. Stokes, in *RCel* xvi. 32 (1895).

35. W. Stokes, ib. xv. 326 (1894).
36. W. Stokes, ib. xvi. 72 (1895).
37. W. Stokes, ib. p. 77.
38. W. Stokes, ib. xv. 295 (1894).
39. W. Stokes, ib. p. 434.
40. W. Stokes, ib. i. 256 (1870).
41. *LL* 82 *b*, 86 *b*; Windisch, *Táin*, pp. 477, 547 (cf. also pp. 338, 366).
42. *Fled Bricrend*, ed. G. Henderson, London, 1899, p. 84 (*ITS*).
43. N. O'Kearney, in *TOS* i. 107 (1853).
44. Cf. *supra*, p. 34.
45. *LL* 76 *a*, 69 *a*; Windisch, *Táin*, pp. 338, 191.

CHAPTER XI

1. Sébillot [a]; cf. also the same scholar [b].
2. See *supra*, p. 73, and cf. p. 135.
3. For these see the Rennes *Dindsenchas*, ed. and tr. W. Stokes, in *RCel* xv. 429 f., 483 (1894), xvi. 50, 65, 146, 153, 164 (1895).
4. W. Stokes, ib. xv. 302 (1894).
5. See MacCulloch [a], pp. 167 ff.
6. Windisch, *Táin*, pp. 869, 886.
7. D'Arbois, *Cours*, v. 10.
8. W. Stokes, in *RCel* xv. 460, 284, xvi. 44, xv. 279 (1894-95).
9. *LL* 16 *b*.
10. See *supra*, pp. 42, 81.
11. W. Stokes, in *RCel* xii. 95 (1891).
12. W. Stokes, ib. p. 71.
13. O. Connellan, in *TOS* v. 96 (1860); S. O'Grady, i. 84.
14. W. Stokes, in *RCel* xv. 279 (1894).
15. See *supra*, p. 75.
16. W. Stokes, in *RCel* xvi. 51 (1895).
17. See *supra*, pp. 54-55, 87, 131.
18. W. Stokes, in *RCel* xv. 421 (1894), xvi. 279 (1895).
19. D. Fitzgerald, ib. iv. 185 (1879).
20. See *supra*, pp. 9-17.

CHAPTER XII

1. E. Windisch, in *IT* i. 210.
2. D'Arbois, *Cours*, v. 14; K. Meyer, in *RCel* vi. 174 (1884).
3. *Cóir Anmann*, ed. W. Stokes, in *IT* iii. 393.
4. See *supra*, pp. 64-65, 83.

5. *LL* 58 *a*; W. Stokes, in *IT* iii. 282.

6. E. Windisch, in *IT* i. 211.

7. *LU* 101 *b*; *LL* 123 *b*.

8. Windisch, *Táin*, pp. 345, 669.

9. ib. p. 106 f.

10. *LU* 59 *b*.

11. Windisch, *Táin*, p. 118.

12. For the meaning of this term cf. *Mythology of All Races*, Boston, 1916, x. 17 ff.

13. *Ériu*, vii. 208 (1914).

14. Cf. *Fled Bricrend*, ed. G. Henderson, London, 1899, p. 67 (*ITS*); Caesar, *De bello Gallico*, vii. 47.

15. Windisch, *Táin*, p. 130 f.

16. In his conversation with Emer, Cúchulainn boasted of his greatness, trustworthiness, and wisdom, and said that, taught by Cathbad, he was "an adept in the arts of the god of Druidism."

17. Cf. *Mythology of All Races*, Boston, 1916, i. 34–35.

18. Two versions are here combined — "The Wooing of Emer" (*Tochmarc Emire*), ed. K. Meyer, in *RCel* xi. 442 f. (1890), and "The Training of Cúchulainn" (*Foglaim Chonculaind*), ed. W. Stokes, ib. xxix. 109 f. (1908).

19. W. Stokes, ib. xvi. 46 (1895).

20. See *Mythology of All Races*, Boston, 1917, vi. 332.

21. See *supra*, pp. 124–25; E. Windisch, in *IT* i. 96 f.; A. H. Leahy, i. 41.

22. Athenaeus, *Deipnosophistai*, iv. 40.

23. Poseidonius, in Athenaeus, *Deipnosophistai*, iv. 40.

24. *Fled Bricrend*, ed. G. Henderson, London, 1899 (*ITS*); E. Windisch, in *IT* i. 235; d'Arbois, *Cours*, v. 81 f.

25. See *Mythology of All Races*, Boston, 1917, xii. 41, 49.

26. E. Windisch, in *IT* ii. 173; d'Arbois, *Cours*, v. 149 f.

27. G. Keating, ii. 223 (*ITS*); O'Curry [b], iii. 81.

28. J. O'B. Crowe, in *JRHAAI* IV. i. 371 f. (1870); cf. *supra*, pp. 131–32.

29. Keating, ii. 223 f. (*ITS*).

30. W. Stokes, in *RCel* xv. 449 (1894); Keating, ii. 235 (*ITS*).

31. R. Thurneysen, in *ZCP* ix. 189 f. (1913); J. Baudiš, in *Ériu*, vii. 200 f. (1914); cf. MacCulloch [a], ch. v.

32. Skene [a], i. 254; cf. Loth, *Mabinogion*, i. 261.

33. R. I. Best, in *Ériu*, iii. 163 (1907).

34. O'Curry [b], ii. 97.

35. See *supra*, p. 127.

36. See *supra*, pp. 73–74.

37. See *supra*, p. 71.

38. See *supra*, pp. 64–65.

39. See *supra*, pp. 130–31.

40. Text and translation of the version in *LL* by Windisch, *Táin*; text of the version in *LU* and *Book of Lecan*, ed. J. Strachan and J. G. O'Keeffe, in *Ériu*, i. (1904), translation by L. Winifred Faraday, *The Cattle Raid of Cualnge*, London, 1904. See also Hull [c]. For references in the *Dindsenchas* see W. Stokes, in *RCel* xv. 464, xvi. 156 (1894–95).

41. See *supra*, pp. 31, 100.

42. Text and translation by W. Stokes, in *RCel* iii. 175 f. (1877); cf. d'Arbois, *Cours*, v. 330 f.; Hull [c], p. 253 f.

43. O'Curry [a], p. 479.

44. ib.

45. W. Stokes, in *RCel* xv. 472 (1894); S. H. O'Grady, ii. 525.

46. W. Stokes, in *RCel* viii. 49 f. (1887); O'Curry [a], p. 637; Hull [c], pp. 87, 267.

47. Rhŷs [e], p. 316.

48. D'Arbois [b], pp. 25, 65 f., *RCel* xx. 89 (1899).

49. D'Arbois [b], p. 63, *RCel* xix. 246 (1898), xxviii. 41 (1907); cf. S. Reinach, in *RCel* xviii. 253 f. (1897).

50. Caesar, *De bello Gallico*, vii. 65; d'Arbois [b], p. 49, and *RCel* xxvii. 324 (1906).

51. Diodorus Siculus, iv. 56; for the Dioscuri see *Mythology of All Races*, Boston, 1916, i. 26–27, 247, 301–02.

52. D'Arbois [b], p. 57 f.; cf. *supra*, p. 129.

53. See *supra*, pp. 28–29.

54. Caesar, *De bello Gallico*, vi. 17; d'Arbois [b], p. 39 f., and *RCel* xxvii. 313 f. (1906); cf. S. Reinach, in *RCel* xi. 224 (1890).

CHAPTER XIII

1. N. O'Kearney, in *TOS* i. 32 f. (1853).

2. MacInness and Nutt, p. 407; MacNeill, i., p. xxvi (*ITS*).

3. MacNeill, i., p. xxxii (*ITS*).

4. *LU* 16 *b*; *LL* 4 *b*, 127 *a*; W. Stokes, in *RCel* xv. 300 (1894).

5. Ed. and tr. D. Comyn, Dublin, 1902, and J. O'Donovan, in *TOS* iv. 281 ff. (1859).

6. S. H. O'Grady, ii. 203.

7. Comyn, p. 18 f.

8. *LU* 41 *b*; W. M. Hennessy, in *RCel* ii. 86 f. (1873).

9. See *supra*, p. 25.

10. S. H. O'Grady, ii. 131, 225, 245.

11. D'Arbois [b], p. 53; Holder, *s. v.* "Camulos"; K. Meyer, in *RCel* xxxii. 390 (1911).

12. MacNeill, i. 33, 133 (*ITS*).
13. Comyn, p. 23 f.
14. MacNeill, i. 134 (*ITS*).
15. S. H. O'Grady, ii. 142 f.
16. *LU* 41 *b*.
17. Comyn, p. 41 f.; cf. K. Meyer, in *RCel* v. 201 (1882); N. O'Kearney, in *TOS* ii. 174 (1855).
18. See *supra*, pp. 109–10.
19. J. Grimm, *Teutonic Mythology*, London, 1879–89, p. 690; J. G. Frazer, in *AR* i. 172 f. (1888); M. R. Cox, *Cinderella*, London, 1893; Miss Buckland, in *JAI* xxii. 29 (1893); W. H. Dall, *Third Annual Report of the Bureau of American Ethnology* (1884).
20. K. Meyer, in *RCel* xxv. 345 (1904).
21. Comyn, p. 50.
22. Curtin [a], p. 204.
23. J. F. Campbell [b], i. 33 f., [a], iii. 348 f.; J. G. Campbell [c], p. 16 f.
24. S. H. O'Grady, ii. 172.
25. N. O'Kearney, in *TOS* i. 13 (1853); S. H. O'Grady, ii. 221.
26. J. F. Campbell [b], i. 198.
27. S. H. O'Grady, ii. 163.
28. W. Stokes, in *RCel* xv. 333 (1894).
29. N. O'Kearney, in *TOS* ii. 167 f. (1855).
30. K. Meyer, in *RIA:TLS* xvi. 22 f. (1910); cf. *supra*, p. 145.
31. N. O'Kearney, in *TOS* ii. 161 (1855).
32. Text and translation by W. Stokes, in *RCel* vii. 289 (1886); cf. MacNeill, i. 28, 127 (*ITS*).
33. Joyce [a], p. 177.
34. J. G. Campbell [c], p. 74.
35. O'Curry [b], ii. 345; MacNeill, i. 207 (*ITS*).
36. MacNeill, i. p. xxxvii (*ITS*).
37. J. G. Campbell, in *SCR* i. 115, 241 (1881); J. F. Campbell [b], i. 68; J. G. Campbell [c], p. 131.
38. J. G. Campbell, in *SCR loc. cit.*; A. MacBain, in *CM* ix. 130 (1884).
39. Aristotle, *Nicom. Ethics*, iii. 77, *Eud. Ethics*, III. i. 25; Stobaeus, *Eclogae*, vii. 40; Ælian, *Varia Historia*, xii. 22.
40. A. Kelleher and G. Schoepperle, in *RCel* xxxii. 184 f. (1911).
41. MacNeill, i. 30, 130 (*ITS*).
42. ib. i. 38, 140; see *supra*, pp. 68–69.
43. See *supra*, p. 128.
44. S. H. O'Grady, ii. 292 f.; Joyce [a], p. 253 f.
45. See *supra*, p. 102.
46. S. H. O'Grady, ii. 222–31.
47. ib. ii. 247 f.

48. S. H. O'Grady, ii. 141, 146.
49. ib. ii. 300; O. Connellan, in *TOS* v. 69 (1860).
50. MacNeill, ii. 5, 101 (*ITS*).
51. S. H. O'Grady, ii. 331; W. Stokes, in *RCel* xvi. 147 (1895).
52. MacNeill, i. 21, 118 (*ITS*); Comyn, p. 20.
53. See *supra*, p. 29; MacNeill, ii. 34, 134 (*ITS*).
54. *Cath Finntrága*, ed. and tr. K. Meyer, Oxford, 1885, pp. 13, 32.
55. J. F. Campbell [b], i. 65; MacDougall, p. 268.
56. K. Meyer, in *RIA:TLS* xvi. 51 (1910).
57. ib. p. xxiii.
58. J. H. Lloyd, O. J. Bergin, and G. Schoepperle, in *RCel* xxxiii. 40 f. (1912).
59. J. H. Lloyd, O. J. Bergin, and G. Schoepperle, ib. p. 160.
60. ib. p. 157.
61. According to Keating, the Tuatha Dé Danann, when in Greece, quickened dead Athenians by their lore, sending demons into them.
62. Text and translation by S. H. O'Grady, in *TOS* iii (1857).
63. MacNeill, i. 45, 149 (*ITS*).
64. J. F. Campbell [a], iii. 49.
65. W. Stokes, in *RCel* xv. 448 (1894).
66. J. G. Campbell [c], p. 53 f.
67. K. Meyer, in *RCel* xi. 131 (1890).
68. MacNeill, i. 120, 121, 165, 200 (*ITS*); J. F. Campbell [b], i. 164.
69. N. O'Kearney, in *TOS* i. 68 f. (1853); J. F. Campbell [b], i. 182.
70. S. H. O'Grady, ii. 98.
71. K. Meyer, in *RIA:TLS* xvi. 69 (1910); cf. introd., p. xxv.
72. S. H. O'Grady, ii. 167.
73. J. F. Campbell [a], iv. 242, [b], i. 195; MacDougall, pp. 73, 283.
74. Nutt [c], i. 51.
75. S. H. O'Grady, ii. 102, 158–59.
76. J. F. Campbell [b], i. 198.
77. J. O'Daly, in *TOS* iv. 233 (1859).
78. Curtin [a], p. 327 f.
79. N. O'Kearney, in *TOS* i. 20 f. (1853); J. O'Daly, ib. iv. 243 f. (1859).
80. N. O'Kearney, ib. i. 131 f. (1853).
81. S. H. O'Grady, ib. iii. 230 f. (1857).
82. N. O'Kearney, ib. i. 93 (1853); S. H. O'Grady, ib. iii. 257, 291 (1857); for other poems see the other volumes of this series, as well as K. Meyer, in *RIA:TLS* xvi (1910); *Dean of Lismore's Book*, ed. and tr. T. McLauchlan, Edinburgh, 1862.
83. D. Hyde, in *RCel* xiii. 417 f. (1892).

CHAPTER XIV

1. *Historia Britonum*, § 50.
2. *De excidio Britanniae*, § 26.
3. *Historia regum Britanniae*, viii. 19 ff.)
4. See *supra*, pp. 62–63.
5. See *supra*, pp. 66–67.
6. E. Anwyl, in *ERE* ii. 1.
7. Holder, *s. vv.* "Artaios," "Artos"; Rhŷs [c], p. 39 f.
8. Loth, *Mabinogion*, i. 243 f.
9. See *supra*, p. 181, on the king of *Tír na nOg*.
10. See *supra*, pp. 28–29.
11. Loth, *Mabinogion*, i. 256.
12. MacInness and Nutt, p. 53.
13. Skene [a], i. 261 f., ii. 458; Loth, *Mabinogion*, i. 310.
14. Skene [a], i. 295.
15. See *supra*, p. 111.
16. Loth, *Mabinogion*, i. 328, 337. In Geoffrey (ix. 4) Prytwenn is Arthur's shield.
17. Skene [a], i. 265; J. G. Evans, *Llyvyr Taliesin*, p. 127.
18. See *supra*, p. 151.
19. Loth, *Mabinogion*, i. 307, 334.
20. ib. i. 305; see also *supra*, pp. 112, 120.
21. ib. i. 259, 269.
22. ib. i. 278.
23. ib. i. 260.
24. Cf. *supra*, pp. 130–31, 154.
25. Weston [f], ii. 205 f.
26. Rhŷs [c], p. 335.
27. See *supra*, pp. 180–81.
28. Weston [f], ii. 111.
29. Layamon, *Brut*, ed. F. Madden, ii. 144, 384.
30. *Otia Imperialia*, ed. F. Liebrecht, p. 12.
31. Stuart-Glennie [a]; Hartland [a], p. 207; Nutt [b], p. 198.
32. Cf. E. Anwyl, in *ERE* ii. 5.
33. Weston [f], i. 287.
34. ib. i. 288 f., ii. 250, [e], p. 81 f.; Loth, *Mabinogion*, i. introd., p. 72.
35. See Windisch, *Táin*, p. xxxix.
36. Loth, *Mabinogion*, i. 288.
37. Weston [a], p. 32 f.
38. ib. ch. viii, [b], p. 46 f.

39. F. Madden, *Sir Gawayne*, p. xxxii.
40. Rhŷs [c], p. 21; Malory, *Morte d'Arthur*, i. 19.
41. Loth, *Mabinogion*, i. 274, 286.
42. ib. i. 286 f., 318 f.
43. ib. i. 330, 338.
44. Rhŷs [c], p. 59.
45. *Historia regum Britanniae*, ix. 11, x. 3.
46. Loth, *Mabinogion*, i. 286.
47. *Historia regum Britanniae*, x. 3, 9.
48. *Historia Britonum*, § 40 f.
49. Gildas, *De excidio Britanniae*, § 25.
50. Geoffrey, *Historia regum Britanniae*, vi. 17–viii. 20.
51. Weston [f], ii. 112.
52. See *supra*, p. 165.
53. See *supra*, pp. 72, 52.
54. Weston [g].
55. Weston [f], i. 330 f., ii. 249 f.; cf. also [e], p. 75 f.
56. K. Meyer, "Eine verschollene Artursage," in *Festschrift Ernst Windisch . . . dargebracht*, Leipzig, 1914, pp. 63–67, believes that he has found allusions to Arthur in Irish literature.

CHAPTER XV

1. *LL* 4 *b*, 12 *a*.
2. *LL* 4 *b*; J. O'Daly, in *TOS* iv. 244 f. (1859); d'Arbois, *Cours*, ii. 76 f.
3. *LU* 15; Harleian MS. 3. 18, p. 38.
4. See *supra*, pp. 109–10, 112, 57–59.
5. See *supra*, pp. 51–52.
6. *Book of Fermoy*, p. 111 f.; in *RIA:IMS* i. 46 f. (1870).
7. J. O'B. Crowe, in *JRHAAI* IV. i. 94 f. (1870).
8. D'Arbois, *Cours*, v. 18; Hull [c], p. 4; O'Curry [a], p. 637 f.; K. Meyer, in *RIA:TLS* xiv. 17 (1906).
9. W. Stokes, in *RCel* iii. 185 (1877).
10. *LU* 37 *a*; J. O'B. Crowe, in *JRHAAI* IV. i. 371 f. (1870).
11. Text and translation by S. H. O'Grady, and by W. Stokes, in *IT* IV. i. 1 ff.
12. S. H. O'Grady, ii. 103 f., 107, 179.
13. ib. ii. 136, 147, 168; other prophecies of Fionn's are given by O'Curry [a], p. 393 f.
14. E. O'Curry, in *Atlantis*, iv. 115 f. (1863); see *supra*, p. 51.
15. Text and translation in Nutt [c], i. 87 f., cf. ii. 8, 30 f.
16. ib. i. 14, 22.
17. E. O'Curry [a], p. 30 f.

18. See *supra*, p. 183.
19. J. O'B. Crowe, in *JRHAAI* IV. i. 371 f. (1870).
20. S. H. O'Grady, ii. 179.
21. Guest, iii. 325.
22. *Kulhwch and Olwen*, in Loth, *Mabinogion*, i. 314.
23. W. Stokes, in *RCel* xv. 468 (1894).